THE
WORLD·WATCH
READER
on
Global
Environmental
Issues

THE

WORLD·WATCH

READER

on

Global

Environmental

Issues

W · W · NORTON & COMPANY

New York · London

Printed in the United States of America.

The text of this book is composed in Compano,
with the display set in Goudy Old Style.
Composition and manufacturing by the Haddon Craftsmen, Inc.
Book design by Jack Meserole.

First Edition.

Library of Congress Cataloging-in-Publication Data

The World watch reader on global environmental issues / magazine
staff: editor, Lester R. Brown; managing editor, James P. Gorman;
senior editor, Mark Cheater; editorial committee, Lester R.
Brown . . . [et al.].
p. cm.
Includes index.
1. Pollution.   2. Environmental protection.   I. Brown, Lester
Russell, 1934–   . II. Worldwatch.
TD174.W68   1991
363.7—dc20   90–26334

ISBN 0-393-03007-5

W. W. Norton & Company, Inc., 500 Fifth Avenue, New York, N.Y. 10110
W. W. Norton & Company, Ltd., 10 Coptic Street, London WC1A 1PU

1 2 3 4 5 6 7 8 9 0

 This book is printed on recycled paper

WORLDWATCH INSTITUTE

CONTENTS

9 *Our Expanding Numbers*

10 *Reclaiming the Future*

FOREWORD

Everyone knows that our current way of life is environmentally unsustainable. The global economy is literally destroying the natural systems that support it. Yet a coherent blueprint of a sustainable economy—where it will get its energy, how it will produce goods and services, how it will transport and feed its population—does not exist in official circles.

Unfortunately, there is not even a vision of an environmentally sustainable economy—not in the White House, not at United Nations headquarters in New York, not at the World Bank, and not in corporate boardrooms. Recognizing this void, the Worldwatch Institute has used the principles of ecological sustainability to design a global economy that could satisfy human needs without destroying its support systems. The *World Watch Reader* aims to provide a vision of the environmentally sustainable society that is now within our grasp.

This anthology—like *World Watch* magazine, on which it is based, and Worldwatch's annual *State of the World*—reflects the Institute's research approach. Working from a vantage point that is both global and interdisciplinary, Worldwatch specializes in identifying trends that would be missed by those concentrating on a particular geographical region or working in a specialized discipline.

For example, Worldwatch's analysis of national transportation systems reveals a fact that startles many people, particularly Americans: The bicycle is the world's leading form of personal transportation. Americans own some 95 million bicycles, but only a tiny fraction of these provide basic transportation. The rest are relegated to weekend recreational use.

However, in "Pedaling into the Future," (p. 246), Marcia D. Lowe tells us that in Asia, home to half the Earth's human population, the bicycle reigns supreme as a transportation machine. In China, where more than a fifth of the world's people live, bicycles outnumber automobiles 540 to 1. The bicycle is becoming an increasingly attractive transportation option worldwide since it addresses many of our environmental problems—increases in greenhouse gases, air pollution, and acid rain—not to mention traffic congestion. The bicycle also satisfies a need for exercise for those who live in more-sedentary societies. For these reasons, more and more bicycles are being produced relative to cars. By 1987, world bicycle production topped 105 million, compared with 33 million for automobiles. To say that the bicycle is the transport vehicle of the future is not a bold projection. It is simply the recognition of an existing reality.

For water use, as for transportation, the global view reveals emerging trends that may not otherwise be obvious. In "Emerging Water Scarcities" (p. 127), Sandra Postel tracks the changing relationship between water supply and demand and observes that water scarcity is hardly a local issue. Since world population is growing by nearly 2 percent a year and the global economy is increasing even faster, demand for water is starting to outstrip supply on every continent.

We see water tables under parts of the North China Plain, where some 200 million people live, falling by 3 to 5 feet a year. In the Soviet Union, a continuation of the recent diversion of water for agriculture will drain the Aral Sea dry within the next 20 years. We see more than one-fifth of the irrigated land in the United States watered by drawing down water tables. And we see a growing competition between cities and farms for fresh water supplies, with farmers almost always losing in this uneven competition. The rapid growth in world irrigation from 1950 to 1980—a near tripling within a generation—came to an abrupt end in 1980. Almost overnight, the volume of irrigation water used per person started to decline—a fall that will probably continue as long as world population continues its rapid growth.

When Worldwatch looks at nuclear power, it analyzes the cost of plant construction and operation as well as the "back-end" costs of waste disposal and decommissioning of worn-out nuclear power plants. It considers nuclear power's threats to public safety and health, plus the link between nuclear power and nuclear weapons proliferation.

In "The Case Against Reviving Nuclear Power" (p. 205), Christopher Flavin seriously questions whether nuclear power belongs in our future. For example, some consider France's nuclear industry a success story. However, Chris points out that the national electricity utility, Electricité de France, has developed a debt of $39 billion, roughly the size of Argentina's foreign debt. He looks at the United States and sees a country where utility executives, responding to market forces, have not ordered a nuclear reactor in 12 years. As older plants begin to close down, we can expect U.S. nuclear power generation to dwindle—starting perhaps as early as 1991. The country that led the world into the nuclear age may well lead it out.

When Worldwatch studies the world food situation, it again uses a global, interdisciplinary perspective. During the early and mid-eighties, most economists surveying world agriculture saw surplus production capacity, mounting stocks, and depressed farm prices. Worldwatch saw these trends too, but it also saw extensive overplowing and overpumping, both of which are by definition unsustainable over the long term.

Today Worldwatch sees a world in which discontinuing the unsustainable use of land and water would drop output far below world consumption. In "Feeding Six Billion" (p. 147), it notes that the effects of environmental destruction are now showing up at harvest time. Nearly every form of environmental degradation—soil erosion, air pollution, acid rain, ozone depletion, the loss of biological diversity, deforestation, and hotter summers as a result of greenhouse gases—are taking their toll on the world food prospect. It sees that the world's farmers are having trouble expanding their output fast enough to feed the projected record 960 million people the nineties will add to today's family of 5.3 billion.

In the final article of this volume, "Vision of a Sustainable World," (p. 299), we summarize the Worldwatch Institute's vision of an environmentally sustainable society. The principal finding: When we are no longer enmeshed in an economic system that is sowing the seeds of its own demise, life will be far more pleasant and satisfying than it is today.

Worldwatch created this book in response to the international hunger for information on global environmental issues, a hunger that reflects the gap between the concern about the future of our planet and the availability of data on its changing condition. Thousands of action-oriented groups are springing up every year throughout the world: Rubber tappers organize to protect the Amazonian rain forest; residents of a Soviet city cooperate to close down an ill-designed nuclear power plant; villagers in India protest the construction of a large dam; and residents of any number of American communities demand the cleanup of a toxic waste site. These groups want information to help them act intelligently.

Governments are having difficulty supplying these grass-roots needs because they themselves lack information and analysis. Not one national government possesses a well-developed global environmental research capability. Governments at all levels, besieged with new environmental problems, often find that they lack the information on which to base wise decisions. The U.S. government has failed to publish any comprehensive analysis of global environmental issues since 1980, when it produced the *Global 2000 Report.* Indeed, Washington has struggled to publish an analysis of even national environmental conditions on an annual basis. Carter administration officials realized that an understanding of global environmental trends—particularly the interaction between environmental and economic conditions—is essential to wise governmental policymaking in fields as seemingly disparate as agriculture and national security. But within months after taking office, the Reagan administration dismantled the interagency machinery constructed to analyze global environmental issues in a systematic fashion.

One of the legacies of the Reagan-Watt-Gorsuch years is that little enlightened systematic thinking now takes place in the U.S. government on global environmental issues. Some exceptional work is done on the individual issues within various agencies, but there is no mechanism for integrating these analyses into a meaningful whole.

Unfortunately, the United Nations does not do much better. Each of the specialized agencies produces its own "State of" report. The Food and Agricultural Organization produces the *State of Food and Agriculture.* The UN Population Fund publishes *State of the World's Population.* The UN Environmental Program, starved for resources, creates a short *State of the World Environment* monograph, and the International Monetary Fund produces an annual *State of the World Economy* report. But the United Nations lacks the capacity to mesh ideas across these specialized fields.

To try and fill this gap, the Worldwatch Institute, with strong support from the Rockefeller Brothers Fund and the keen interest of W. W. Norton, unveiled its own annual *State of the World* report in 1984. Indicative of the demand for environmental information, *State of the World* is now published in all of the world's major languages—Spanish, Portuguese, Arabic, Chinese, Japanese, Indonesian, German, Italian, Polish, French, and Russian, in addition, of course, to English. Widely used by national governments and UN agencies, the report has acquired a semiofficial status.

National political leaders who rely on Worldwatch analyses range the political spectrum. In December 1988, when Mikhail Gorbachev spoke to the United Nations on redefining national security, he drew heavily on the last chapter of *State of the World 1986,* entitled "Redefining National Security." (Its conclusion that Japan was the only winner in the Cold War had struck a responsive chord in Moscow.)

When Margaret Thatcher decided to host an international conference on depletion of the stratospheric ozone layer, she discovered that her own government did not have a comprehensive study of the issue. She therefore distributed to conference participants—representatives of some 60 countries, including several heads of state—Worldwatch Paper 87, *Protecting Life on Earth: Steps to Save the Ozone Layer.*

In addition to the paucity of existing environmental information, the enthusiastic reception to the magazine itself has inspired us to launch this reader. Within two years of the magazine's inception, the English edition had subscribers in some 60 countries. Within its first year of publication, we received inquiries from publishers in other languages about acquiring translation rights. Negotiations were quickly completed for a Japanese edition, which was first published in 1989. Negotiations are now underway for Italian and Russian editions. Our long-term goal is to publish the magazine in all the world's major languages.

The magazine has also been nominated for several awards. During its first year, it was nominated in 2 out of 12 categories in the Utne Reader's Alternative Press Awards. In its second year, it was nominated in 3 categories: investigative reporting, international reporting, and general excellence. It won in the first category, edging out nine other nominees, including magazines of long standing, such as *Harper's.*

This *World Watch Reader* provides a vision of what an environmentally sustainable future might look like and how we can get there. We plan to update the reader periodically and offer fresh examples of successes from this effort. We hope this ongoing analysis will be of interest to those who want to reverse the trends that are undermining not only our future, but that of generations to come.

Lester R. Brown
Editor, *World Watch*

Worldwatch Institute
1776 Massachusetts Avenue, N.W.
Washington, D.C. 20036

ACKNOWLEDGMENTS

Any *Reader* is, by definition, a collaborative effort. This is especially so for the *World Watch Reader,* from the foundations who funded *World Watch* magazine to the research assistants who gathered data for the articles to the designers who artfully composed the pages. Many more worked to select, organize, update, edit, and set into print the articles from the magazine contained in this selection.

Two groups deserve special recognition for their distinctive contribution. First are the foundations who provided specific funding for the magazine, which was launched in January of 1988. These include the George Gund Foundation, the John D. and Catherine T. MacArthur Foundation, the Edith Munson Foundation, and the Rockefeller Brothers Fund. Foundations which support the Institute's research program and thus also contribute indirectly to this *Reader* include the Geraldine R. Dodge Foundation, the William and Flora Hewlett Foundation, the W. Alton Jones Foundation, the Andrew W. Mellon Foundation, Public Welfare Foundation, the Rockefeller Foundation, and the Winthrop Rockefeller Charitable Trust. The Surdna Foundation and the United Nations Population Fund support research on transportation and population issues, respectively, articles of which are found in this *Reader.*

The second group whose names do not appear frequently in print, but who deserve a great deal of credit, are the Institute's administrative staffers who labor cheerfully and tirelessly to keep Worldwatch running. They include Barbara Fallin, Guy Gorman, Gloria Grant, Blondeen Gravely, Joseph Gravely, Heather Hanford, Millicent Johnson, Reah Janise Kauffman, and Steven Kaufman. To them, and to the many others who contributed to this book, but whose names we do not have the space to mention, thanks.

1

*Our Endangered
Earth*

Restoring Degraded Land

By Sandra Postel

Farmers in the north African country of Niger know firsthand that the land they have farmed for decades is worn out. *Kasar mu, ta gaji,* they lament in their native Hausa. "The land is tired." Peasants in western parts of the country strike a more ominous chord in Zarma with *Laabu, y bu,* "The land is dead."

The phrases aptly depict land suffering from what scientists call desertification. While the term conjures up images of Saharan sand dunes engulfing new territories, its most worrisome aspects are less dramatic. Desertification refers broadly to the impoverishment of the land through overgrazing, overcultivation, deforestation, and poor irrigation practices. Under these pressures, land degrades gradually and insidiously toward a desert-like state.

Each year, desertification claims an estimated 15 million acres worldwide—an area the size of West Virginia lost beyond practical hope of reclamation. An additional 50 million acres annually become too debilitated to support profitable farming or grazing. Hundreds of millions of acres lie somewhere on the degradation continuum, between fully productive and hopelessly desertified. Unfortunately, much of this land is sliding down the diminishing productivity side of the scale.

Techniques to restore resilience and productivity to stressed lands exist, but so far the international commitment does not. The majority of people affected are poor, disenfranchised farmers and pastoralists living at society's margins. A lasting victory over land degradation will remain a distant dream if there are not social and economic reforms that give rural people the security of tenure and access to resources they need to improve and protect the land. And, with degradation rooted in excessive human pressures, slowing population growth lies at the heart of an effective global strategy.

Unlike acid rain, toxic contamination, or the nuclear weapons threat, desertification is difficult to rally around and adopt as a cause. Yet its consequences—intensified droughts and floods, famine, declining living standards, and swelling numbers of environmental refugees—could not be more real or packed with emotion.

A world of 5.3 billion people growing by 95 million each year cannot afford to squander its food base. Without good land, humanity quite literally has nothing on which to grow.

How to Make a Desert

Spurred by the devastating drought that struck much of western and north-central Africa from 1968 through 1973, government representatives from around the world gathered in Nairobi, Kenya, during the summer of 1977 for a United Nations conference on desertification. It was the first time the world's attention was focused on the problems and prospects of fragile lands. Out of Nairobi came the Plan of Action to Combat Desertification, which recommended 28 measures that national, regional, and international institutions could take to halt land deterioration.

Sadly, the action plan fell victim to inadequate funding and a lack of sustained commitment by governments. In 1984, when the United Nations Environment Program

(UNEP) assessed progress in implementing the plan, it found not only that little had been accomplished during the past seven years, but that an already daunting problem was worsening rapidly.

According to UNEP, 11 billion acres—35 percent of the earth's land surface—are threatened by desertification and, with them, fully one-fifth of humanity. Three-quarters of this area has already been at least moderately degraded and an astonishing one-third has lost more than 25 percent of its productive potential.

These numbers point toward an unbalanced relationship between people and the land, a predicament all the more tragic because people are both degradation's victims and its unwitting agents. The four principal causes of land degradation—overgrazing on rangelands, overcultivation of croplands, waterlogging and salting of irrigated lands, and deforestation—all stem from human pressures or poor management of the land (see Table 1).

Degradation of rangelands results from excessive grazing by the three billion cattle, sheep, goats, and camels that roam the world's countryside. As the size of livestock herds surpasses the carrying capacity of perennial grasses on the range, less palatable annual grasses and shrubs move in. Eventually, plant cover of all types begins to diminish; this leaves the land exposed to the ravages of wind and water.

In the most severe stages, animal hooves trample nearly bare ground into a crusty layer no roots can penetrate, causing erosion to accelerate. The appearance of large gullies or sand dunes signals that desertification can claim another victory. This process is most pervasive and visible in Africa, home to more than half of the world's pastoralists.

Similarly, cropland left without protective vegetative cover or situated on steeply sloping hillsides is subject to the erosive power of wind and rain. An inch of topsoil takes anywhere from 200 to 1,000 years to form; under the most erosive conditions, that same soil can be swept off the land

TABLE 1   Observations of Land Degradation in Selected
Countries and Regions

Country/Source	Observation
Mali Patricia A. Jacobberger, geologist, Smithsonian Institution, 1986	"On the Landsat maps, there is now—and there wasn't in 1976—a bright ring of soil around villages. Those areas are now 90 percent devoid of vegetation, the topsoil is gone, and the surface is disrupted and cracked."
Mauritania Sidy Gaye, *Ambio*, 1987	"There were only 43 sandstorms in the whole country between 1960 and 1970. The number increased tenfold in the following decade, and in . . . 1983 alone a record 240 sandstorms darkened the nation's skies."
China *Beijing Review,* interview with Zhu Zhenda, Chinese Academy of Sciences, 1988	"Unless urgent measures are taken, desertification will erode an additional 29,000 square miles . . . by the year 2000, more than twice the area of Taiwan."
Indonesia Ronald Greenberg and M.L. Higgins, USAID Jakarta, 1987	"Thirty-six watersheds . . . have critical erosion problems. . . . In Kalimantan, the silt load in streams has increased 33-fold in some logging areas."
Thailand D. Phantumvanit and K.S. Sathirathai, Thailand Development Research Board, 1988	"The pace of deforestation has been accelerating since the early 1900s, but it has moved into a higher gear since the 1960s. . . . [Between 1961 and 1986] Thailand lost about 45 percent of its forests."

in just a few seasons. Crop production suffers over the long term, because those upper layers of soil contain most of the organic matter and nutrients that plants need to grow. Erosion also breaks down the soil's structure and diminishes its water-holding capacity; this is often erosion's most damaging effect, especially in drought-prone regions.

At least 825 million acres of rain-fed cropland—more than a third of the global total—are losing their productive potential in this way. If fertilizers cannot make up the loss, as is often the case among poor subsistence farmers, crop yields decline.

Ultimately, when pastoralists or subsistence farmers can no longer eke out an existence, they leave their homelands in search of more fertile fields or a better life in the already swelling slums and shantytowns of major cities. Nouakchott, the capital of Mauritania—among the countries most severely stricken by desertification—has grown from a population of 20,000 in 1960 to about 350,000 today. More than half these people migrated from the deteriorating countryside, leading some to call that city the largest refugee camp in the world.

Although irrigated lands are well-watered and protected from the ravages of drought, they, too, suffer from a special type of desertification. Over time, seepage from irrigation canals and overwatering of fields will cause the underlying water table to rise. If drainage is inadequate, the root zone eventually becomes waterlogged and inhospitable to plants. Farmers belonging to a large irrigation project in the Indian state of Madhya Pradesh have referred to their once-fertile fields as "wet deserts."

In dry regions, the evaporation of water near the soil surface leaves behind a damaging residue of salt—a process called salinization. UNEP's assessment placed the irrigated area suffering from salinization at 100 million acres. About half of this area is in India and Pakistan, but the problem also pervades the Tigris and Euphrates river basins of Syria and Iraq, California's San Joaquin Valley, the Colorado River basin, China's North Plain, and Soviet Central Asia.

The consequences of desertification on irrigated lands are disproportionately costly. Irrigation represents a hefty investment that typically pays off because it boosts yields by two to three times over those of rain-fed cropland. Roughly a third of the world's food is grown on the 17 percent of cropland that is irrigated. So the destruction—sometimes abandonment—of this land represents a heavy loss of investment, diminished food security, and a further shrinkage of the planet's agricultural resource base.

The Roads to Ruin

While it is easy to ascertain desertification's direct causes, the conditions leading to these pressures are more varied and complex. Generally, they stem from population densities greater than what the land can sustain and, more fundamentally, from social and economic inequities that push people into marginal environments and unstable livelihoods.

In response to mounting concern about environmental deterioration in West Africa, the World Bank set up a special working group led by French agronomist Jean Gorse to study this troubled region in greater depth. Gorse's group focused on a band of seven countries in what are known as the Sahelian and Sudanian zones: Burkina Faso, Chad, The Gambia, Mali, Mauritania, Niger and Senegal. In these countries, annual rainfall increases from north to south— from less than 8 inches in the northernmost zone to more than 30 inches in the southernmost—and so, consequently, does the number of people that can be supported by traditional farming and livestock practices.

Gorse's study found that in parts of the region the rural population in 1980 had already exceeded the number for which the land could sustainably provide sufficient food. Even more important, fuel wood emerged as the limiting

area would therefore feed on itself and become more desert-like.

Tests of Charney's hypothesis using climate models generally confirmed its validity: Large increases in albedo did indeed reduce rainfall. Less clear, however, was how smaller changes in reflectivity would affect rainfall and whether the patchy pattern of desertification could produce albedo changes sufficient to affect rainfall levels. Unfortunately, the global circulation models used in climate studies are not sufficiently fine-tuned to predict changes for specific locations.

Another worrisome link surfaced from the modeling studies Jagadish Shukla and Yale Mintz conducted at the University of Maryland. They examined the effects on rainfall of changes in evapotranspiration, which is the transfer of water vapor from the land to the atmosphere through evaporation or transpiration by plants. For this process to occur, the soil must be sufficiently moist and vegetation must be present to bring that moisture into contact with the air. Presumably, if evapotranspiration is an important source of atmospheric water vapor in a given locale, then rainfall levels would decline as it diminishes. Shukla and Mintz found just that, although, as with Charney's study, their conclusions pertained to changes on a large scale.

Meanwhile, Sharon Nicholson, a meteorologist at Florida State University at Tallahassee, was analyzing rainfall data from roughly 300 sites in some 20 African countries. She established a long-term average from data covering the years 1901 to 1974, and then calculated the annual percentage departures from that long-term average for the years 1901 to 1984.

Between 1967 and 1984, these countries experienced 17 consecutive years of below-normal rainfall, by far the longest series of subpar rains in the 84-year record. Annual rainfall in 1983 and 1984 fell more than 40 percent short of the long-term average. Interestingly, Nicholson also analyzed northern sub-Saharan rainfall levels according to three bands, each running east-west, and found that drought was most persistent in the northernmost, most arid band, where theoretically the albedo and low-evapotranspiration feedbacks would be greatest.

THE WELL GONE DRY

Regardless of whether desertification can actually diminish rainfall, there is little doubt that the water cycle is greatly influenced by the land and its vegetative cover. When rainwater hits the surface, it either immediately runs off into rivers and streams to begin its journey back to the sea, soaks into the subsurface to replenish groundwater supplies, or returns to the atmosphere through evaporation or transpiration.

Land degradation shifts the proportion of rainfall following these pathways. Due to less vegetative cover and hard-packed soils, degraded land suffers from increased runoff and decreased infiltration into the subsurface. The resulting reduction in soil moisture and groundwater supplies worsens the effects of drought, while the increase in rapid runoff exacerbates flooding.

What appear, then, to be consequences and signs of meteorological drought—withered crops, falling groundwater levels, and dry stream beds—can actually be caused in large part by land degradation. Perhaps nowhere has this case been made more convincingly than in India, where a growing number of scientists now blame deforestation and desertification for the worsening of droughts and floods. Jayanta Bandyopadhyay of the Research Foundation for Science, Technology and Natural Resource Policy in Dehra Dun writes: "With an amazing rapidity, acute scarcity of water has grabbed the center stage of India's national life. . . . State after state is trapped into an irreversible and worsening crisis of drought, desertification and consequent water scarcity, threatening plant, animal and human life."

Water shortages plagued some 17,000 villages in the northern state of Uttar Pradesh in the sixties; by 1985, that figure had risen to 70,000. Similarly, in Madya Pradesh, more than 36,400 villages lacked sufficient water in 1980; in 1985 the number totaled more than 64,500. And in the western state of Gujarat, the number of villages short of water tripled between 1979 and 1986, from some 3,840 to 12,250.

Ultimately, drought and desertification reinforce each other by preventing land from recovering from stress. Whereas healthy land will bounce back to its former productivity after a drought, degraded and abused land frequently will not. Areas plagued both by drought and degradation—including much of Africa and India—thus face the prospect of a downward spiral of land productivity, bringing even greater hunger and human suffering than these regions witnessed during the eighties.

RESTORING LIFE TO THE LAND

Halting the spread of desertification is no easy task. Populations are growing fastest in some of the regions most threatened by desertification. The challenge is to restore and protect the land while at the same time meeting the basic needs of growing numbers of people. Here and there—in villages, grass-roots organizations, research institutes, experiment stations, and development agencies—strategies are being devised, tried, and shown to have potential.

The most promising efforts center around measures that concentrate production on the most fertile, least erodible land; stabilize soils on sloping and other marginal land; and reduce rural people's vulnerability to crop failure by diversifying income-generating options at the village level.

One such effort is under way in China's Loess Plateau, a highly eroded area spanning some 150 million acres around the middle reaches of the Yellow River watershed. There, a partnership of scientists, villagers, political leaders, and international development agencies has dramatically altered the use of the land in selected villages and brought soil erosion under control; at the same time living standards have improved.

In the village of Quanjiagou, flat, fertile farmland created with soil-trapping dams and extensive terraces allowed crop production to increase 17 percent between 1979 and 1986, even though the area planted in crops was reduced by half. With the added value from cash-crop tree products and animal husbandry, the village's per-capita income more than doubled (see Table 2).

Similar strategies are being tried in the drought-plagued, degraded highlands of Ethiopia. Simple structures called bunds, really just walls of rock or earth constructed across hillsides, catch soil washing down the slopes. As soil builds up behind the bund, a natural terrace forms, that both diminishes erosion and enhances water infiltration; this has led to higher crop yields.

Between 1976 and 1985, through projects sponsored by the United Nations and various foreign aid agencies, Ethi-

TABLE 2
Effects of Land Rehabilitation Strategy in Quanjiagou, Mizhi County, 1979–85

Effects	1979	1986	Change
Land use	(acres)		(percent)
Cropland	578	289	− 50
Trees	148	274	+ 85
Pasture	40	205	+ 413
Crop production	(tons)		(percent)
	250	293	+ 17
Per-capita income	(yuan[1])		(percent)
	127	313	+ 146

[1]As of April 1991, one yuan exchanged for U.S. $0.19.
Source: Shaanxi Control Institute of the Loess Plateau.

opian farmers built nearly 373,000 miles of bunds and 292,-
000 miles of terraces to stabilize steep slopes. Although impressive, these efforts are but a start: Just 6 percent of the
threatened highlands are now protected.

SOME SIMPLE SOLUTIONS

Whatever strategy is devised, successful land reclamation
hinges on simple techniques that add nutrients and moisture
to the land while holding the soil in place. Work at the International Institute of Tropical Agriculture in Ibadan, Nigeria,
has shown, for example, that applying a mulch of crop residues in amounts of 2.4 tons per acre (a very thin layer) can
control erosion nearly completely on slopes of up to 15 degrees and make sustainable cropping possible. In field trials,
yields increased over nonmulched plots by 83 percent for
cowpeas, 73 percent for cassava, and 23 percent for maize.

Alley cropping, in which food crops are planted between
hedgerows of trees, holds promise for tropical regions.
Hedgerow trimmings provide a good mulch for the crop and
offer fodder for animals and fuel wood for cooking. Legumi-
nous trees that fix nitrogen are especially useful since they
improve and maintain soil fertility. Sudanese farmers who
leave native *Acacia senegal* trees on their cropland have
learned this over time and find they can grow millet continuously for 15 to 20 years, compared with three to five
years if the trees are removed.

Another promising approach for fighting land degradation is planting a densely tufted, deep-rooted plant called
vetiver grass. Native to India and known there as *khus,*
vetiver grass can be put to work on erosive land for between
1 and 10 percent of the cost of bunds and earthen walls, and
it requires no maintenance. When closely spaced along the
contours of a hillside, vetiver grass forms a vegetative barrier
that slows runoff and thus gives rainfall a chance to spread

out and seep into a field. It also traps sediment behind it, which gradually forms a natural terrace. Farmers only need to give up a 20-inch strip of cropland for each contour hedge of vetiver and, since yields typically increase by 50 percent, the conservation gains far outweight the loss from the small amount of land taken out of production.

Unfortunately, successes in rehabilitating degraded rangelands and salinized irrigated lands make for a rather short list. Perhaps the clearest advance in rangeland restoration comes from the revival of the ancient "Hema" system of management in Syria. There, cooperatives are established that have the sole right to graze demarcated sets of range. Families in a cooperative are then granted a license to graze only a certain number of sheep. By reducing overgrazing, the system has enabled the revegetation of 17 million acres of rangeland.

Among the countries most affected by salinization, Pakistan has perhaps tried hardest to tackle it, but has achieved only mixed results. In 1960, the government committed itself to draining salt-affected lands by installing vertical tube wells. Two decades and more than 12,000 tube wells later, the area reclaimed still falls far short of the target. The Five Year Plan for 1983 to 1988 allocated an astonishing 43 percent of the total water budget to drainage activities and provided for credits and subsidies to foster more private development of tube wells.

In Egypt, a proposed drainage system covering only a small portion of the Nile Delta has been priced at $1 billion. Such high sums partly explain why governments tend to ignore the problem and why preventing salinization through careful water management is so crucial.

Sizing Up the Opponent

Why, more than a decade after a global goal was set to stop desertification by the year 2000, are we losing more trees, more topsoil, and more grazing land than ever before? The easy answers are that governments fail to grasp the severity of the threat, lack the political will to give it priority, and underfund efforts to combat it.

But a more fundamental reason may lie in the very nature of "desertification control" itself. It crosses all traditional disciplinary and bureaucratic boundaries to tie in agriculture, forestry, water management, and pastoralism. Lasting solutions will be rooted as much in social and economic reforms as in effective technologies.

All the elements needed to halt land degradation exist, but they have not been joined effectively in the battle or given the resources needed to mount an adequate fight. In the United Nations Environment Program and its executive director, Mostafa Tolba, desertification control has a strategic headquarters and a strong, committed leader. But the amount of funding mobilized over the last decade has fallen far short of UNEP's estimated investment needs of $4.5 billion per year to bring desertification under control within 20 years. Several countries have developed the national plans of action called for by the 1977 Nairobi conference, but only three—Burkina Faso, Mali, and Tunisia—have drummed up sufficient support to begin implementing them.

While this top-down approach proceeds at a snail's pace, efforts starting at the village level have produced numerous, albeit small, successes. In western Kenya, 540 local organizations—mostly women's groups and primary schools—are working with the U.S.-based organization CARE to promote reforestation. CARE provides the materials needed to establish nurseries, as well as training and extension services, but local people do the planting. Each group plants between 5,000 and 10,000 seedlings a year; collectively this amounts to nearly a third of the plantings that the government estimates are needed.

Projects such as this demonstrate that the greatest hope for reversing land degradation lies in marrying the commitment and experience of organizations operating at the local level with stepped-up international support and technical guidance through United Nations agencies, bilateral and multilateral donors, and national governments.

UNEP has begun to recognize that community-based initiatives have higher success rates and more lasting impacts than top-down projects and is now strengthening its cooperation with nongovernmental organizations (NGOs). The agency currently supports several grass-roots projects through the Nairobi-based African NGO Environmental Network and also has helped launch the Deforestation and desertification Control NGO Network in the Asia-Pacific region. Among the groups that have benefited from UNEP's new approach is the Millions of Trees Club, which has set up "people's nurseries" and training centers for reforestation in southern India. UNEP's infusion of $35,000 over two years helped local people plant more than two million trees and shrubs.

Credit Where It Is Due

Until governments and donor agencies begin giving farmers the incentives they need to invest in land productivity, there is little hope of making more than a dent in desertification. As noted earlier, reforming land ownership and tenure policies and providing access to credit for small landholders is crucial to the reversal of land degradation. Special emphasis needs to be placed on the status of women, especially in Africa, where the disparity between the work women do and the rights they have is greatest.

Of the multilateral development organizations, the International Fund for Agricultural Development (IFAD) is heads above the others in more thoroughly incorporating these needs into its projects. This decade-old UN agency has now carried out some 190 projects and, in the words of IFAD president Idriss Jazairy, they are "people-oriented" and built upon the philosophy that development involves the "liberation of [people's] creative potential."

An IFAD project in Kenya, for example, operates through women's savings clubs and other community groups to enhance access to credit, farm supplies, and extension services. Another project in The Gambia works to uphold traditional female cultivation rights under a new land-distribution scheme and establishes day-care centers for children of women whose work loads have increased with the introduction of double-cropping. While the provision of child-care services may seem far removed from desertification control, freeing women to do the work of boosting land productivity could, in fact, be an essential first step.

More research into crop varieties and production systems appropriate for the lands and people at risk is also needed. With the high-yielding, "green revolution" package of technologies commanding the research limelight over the last several decades, efforts to improve the productivity of subsistence farming are just beginning to get the attention they deserve. Research on cowpeas, for example, an important legume grown in Africa, has led to varieties harvestable in 50 to 60 days instead of 90 to 100. That paves the way for double- or even triple-cropping in some regions, which would reduce pressures to extend cultivation to marginal lands.

Finally, with much of degradation stemming from excessive human pressures, reversing it will require a dramatic slowing of population growth. If current growth rates persist, Africa's worn-out lands will need to support an additional 263 million people by the year 2000—more people than currently live in the United States. India will grow by nearly 200 million people, or 24 percent, and the Philippines, with the fastest growth rate in Southeast Asia, by more than a third. No matter how much funding comes forth, how fast effective technologies spread, or how diligently governments implement land reforms, a lasting victory over land degradation will remain out of reach until population pressures ease.

THE OCEAN BLUES

By Nicholas Lenssen

The last few years have been rough on the oceans. Hundreds of beaches along the Italian Adriatic were off limits due to an infestation of algae. Medical waste washing ashore closed beaches in many areas of the eastern United States. Thousands of seals died in the North Sea, possibly due to a combination of disease and pollution. A similar fate befell dolphins off the U.S. Atlantic coast. And in Alaska, a supertanker hit a reef and dumped a quarter million barrels of oil into one of the world's richest fishing grounds.

Once thought to be so vast and resilient that no level of human insult could damage them, the oceans are now crying out for attention. While the public eye is periodically turned to large disasters such as the ones mentioned above, it is routine assaults that most threaten the marine environment. Daily chemical and biological pollution is damaging the oceans at a frightening rate, while ongoing coastal development and overfishing hamper their ability to recuperate.

Gone with pristine waters are futurists' dreams of a world fed by the sea's abundance. In their place is the reality of stagnating oceans; shrinking wetlands, coral reefs, and mangroves; and falling fish catches that jeopardize a key source of protein for the world's poor. Unless we act soon,

43

reversing these worsening conditions will only become more difficult.

Too Much of a Good Thing

One of the chief oceanic pollutants is human sewage. Properly handled on land, human waste makes a good fertilizer that has a balanced complement of nutrients to promote plant growth. Flushed into streams and rivers, these same nutrients can lead to eutrophication, the overenrichment of water. Additional nutrients wash into the sea from fertilized farmland and from acid rain, which contains nitrogen compounds released in fossil-fuel combustion. Algae feed on this windfall of nutrients and multiply at an incredible rate until they form what are called "blooms."

As these tiny organisms decompose, they leave surrounding waters oxygenless and lifeless. In Australia, Chile, Nigeria, Pakistan, the Soviet Union, and the United States, the story is the same: Nutrient overload has left beaches unusable and large areas of water temporarily dead.

Even worse, there is a growing epidemic of algae blooms that are toxic. These "red tides" can poison marine life and throw whole ecosystems off balance. Until recently, scientists thought red tides were entirely natural events. Theodore Smayda of the University of Rhode Island and Donald Anderson of the Woods Hole Oceanographic Institution now have found a strong correlation between the occurrence and location of these blooms and increased nutrient levels.

European waters are in particularly bad shape. Nearly half of the Baltic Sea's bottom waters have become oxygenless; algae blooms in the Adriatic Sea killed fish in areas as large as 400 square miles; and the North Sea coasts of Denmark and Germany experienced a 400 percent increase in major blooms.

In May 1988, a particularly devastating toxic algae bloom dominated the Skagerrak, which connects the North Sea to the Baltic Sea, and killed nearly all marine life to a depth of 50 feet, including fish valued commercially at $200 million. Norway's Bergen Scientific Center found that the bloom was caused at least in part by urban and agricultural pollution. It warns that as long as such nutrient discharges continue, similar blooms can be expected.

Red tides were once rare events along the East Coast of the United States, but since 1972 waters from Massachusetts to North Carolina have been plagued by six major toxic blooms. A bloom of the algae *Ptychodiscus brevis,* normally found in the Gulf of Mexico, struck near Cape Hatteras, North Carolina, in October 1987 and inflicted $25 million in losses on the fishing and tourist industries. This bloom created a political uproar when a government report implicated it in the deaths of 3,000 dolphins, many of which had washed up on public beaches along the eastern seaboard. Some scientists and members of Congress remain skeptical about the causes of the dolphin deaths; they contend that extremely high levels of PCBs and pesticide residue found in the dead mammals were a contributing factor.

The increase in blooms and their toxicity has created problems for fishers and consumers of sea products. Guatemala and the Philippines have reported deaths from bloom-contaminated shellfish, an event unknown until this decade.

Sewage discharges can lead to health problems even when blooms don't occur. In Shanghai, nearly 300,000 people came down with hepatitis A in a three-month stretch in 1988, due to contaminated clams; 47 victims died. Industrial countries generally have better controls that keep contaminated seafood from market, which means that at any one time one-third of the U.S. shellfish beds are closed because of pollution.

Oil and Water Don't Mix

The wreck of the supertanker *Exxon Valdez* in Alaska's Prince William Sound on March 24, 1989, was the most dramatic oceanic disaster in recent memory. By mid-May, crude oil covered more than 730 miles of wilderness coast, in some places 3 feet deep. The spill created an environmental disaster that will linger for decades, for oil does not break down as fast in Alaska's cold climate as it does in warmer regions. Also, since much of the oil either fell to the bottom of Prince William Sound or dissolved into the water, diseases or damage to animal reproduction will occur irregularly as hydrocarbons seep out and move up the food chain.

Amidst the bungled cleanup effort, Exxon executive Don Cornett claimed the spill was "just another cost of doing business." For the oil industry, with its vast economic resources, this may be true, but not so for the Alaskan fishing and tourist industries, whose losses could approach $250 million. Fishing is a $130-million-a-year business in Prince William Sound, and the spill's effects on salmon, herring, shrimp, and other populations will be felt for years to come.

The Alaska spill capped an extremely messy year for the oil industry. Antarctica's coast was fouled by two petroleum spills in a month, and oil coated shorelines in Belgium, the Netherlands, Florida, Hawaii, and on Washington State's Olympic Peninsula. Recent research findings from Panama show that oil in warmer, tropical waters has a far greater impact than previously thought; it now is seen as particularly deadly to coral reefs and mangroves.

Although large spills get media attention, far more oil silently finds its way into the oceans via street runoff, ships flushing their tanks, and effluent from industrial facilities. A 1985 U.S. National Research Council (NRC) study, *Oil in the Sea*, estimated that 21 million barrels of oil annually enters the seas this way, many times more than the 600,000 barrels accidentally spilled on average each year last decade. The NRC also warned that there is a special concern for areas suffering chronic exposure, since as little as one part of oil for every 10 million parts of water has serious effects on the reproduction and growth of fish, crustaceans, and plankton.

A petroleum derivative, plastic, also takes a heavy toll on marine life. Each year, 30,000 northern fur seals die as they become entangled in plastic bags or lost fishing nets, as do hundreds of thousands of other marine mammals, seabirds, and fish. It's estimated that up to a half million plastic containers are dumped into the seas from merchant ships every day and that untold miles of fishing gear, including whole nets, are accidentally set adrift.

A Thin Layer of Death

Chemical pollutants constitute another assault on the marine environment, especially in the uppermost layer of water. The tiny phytoplankton and zooplankton that form the base of the oceanic food chain congregate in the microlayer, which is 1/100th of an inch thick, as do certain fish and shellfish in early stages of their lives.

Unfortunately, that's not all that concentrates there. John Hardy, a biologist at Oregon State University, has found toxic chemicals and such heavy metals as copper, lead, and zinc in the microlayer in concentrations 10 to 1,000 times greater than in the rest of the water. Scientists are trying to determine what role the contaminated microlayer has in diminishing fish and shellfish populations in coastal waters.

These chemicals come from a variety of sources—industries, airborne pollutants, shipping accidents, pesticide runoff, mine tailings, and waste incineration. Once toxics enter the marine environment, it's very hard to get them out, since they seep into the sediments, enter the food chain, or simply flow with the currents. More than 2.1 million tons of liquid chemical waste is poured into the North Sea alone each year, and the shipboard incineration of more than 100,000 tons of hazardous wastes adds an unspecified amount of toxic ash. The intergovernmental North Sea Scientific Commission has found that although several opportunistic species have thrived under these conditions, the overall diversity of marine organisms is reduced by these discharges.

From 1988 to early 1989, 17,500 seals in the North and Baltic seas died mysteriously; this has worried citizens and politicians in bordering countries. While scientists have blamed a new virus for the epidemic, the role the poisoned waters have played in wiping out three-quarters of the North Sea's seal population is hotly debated. Marine biologists agree, however, that chemicals will impede the recovery of the seals, as up to 80 percent of female seals in the Baltic are believed to be sterile due to polychlorinated biphenyls (PCBs).

Chemical pollutants are doing damage in other bodies of water as well. High levels of PCBs, DDT, mercury, cadmium, and other chemicals are blamed for the collapse of beluga whale populations in Canada's Saint Lawrence River. Autopsies of 72 dead whales have found tumors, ulcers, respiratory ailments, and failed immune systems. Joseph Cummins, genetics professor at the University of Western Ontario, believes that the "beluga is the most polluted mammal on earth" and that marine mammals around the world face extinction from PCBs.

These chemicals move through the food chain and can also end up in humans. Between 1953 and 1968, some 649 residents of Minamata, Japan, were killed after they consumed seafood contaminated by industrial mercury. Seafood from Minamata Bay still cannot be eaten. In the United States, lobsters containing up to 20 times the allowable limit of PCBs have been caught off the Massachusetts coast. Fish with tumors from unknown causes also are being caught with greater frequency along the eastern seaboard of the United States, as are fish in Florida with high levels of mercury.

ROBBING THE CRADLE

As chemical threats grow, the marine habitats that nurture ocean life are disappearing. That's bad news for the future of the oceans, since coral reefs, mangroves, and sea grasses are the "nurseries" and feeding grounds for much of marine life, supporting as they do the sea's richest areas of biological diversity and productivity (see Figure 1).

Coral reefs are home to an estimated one million species, including 2,000 fish species, and are considered the tropical rain forests of the oceans. They also happen to be the ecosystems most sensitive to changes in temperature and light. Healthy coral reefs are becoming hard to find. Rivers choked

FIGURE 1   Productivity of Marine Habitats per Cubic Meter Annually

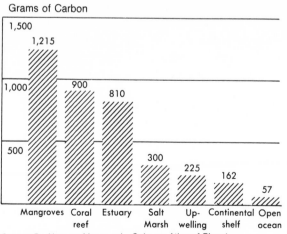

Source: Dr. Norman Myers, ed., *Gaia, an Atlas of Planet Management* (Garden City, NY: Anchor Press/Doubleday, 1984).

with sediment from deforested lands or eroded agricultural fields cloud coastal waters and kill reefs by blocking sunlight. Along Costa Rica's Caribbean coast, sediments from local rivers have killed 75 percent of the reefs. Local fishers in Indonesia, Kenya, and elsewhere add to the damage by using dynamite to kill and collect fish that hide in coral reefs. Also, reefs throughout the world are mined for construction material or ornamental pieces.

By 1981, 70 percent of the reefs in the Philippines had been damaged, many beyond recovery, by the cumulative effect of poisoning from cyanide, mine tailings, pesticides, and erosion. Particularly damaging is the use of cyanide in collecting tropical fish for the commercial aquarium business. Fishers squirt sodium cyanide into reef hideaways to stun valuable species. Even though the cyanide is not intended to kill the fish, it frequently does. It also kills the coral.

The natural and economic losses from this destruction are vast. More than 100,000 jobs, as well as $80 million in potential fish catches, are lost each year as coral reefs disappear, estimates Don McAllister, curator of the National Museums of Canada and director of the International Marinelife Alliance (IMA). "Due to lowered fish production from destroyed coral reef, more than five million Filipinos do with less than enough seafood; many starve," says McAllister. Already between one-fourth and one-half of the children living in coastal settlements in the Philippines are malnourished. The continuing loss of coral reefs and fish will only increase this figure. Encouragingly, IMA and the Philippine Ministry of Agriculture, with funding from the Canadian government, have initiated programs to assist fishers in returning to sustainable harvesting methods.

The salt-tolerant mangrove trees that inhabit low-lying areas of the tropics and subtropics are also threatened. Even richer breeding, nursery, and feeding grounds than coral reefs, mangrove forests are nonetheless being rapidly cut to make charcoal and pulp and to clear the way for salt-making and aquaculture ponds. Between 1963 and 1977, almost half of India's mangroves were cut down; one-third of Ecuador's mangroves have been converted to ponds for a rapidly growing shrimp-farming industry; and 10 years is all Philippine mangroves are given before aquacultural expansion wipes them out. On a positive note, Tanzania recently banned the destruction of its remaining 200,000 acres of mangroves.

BOUNTY OF THE SEA

Along with pollution, overfishing threatens the future productivity of the seas, warned Edouard Saouma, director general of the United Nations Food and Agriculture Organization (FAO) in April 1989. Paradoxically, his statement came as the worldwide commercial catch reached a record level of 84.5 million tons in 1987, up from 21 million tons in 1950. Fish account for more than 40 percent of the animal-protein supply for two billion people in the developing world, although only 24 percent for the world as a whole. Fish supplies are not unlimited, however; after nearly doubling between 1950 and 1970, the per-capita fish catch of 40 pounds has advanced little since (see Figure 2).

The global commercial fish catch is nearing the maximum sustainable yield of 100 million tons that FAO scientists think the oceans can produce. Indeed, the total catch may exceed that level, since subsistence fishers net another 24 million tons. Trends in particular fish species confirm this. Of the 280 fish stocks monitored by the FAO, only 25 are considered slightly to moderately exploited. Meanwhile, at least 42 stocks are already overexploited or depleted.

The recent upswing in catches is attributed to the use of more-efficient fishing techniques and the increased exploitation of less desirable species in the herring and sardine family. Also, the world's fishing fleets have intensified their ex-

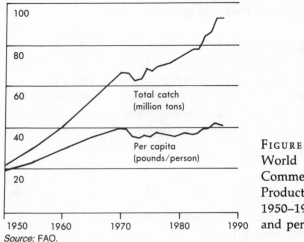

FIGURE 2
World
Commercial Fish
Production
1950–1987: Total
and per Capita

Source: FAO.

ploitation of remote regions in the southern Pacific Ocean. As fisheries decline, family income and even food intake will head downward for the more than 100 million people who depend on the oceans for their livelihood. In Costa Rica, the Philippines, and elsewhere, hunger is driving fishing families away from the sea and thus adding to bulging urban populations.

For more than two decades, scientists and policymakers have worked to manage fishing, particularly that by long-range trawler fleets, better through stronger national responsibility and management of fish stocks. A potential solution was agreed to during negotiations at the United Nations Conference on the Law of the Sea in the seventies. The treaty extended national economic boundaries out to 200 miles from the shoreline—an area that yields more than 90 percent of the ocean's fish catch.

Although more than 70 countries have declared these "exclusive economic zones" (EEZs), that in itself is not enough to protect national fisheries. Developing nations with small navies or coastal patrols are having an especially difficult time enforcing stringent controls on fishing. Vlad Kaczynski, a research associate at the University of Washington's Institute for Marine Studies, finds that West African countries, such as Guinea, Mauritania, and Senegal, are unable to police the predatory trawlers from South Korea, Spain, the Soviet Union, and others. Indonesia hopes to discourage foreign poaching through its recent announcement that illegal fishers will be tried for treason, a crime that carries the death penalty.

Beyond the 200-mile zones, huge trawlers are catching up, reducing, and moving on from one fish species to another. In the northern Pacific, more than 700 Japanese, South Korean, and Taiwanese fishing boats equipped with 20- to 40-mile-long drift nets sweep an area of sea the size of Ohio each night. These vessels ostensibly fish for squid, but all marine life, including fish, mammals, and birds, gets tangled in the nets.

Scientists blame driftnetters for the 1988 crash in the Alaska pink salmon fishery, in which only 12 million fish of an expected 40 million were taken by Alaskans. The vast reach of driftnet ships is also being felt in the southern Pacific, where it is expected that albacore tuna's sustainable yield will be surpassed by as much as 600 percent.

What happens in the open seas can foil even the best efforts to protect native fisheries. When Canada declared a 200-mile zone in 1977, it hoped to regulate a sustainable harvest of Atlantic cod, a species that accounts for nearly one-third of the country's total catch. Since the cod's migration takes it outside Canadian waters, however, foreign fishers continued to prey on the fish; this led to a steep drop in its population. Past errors in estimating the cod's mortality rate haven't helped matters. To compensate, the Canadians ordered cuts in their own cod catches for 1989; they expect further reductions in the future.

With cod supplies down, Pacific Ocean pollock will face more pressure from the Canadian fleet, but that fish already is showing signs of stress from overfishing, particularly in the international waters of the Bering Sea. There, the catch has increased from 100,000 tons in 1984 to 1.3 million tons in 1988—a level that marine scientists think is unbearable.

Fish is becoming a more expensive food source as supply falls behind demand. In the United States, fish prices have more than doubled in real terms since the mid-sixties, while beef and pork have held constant and chicken has declined. Higher prices in the industrial world can and probably will lead to higher prices in, and more exports from, developing countries. In fact, between 1974 and 1987, the volume of fish exported from cash-starved, protein-deficient developing countries nearly quadrupled.

For a world with limited fish stocks, a growing population that needs more protein, and a rising demand for fish in the industrial world, more protein malnutrition among the fish-dependent poor becomes inevitable.

As If That Weren't Enough

Decreased global stratospheric ozone—and an anticipated 5 to 20 percent increase in ultraviolet radiation over the next 40 years—poses another threat to marine life. Too much ultraviolet radiation slows down photosynthesis and growth by phytoplankton and can alter their genetic makeup. Globally, a 2 percent decrease in ozone has occurred, but the Antarctica "ozone hole" gives us an idea of what future losses will lead to. In 1988, Antarctica suffered a 15 percent loss of ozone and a 15 to 20 percent decline in the population of surface phytoplankton. While negligible declines in phytoplankton numbers were recorded below 35 feet, scientists expect impacts as deep as 100 feet in the future.

At stake is the oceanic food chain itself. As ultraviolet radiation increases, changes in the species of algae are bound to follow; ultraviolet-resistant strains will gain and less resistant strains will disappear. The most severe consequences are predicted for tropical and subtropical regions, where the high angle of the sun will allow more ultraviolet radiation to enter.

The seas will also be affected by another global environmental threat—the greenhouse effect. The seas now act as a brake on global warming because they absorb much of the excess heat produced by this phenomenon and capture much of the carbon dioxide that drives it. They store more than 90 percent of the planet's actively cycling carbon and are thought to absorb 45 percent of the carbon dioxide—the prime agent of warming—emitted by the burning of coal and oil. However, scientists are concerned that predicted changes in climate could warm the oceans and eventually alter their circulation and currents, and this, in turn, would alter global climatic patterns.

The oceanic influence on planetary health goes even deeper. A decrease in plankton productivity could accelerate the warming. Via photosynthesis, plankton capture carbon dioxide that otherwise would contribute to the greenhouse effect; they split the carbon molecule from the oxygen, use it as food, and then sink it to the ocean bottom when they die.

The ocean's ability to absorb carbon dioxide already is diminishing, due to increased saturation of surface waters with the gas and to warmer oceanic temperatures. In fact, the U.S. government released findings in April 1989 showing that the oceans warmed at a far faster rate in the eighties than previously anticipated. The greenhouse effect will also cause the seas to expand and rise, creating a 2- to 3-foot increase in sea level by the end of the next century that threatens to flood important estuary and coastal habitats.

STEWARDS OF A SHARED RESOURCE

The steady deterioration of the world's oceans stems largely from the fact that these waters are a huge commons that individual citizens and nations have little incentive to protect. Like the village commons that is overgrazed because it is shared property, the oceans could lose their vitality if governments and international bodies don't soon develop rules and regulations that encourage people to become stewards of a shared resource, rather than plunderers of a common frontier.

The world is in the early stages of a fundamental transition in the way it views and treats the oceans. Since the seventies, a growing array of local, national, and international laws has been adopted to protect the marine resource base. While not all of these efforts have met with immediate success, they have formed an important groundwork for progress in the future.

In the United States, several state governments have taken action to improve the health of coastal waters. In 1987, Maryland, Pennsylvania, Virginia, and the District of Columbia committed themselves to an ambitious and comprehensive program to cut the nutrient discharge into Chesapeake Bay by 40 percent by 2000. The four governments that jointly pollute the Chesapeake have pledged to work toward a toxic-free bay and to achieve an increase in wetland habitats in the region.

Some industrial-country governments are also moving to protect marine habitats. The U.S. Congress, for example, has adopted a goal of "no net loss" of wetlands. The Japanese government, meanwhile, has decided not to construct a controversial airport runway atop the largest blue coral reef in the world.

In developing countries, the connection between marine habitats and the health of fisheries is still being realized, but such awareness could be accelerated with the encouragement of development agencies. In Ecuador, Sri Lanka, and Thailand, for example, the U.S. Agency for International Development is training scientists and fishers to manage wild shrimp stocks and slow the destruction of coastal resources as economic development continues.

One of the most important steps in protecting the oceans is for individual nations to gain better control of their waste streams. As with land-based waste problems, polluted oceans will not become clean until less garbage is produced and the recycling of sewage and other wastes is encouraged. Banning ocean dumping of all wastes by the year 2005 would be a first step.

THE INTERNATIONAL CHALLENGE

The world is also moving to adopt international agreements that manage the oceanic commons. To date, 39 nations have ratified an international treaty known as Annex V of MARPOL, which bans the discharge of plastics by ships. The ban went into effect in January 1989. The London Dumping Convention, signed in 1972, has led to a ban on the dumping of extremely hazardous materials, including radioactive wastes, heavy metals such as cadmium and mercury, and synthetic materials, in the oceans. In 1988, 63 signatories of the London accord also approved a ban on ocean incineration of toxic substances by 1994.

The eight countries bordering the North Sea agreed in 1987 to reduce nutrient and toxic discharges by half by 1995. The Netherlands, West Germany, and Norway are moving ahead to finance improvements in sewage treatment and reduce the agricultural runoff of nitrogen fertilizers. A similar accord has been signed by the seven Baltic Sea nations.

To make these agreements effective, it may be necessary to provide an international transfer of financial resources. The Nordic Investment Bank, for example, is considering providing credits to Poland for reducing discharges of industrial and municipal pollutants into the Baltic. This precedent could be carried over to developing countries, which have been severely constrained in their ability to pay for pollution prevention measures.

In protecting fisheries, the problem of the commons is

particularly evident, since migrating fish move freely between various countries' national waters. The advent of exclusive economic zones offers a promising start at controlling overfishing, since it gives national governments clear responsibility for their own fisheries.

EEZs are a necessary but insufficient condition of fishery regulation, since many governments have failed to enforce compliance with existing controls on fishing. However, governments seem to be taking fishery management more seriously now and the U.S. government has even threatened trade sanctions against Asian countries that allow their fleets to intercept migrating salmon.

"The most significant initial action that nations can take to protect the ocean's threatened life-support system is to ratify the Law of the Sea Convention," says the UN World Commission on Environment and Development. Completed in 1982, the Law of the Sea offers an integrated management regimen, or "constitution," for the world's oceans. It was negotiated with the belief that the seas are "the common heritage" of humanity. Besides the 200-mile exclusive economic zones that entrust most fisheries to national governments, this constitution includes provisions on seabed mineral resources, protection of the marine environment, and navigation rights.

Yet, of the 159 countries that have signed the treaty, only 40 have ratified it; this leaves 20 to go before it can enter into force. Particularly crucial is the support of key nations such as the United States, the United Kingdom, and Germany, which have so far refused to sign or ratify the convention. There is, however, a good chance that recent maritime crises will increase support for the Law of the Sea and lead to new efforts to make it work.

If government leaders do not respond soon, popular concern for the health of the sea may become more strident. Citizens the world over are beginning to demand changes. In 1988, 30,000 people formed a 25-mile chain in Sylt, West

Germany, to protest North Sea pollution; 40,000 volunteers cleaned up beaches in the United States; and as many as 100,000 Estonians, Lithuanians, and Latvians linked hands along the Baltic Sea to call for a cleaner environment. In the United States, an organized campaign led thousands of consumers to mail their EXXON credit cards back to the company following the 1989 oil spill.

These public events demonstrate a growing political backing for better protection of the oceans and a dissatisfaction with the weak policy measures of the past. It's time for governments to hear the message and act.

Mending the Earth's Shield

By Cynthia Pollock Shea

The Montreal Protocol on Substances that Deplete the Ozone Layer was considered a remarkable diplomatic achievement when it was signed by 24 nations in September 1987. The ink had hardly dried, however, when new studies revealed that erosion of this vital shield is occurring far more rapidly and is more widespread than had been anticipated. Indeed, more depletion has already taken place than negotiators assumed would happen in the next 100 years.

Alarming though the latest ozone measurements are, they reflect only the reponse to ozone depleting chemicals— chiefly chlorofluorocarbons (CFCs) and halons—released through the early eighties. Gases now rising to the stratosphere and those contained in millions of appliances will continue to erode the ozone layer for years to come.

As a result, even with the agreement, ozone loss could lead to 5 to 20 percent more ultraviolet radiation reaching populated areas in the next 40 years. Scientists originally believed that between 1969 and 1986 the average concentration of ozone in the stratosphere fell by approximately 2 percent. More accurate measurements from NASA now show that an even greater depletion of 4 to 6 percent in mid-latitude regions has occurred—enough to allow for 8 to 12 percent more radiation to reach the earth's surface. Exposure resulting from an ozone loss of 10 percent would correspond to moving 30 degrees closer in latitude to the equator—like moving New York City to Caracas, Venezuela. The planet's food chains, both on land and in the oceans, could be seriously affected. Human health would also suffer as more people would be afflicted with skin cancer, cataracts, and depressed immune systems.

At the time of its signing, the treaty was so riddled with loopholes that the protocol would not even accomplish its limited objectives of halving CFC consumption by 1998 and freezing halon consumption by 1992. To make matters worse, several chemicals that are major threats to the ozone layer were not regulated by the agreement.

Shortly after the treaty was signed, the U.S. Environmental Protection Agency concluded that even with 100 percent global participation in the protocol, concentrations of chlorine—the ozone destroying component of CFCs—would triple by 2075. The level of halons—used primarily in fire-fighting equipment—would increase even more dramatically. Halons contain bromine, which is a more effective ozone destroyer than chlorine.

Another meeting of the Montreal Protocol was held in June 1990. At the meeting, 93 nations agreed to halt the production of most CFCs by the year 2000. In addition, two commonly used solvents—methyl chloroform and carbon tetrachloride—were added to the list of chemicals restricted by the protocol. Also, an international fund was created to help developing countries acquire the technologies needed to phase out CFC use.

But given the recent NASA data showing greater-than-expected ozone damage, even these measures may not be enough. The technology already exists to do away with CFC and halon emissions almost entirely. The challenge is for governments to muster the political will to do so. The speed with which stricter controls are introduced will determine the extent of ozone depletion in the years ahead.

Our Global Sunscreen

Protecting ozone is so crucial because it is the only gas in the atmosphere that limits the amount of harmful solar ultraviolet radiation reaching the earth. Without it, life on earth would be impossible.

Under normal conditions, chemical reactions triggered by sunlight continuously destroy and replenish ozone. But humanity has upset that balance with the introduction of chlorine- and bromine-containing chemicals that can survive intact in the atmosphere for a century. When these compounds do break down, each chlorine and bromine atom can destroy tens of thousands of ozone molecules.

The life-threatening consequences of ozone depletion are being ushered in by our demand for aerosol spray cans, artificial cooling, soft seat cushions, squeaky-clean computer chips, and space-saving foam insulation. The versatility and low cost of CFCs resulted in their extensive use in these applications before scientists realized the harm that they pose to the ozone layer.

Beside allowing more ultraviolet radiation into the earth's atmosphere, these chemicals prevent infrared radiation from escaping it. Because they are such effective greenhouse gases, they will account for 15 to 20 percent of the global warming that many scientists believe has already started. However, since they are synthetic chemicals for which substitutes exist or can be developed, they are the easiest greenhouse gases to control.

Where to Start Reducing

Chemical substitutes, redesigned technologies and manufacturing processes, and a new approach to equipment maintenance and disposal could obviate the need for ozone depleting chemicals. Some of these measures will be required just to comply with the protocol, but their adoption could be speeded. Moving more quickly to curb emissions requires individual countries to target the largest domestic sources of these chemicals. Global chemical use and emissions are shown in Table 1, but consumption patterns differ widely among nations.

Some chemical uses are easier and less expensive to control than others. Immediate reductions in CFC emissions can be achieved by banning CFC propellants in aerosols and by eliminating the rapid evaporation of chlorine-based cleaning solvents. Intermediate savings are obtainable by capturing the CFC blowing agents that are used to inflate flexible foams, by plugging the leaks in refrigeration and air conditioning systems, and by recovering the refrigerants drained when cooling systems are serviced and repaired. Long-term reductions call for alternative disposal methods for junked appliances, use of substitute chemicals, and development of technologies that do not rely upon ozone-depleting substances.

A track record already exists for making a dent in one CFC use. Back in the seventies, public concern about the ozone layer prompted Canada, Norway, Sweden, and the United States to ban CFC propellants from 90 percent of their aerosol products. Since a majority of CFC-11 and CFC-12 production was used in aerosols, spray cans were an obvious target.

In 1980, the European Community took a similar, but less significant step. It agreed to freeze its production capacity for these two CFCs and to cut back their use in aerosol propellants by 30 percent in two years. Cumulative reductions in CFC-11 and CFC-12 emissions from the United States and the European Community are equal to six years of current CFC-11 production and one year of CFC-12 output.

Denmark banned CFC propellants in 1987, and industries in Belgium, the Netherlands, Switzerland, the United

Our Endangered Earth

TABLE 1   Use and Emissions Profiles of Commonly Used Chemicals, 1985

Chemical	Emissions	Atmospheric Lifetime[1]	Applications	Annual Growth Rate	Share of Contribution to Depletion[2]
	(thousand tons)	(years)		(percent)	(percent)
CFC-12	454	139	Air conditioning, refrigeration, aerosols, foams	5	45
CFC-11	262	76	Foams, aerosols, refrigeration	5	26
CFC-113	152	92	Solvents	10	12
Carbon tetrachloride	73	67	Solvents	1	8
Methyl chloroform	522	8	Solvents	7	5
Halon 1301	3	101	Fire extinguishers	n.a.	4
Halon 1211	79	22	Refrigeration, foams	11	0

[1]Time it takes for 63 percent of the chemical to be washed out of the atmosphere. [2]Total does not add to 100 due to rounding. Contribution of HCFC-22 rounds to zero. *Sources:* U.S. Environmental Protection Agency and Investor Responsibility Research Center.

Kingdom, and West Germany announced they would voluntarily cut back their use of CFC propellants by 90 percent by the end of 1989. British and Swiss manufacturers will also label their products so consumers will know they are "ozone friendly." The Soviet Union has declared its intention to switch to non-CFC aerosol propellants by 1993. The junior member of the CFC family, CFC-113, is now the fastest growing. Because the chemical is used to clean computer chips, metals, and fabrics and is not incorporated into final products, its emissions are some of the easiest and most economical to control. There are strong incentives to recover and recycle this solvent, not the least of which is the fact that it costs about twice as much as other CFCs.

Rapid progress in emissions reductions over the past several years bodes well for more short-term savings in the fight to keep CFCs grounded. Hirotoshi Goto, director of the Stratospheric Protection Program in Japan, expects industries that use CFC solvents in his country to achieve recycling rates of 95 percent. An IBM plant near Stuttgart, West Germany, has installed an on-site recycling system that recovers 70 to 90 percent of the CFCs it uses. Similar rates are being achieved by AT&T in the United States. An option for smaller electronics firms, for whom in-house recycling may be too expensive, is to sell used solvents to commercial recyclers or back to their producer.

MIDTERM SOLUTIONS

The manufacture of flexible foams—to make softer furniture cushions, carpet padding, and automobile seats—also results in the immediate release of CFCs. However, new ventilation systems can recover from 40 to 90 percent of the CFCs that would otherwise get away.

A system operating in both Denmark and Norway traps CFCs at the blowing stage and recovers 40 to 45 percent of total emissions. A more comprehensive system designed by Hyman Development in the United Kingdom is able to recover almost twice as much. By reducing the curing time for flexible foam from several days to 40 minutes and doing so in an enclosed area, virtually all the CFC is captured. Unifoam, a Swiss company, is marketing a similar technology that can recover 85 percent of the blowing agent for reuse.

The refrigeration and air conditioning industry—consumer of half the CFC-12 produced each year—is another source from which emissions could be greatly reduced. Relatively simple housekeeping measures are the first step. Many countries are devising worker training programs and intend to limit maintenance to authorized personnel. Installing leak detection systems is another easy way to curb emissions.

Careful study of the automobile air conditioning market, the largest user of CFCs in the United States, has found that 34 percent of emissions can be traced to leakage, 48 percent occurs during recharge and repair servicing, and the remainder happens through accidents, disposal, and manufacturing, in that order. Designing equipment with better seals and hoses would reduce leaks and require less system maintenance.

Until such equipment is available, however, better maintenance practices are the key to reducing emissions. It is now standard practice when servicing car air conditioners to drain the refrigerant and let it evaporate. Several companies have seen the folly of this approach and designed recovery systems, known as "vampires," that pump coolant out of the compressor, purify it, and reinject it into the automobile. Because coolant generally contains few contaminants, up to 95 percent can be reused. Potential users of the vampires include mass transit companies, airplane manufacturers, government agencies, automobile dealerships, and high-volume car repair stations.

Recovering CFCs from junked automobiles and appliances presents a greater problem. Providing a collection system or offering bounties to scrap dealers may be the answer. Several towns in West Germany have begun collecting discarded household refrigerators to keep CFCs in the coolant and the foam insulation from escaping. The refrigerant will be recycled and the foam will be incinerated in high-temperature furnaces.

Although a few other countries are eyeing this approach, most view it as economical only for large commercial and industrial units, not for the small volumes that would be recovered from household appliances.

CAPABLE UNDERSTUDIES

Over the longer term, phasing out the use and emissions of CFCs will require the development of chemical substitutes that do not harm the ozone layer. The challenge is to find alternatives that perform the same function for a reasonable cost, do not require major equipment modifications, are nontoxic to workers and consumers, and are environmentally benign.

This is a difficult task, but some advances do appear promising. Petroferm, a small company in Fernandina Beach, Florida, has developed a substitute solvent, called BioAct EC-7, made from terpenes found in citrus fruit rinds. The chemical is biodegradable, nontoxic, and noncorrosive. BioAct EC-7 has been tested by AT&T at three of its plants and was found to be effective and economically competitive, even allowing for the cost of replacing machinery. AT&T, which used roughly 1,500 tons of CFC-113 in 1986, expects to displace about one-fourth of its CFC use with BioAct EC-7 in the next two years. An outside analysis estimates that the new compound could substitute for 30 to 55 percent of total projected CFC-113 use in the U.S. electronics industry.

Du Pont and Imperial Chemical Industries (ICI), the world's two largest CFC producers, appear convinced that the replacement chemical for CFC-12 in air conditioners and refrigerators will be chlorine-free HFC-134a. Du Pont is now investing heavily in alternatives. A $25 million plant in

Corpus Christi, Texas, will be the company's fourth and largest facility for producing HFC-134a, and the seventh in the company's overall program to develop CFC alternatives.

Many of the major chemical manufacturers are hoping to find new foam blowing agents among the HCFC family of compounds, whose members—22, 123, 141b, and 142b—have an added hydrogen atom that makes their ozone depleting potential only 5 percent that of the chemicals they would replace. Their cost, on the other hand, would be three to five times greater.

One major delay associated with the commercialization of new chemicals is the need for extensive toxicity testing. To expedite this five- to seven-year process, 14 countries have pooled their efforts in a multimillion-dollar joint testing program. HCFC-22 has already passed; HCFC-123 and HFC-134a are now undergoing tests. Results will be shared among members and, if promising, ought to be passed along to regulatory agencies to speed the approval process.

Ultimately, new product designs may eliminate or reduce the need for CFCs and substitute chemicals. In automobiles, for instance, side vent windows, window glazings that slow solar absorption, and new solar ventilation systems can reduce interior heating and curb or eliminate the need for air conditioning.

Helium-cooled refrigerators, long used for space and military applications, have been adapted for civilian use in trucks and homes. Cryodynamics, a New Jersey–based company, will soon produce 9 million of these refrigerators in Shanghai, China. They have the added benefit of using less than half the energy of conventional appliances.

Rigid-foam insulation in refrigerators and freezers may someday be replaced by vacuum insulation, the type used in thermos bottles. Work done at the U.S. Solar Energy Research Institute in Golden, Colorado, indicates that vacuum panels take up less space than foams and make appliances more energy efficient. Today, the foam walls of a household refrigerator contain five times as much CFC as is used for cooling.

Results of the most current research, as well as new technologies and processes, need to be shared with the developing countries. Ozone depletion is a global problem that requires a coordinated response. Unless the most recent advances are shared with these nations—where CFC emissions are growing the fastest—they will continue to use environmentally damaging equipment for years to come.

THE OTHER CULPRIT

Halons, which contain bromine, are another member of the ozone-destroying team. Although there are no promising substitutes on the horizon, their emissions appear relatively easy to curtail. Because halons are nontoxic and can be applied directly to sensitive equipment without causing damage or leaving a residue, they have become the favored chemical for fighting fires. But most halons never need to be used, they just need to be available in case of an emergency.

At present, halon flooding systems—designed for enclosed areas with valuable contents, such as computer rooms, telephone exchanges, museums, and bank storage vaults—are tested when first installed by releasing all the gas in the system. Discharge testing now contributes more emissions than fire fighting does. Using alternative chemicals or other testing procedures and eliminating accidental discharges would cut annual emissions by two-thirds.

Another large source of halon emissions is fire-fighter training. The U.S. military, with one of the world's biggest programs, has recently introduced the use of simulators that do not require actual chemical release. ICI is establishing a recycling service for halon 1211 so that contaminated supplies, and those that would otherwise be disposed of, can be recovered.

A MODEL APPROACH

The approach taken to reducing CFC and halon emissions varies greatly among nations and industries. The major chemical producers in France, Japan, the United Kingdom, the United States, and Germany have typically viewed emissions controls as a threat to their international competitiveness. They have been loath to go along with unilateral control measures for fear of losing their market share. Companies in Sweden, on the other hand, view the development of alternative products and processes as an economic opportunity. They are poised to seize new international markets in a changing global economy.

Sweden was one of the first countries to pursue aggressively a phaseout of CFCs. In June 1988 the Swedish Parliament passed legislation that includes specific deadlines for banning the use of CFCs in new products. Consumption is to be halved by 1991 and virtually eliminated by 1995.

To meet that deadline, the small quantities of CFCs used as sterilants and aerosol propellants were to be phased out by the end of 1988. Use in packaging materials was to cease in 1989. CFCs used as an engineering solvent and for blowing flexible and extruded polystyrene foams are to be discontinued by 1991. Blow molding of rigid foams and dry-cleaning and coolant uses are to cease by the end of 1994 at the latest. Under no circumstance may CFCs be replaced with chemicals that pose environmental or health hazards.

If it becomes possible to phase out any of these uses sooner, Swedish industries will be required to do so. In the interim, the Swedish government plans to offer incentives and provide financial support for the research and development of recovery and recycling technologies, of alternative products, and of means to keep discarded CFCs from reaching the atmosphere. The latter includes collection systems for coolants and incineration technologies for rigid foams.

Sweden is currently responsible for less than 1 percent of global CFC use, so its approach will have to be adopted by many more countries before a significant dent is made in global emissions.

Levying a tax on newly manufactured CFCs and other ozone-depleting substances is one way governments can cut emissions and accelerate the adoption of alternative chemicals and technologies. If the tax increased in step with mandatory production cutbacks, it would eliminate windfall profits for producers, encourage recovery and recycling processes, stimulate use of new chemicals, and provide a source of funding for new technologies and for needed research. Such a tax already exists in the United States. Promoting investments in recycling networks, incinerators for rigid foams, and collection systems for chemicals that would otherwise be discarded could substantially trim emissions.

Governments may also need to step in and support research on new refrigeration, air conditioning, and insulation processes, because although CFC manufacturers are boosting their spending on chemical substitutes, they have no interest in pursuing alternative product designs that cut into their markets.

PICKING UP THE PACE

Under the Montreal Protocol, a scientific assessment of current ozone depletion occurred from April to August of 1989. This was followed by a meeting of treaty negotiators that strengthened the original protocol. But recent scientific evidence shows that a complete phaseout of ozone-depleting chemicals cannot happen too soon.

Time is of the essence in moving to phase out CFCs, halons, and other ozone depleters. Analysts at EPA examined the effects of a 100 percent CFC phaseout by 1990 and a 95 percent phaseout by 1998. Peak chlorine concentrations under the two scenarios would differ by 0.8 parts per billion—nearly one-third of current levels. With the slower approach, atmospheric cleansing would be delayed considerably; chlorine concentrations would exceed the peak attained with the accelerated schedule for at least 50 years.

The scientific fundamentals of ozone depletion are known. Although models of future change vary in their predictions, the evidence is clear enough to warrant an immediate response. Because valuable time was lost when governments and industries relaxed their regulatory and research efforts during the early eighties, a crash program is now essential.

Most of the control strategies outlined here are already cost-effective, and more will become so as regulations push up the price of ozone-depleting chemicals. How quickly stricter controls are adopted will determine the extent of ozone depletion in the years ahead and when healing of the ozone layer will begin. Human health, food supplies, and the global climate all hinge on putting an end to chlorine and bromine emissions.

2

The Greenhouse Effect

THE HEAT IS ON

By Christopher Flavin

The scene was a cool, air-conditioned U.S. Senate hearing room, but outside, temperatures were soaring through the nineties as Dr. James Hansen began his testimony. Hansen, who directs NASA's Goddard Institute for Space Studies, had a simple message: "Global warming has begun." The date was June 23, 1988, and human-induced global warming had emerged as a threat and public concern that policymakers could no longer ignore.

Only rarely are public-policy turning points so clearly marked. Scientists had accumulated empirical evidence for a phenomenon with the potential to fundamentally alter life on earth. Although much of the key data had been developed and even published in preceding months, Hansen's testimony was more definitive. A sober government scientist was publicly stating his firm conclusion that greenhouse warming is under way.

The senators and reporters present at the hearing were undoubtedly swayed in part by the fact that Washington temperatures that day were oppressively hot, and a devastating drought was searing the Midwest. The harsh summer weather that some areas of the world experienced in 1988 cannot be directly attributed to global warming, but climate scientists now believe that it was typical of the oppressive

conditions likely to become commonplace as early as the
nineties. In later years, conditions could grow far worse. The
summer of 1988 was at minimum a mild preview and timely
reminder of the costs of inaction.

From national news magazines to casual conversations,
the gloomy prospect of hotter summers, recurrent droughts,
more intense hurricanes, and flooded cities has edged into
the public consciousness. Millions of people, many with
only a vague sense of what the "greenhouse effect" is, experienced the uneasy sense of a world out of control and a
human race that is irrevocably altering the very conditions
that made modern societies possible.

Indeed, conditions that are essential to life as we know it
are now at risk. By the middle of the next century, cities
such as New Orleans and Venice could be flooded and abandoned. Intense heat may well cause a vast reversal of sunbelt
migration as people seek out the more temperate regions of
the Yukon and Siberia.

Several decades from now, Bangladesh and the Netherlands may be struggling with vast seawalls to preserve what
little remains of their landscapes. The Maldives, a small,
low-lying nation in the Indian Ocean, could simply cease to
exist. Much of the parched American farmbelt may have
been converted to meager rangeland, with ghost towns
standing as the only reminder of the thriving farm economy
the region once supported.

It remains to be seen whether global anxiety over climate
change can be translated into effective policies to forestall
the looming heat wave. Already, an impressive start has
been made. By 1991, 22 nations had made commitments to
limit emissions of carbon dioxide. The United States, however, not only continues to resist making a national pledge to
reduce emissions, but even fails to recognize the gravity of
the threat.

Only a broad international effort to slow the buildup of
greenhouse gases will be sufficient to protect the climate.

Encouragingly, an international conference sponsored by the government of Canada, and held just days after Hansen's testimony, reached consensus on the urgency of the problem. Negotiations for an international global warming treaty are now in progress and should culminate at the United Nations Conference on Environment and Development to be held in Brazil in 1992.

These stirrings of activity should not lull the world into complacency. Commitment to the issue could fade as quickly as the seasons change. Neither politicians nor ordinary citizens have come to grips with the profound changes in global energy and forestry trends needed to forestall global warming. By comparison, the bitterly contested clean air regulations and water pollution control legislation of the seventies were child's play.

THE GLOBAL HOTHOUSE

The earth's climate is the product of a delicate balance of energy inputs, chemical processes, and physical phenomena. On Venus, a human being's blood would boil. On Mars, a person would instantly freeze to death. This difference in temperatures is largely due to the widely varying chemical compositions of each planet's atmosphere.

All three planets receive huge quantities of solar energy, but the amount of energy that is radiated back into space in the form of heat depends on the gases in the atmosphere. Some gases such as carbon dioxide and methane tend to absorb this heat in the lower atmosphere in the same way that glass traps heat in a greenhouse and allows temperatures to build up.

The scorching temperatures of Venus are the product of an atmosphere that is composed largely of carbon dioxide, which leads to an uncontrolled greenhouse effect. Mars has too little carbon dioxide or other greenhouse gases to support above-freezing temperatures. Earth, on the other hand, has a nitrogen-based atmosphere, only 0.03 percent of which is carbon dioxide—a share that has varied only slightly over the past several million years.

The notion that human activities might disrupt this delicate balance was first proposed by the Swedish chemist Svante Arrhenius in 1896. Coal and other carbon-based fuels, such as oil and natural gas, release carbon dioxide as the basic product of their combustion. Arrhenius theorized that the rapid increase in the use of coal in Europe during the Industrial Revolution would increase carbon dioxide concentrations and cause a gradual rise in global temperatures.

The Swedish chemist's theory gathered dust for six decades; it appeared to be little more than an academic's musings. For one thing, no one was sure whether carbon dioxide concentrations were actually increasing. Then, a 1957 study by the Scripps Institute of Oceanography in California suggested that half the carbon dioxide released was being permanently trapped in the atmosphere. Humanity, stated the study, was "engaged in a great geophysical experiment."

Still, solid evidence was needed. A young graduate student by the name of Charles Keeling was given the task of setting up a carbon dioxide measuring station on the Hawaiian volcano of Mauna Loa to test the pollution-free air in the middle of the Pacific. From 315 parts per million in 1958, Keeling has measured an increase in atmospheric carbon dioxide concentration of 10 percent—to 349 parts per million. Measurements taken from air bubbles trapped in the cores of glacial ice suggest that this is substantially above the highest such concentrations the earth has experienced during the past 160,000 years.

Satellite reconnaissance, improved understanding of the oceans, and more sophisticated computer models have in recent decades greatly deepened understanding of the complex forces at work in the world's climate. However, in a field in which accurate three-day weather forecasts are still elusive, it is hardly surprising that long-term climate trends defy simple analysis.

Among the most effective tools of analysis are the "global circulation models" that run on large computers and simulate the many complex phenomena that make up the global climate. By the early eighties, these models had established a fairly solid consensus about the amount of warming that could be expected if carbon dioxide buildup continues for the next 100 years—and they were surprisingly close to Arrhenius's 1896 prediction.

However, during the eighties disturbing new evidence emerged. Measuring stations reported a steady increase in other even more potent greenhouse gases, notably methane, nitrogen compounds, and chlorofluorocarbons (CFCs). Although each of these exists in the atmosphere in far smaller quantities than does carbon dioxide, their strong heat-absorbing properties mean that together their growth in the atmosphere may have as much greenhouse potential as does carbon dioxide. Further, they are complementary, because they each tend to trap different spectra of thermal radiation.

It now appears that the world is warming at twice the rate projected just five years ago. Scientists believe that by the year 2030 global average temperatures will be between 3 and 8 degrees Fahrenheit higher than they have averaged between 1950 and 1980, or warmer than the earth has been for the past two million years.

THE EVIDENCE MOUNTS

Politicians and the public have largely ignored these warnings. The reason, in essence, is the lack of an obvious record of change—that is until recently. The most compelling evidence offered by James Hansen at the 1988 hearings in Washington was a 108-year series of global average temperature figures that have been assembled by scientists in the United States and Great Britain.

These figures are based on readings taken all over the world and corrected for possible inaccuracies. Although pre-1900 figures are considered somewhat less solid, the overall trend is clear. Whereas the global average temperature in the 1890s was about 58.2 degrees, by the 1980s it had climbed to about 59.4 degrees. While temperatures had leveled off between 1940 and 1970, the accelerating rise of temperatures during the eighties has more than offset this lull (see Figure 1).

Remarkably, six of the seven warmest years since 1850 have all occurred since 1980, and 1990 was the warmest since scientists began measuring the earth's temperature. The chances against this clustering of warm years being a coincidence are overwhelming.

There is an uncanny correlation between the approximately 1 degree warming observed so far and the predictions of the climate models. Other evidence also points to greenhouse warming. The upper atmosphere is becoming cooler

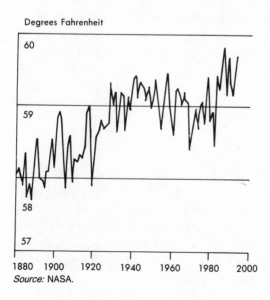

Degrees Fahrenheit

60

59

58

57

1880 1900 1920 1940 1960 1980 2000

Source: NASA.

FIGURE 1
Global
Temperature,
1880–1987.

while the lower atmosphere warms, and temperatures at higher latitudes are increasing faster than they are at the equator, both in accordance with model predictions. Although it is difficult to predict the regional effects or the extent of damage caused by climate change, most scientists agree that the build-up of carbon dioxide in the atmosphere has the potential to be devastating. The Intergovernmental Panel on Climate Change (IPCC), convened by the United Nations in 1988 to review the existing scientific evidence on global warming, confirmed in 1990 that human activities are altering the atmosphere.

The panel's report, prepared by a group of 300 scientists from more than two dozen countries, projects that by the end of the 21st century global average temperature will increase by 5.4 degrees Fahrenheit—a rate of temperature change not seen for tens of thousands of years.

Where Are We Headed?

Some might argue that we are already experiencing climate change. Africa's Sahel has suffered extraordinary drought during much of the past decade. Western North America has had two serious droughts since the late seventies, and eastern North America has had a string of hot summers—as well as some very cold winters—during the eighties. In 1987, India experienced one of the most serious monsoon failures in recent history, and in 1988 China suffered a serious drought.

Weather is by its nature erratic, and there is no solid evidence linking these events to climate change. It is striking, however, that some of the apparent aberrations in recent weather are consistent with the greenhouse predictions of global circulation models. These include hotter summer temperatures and more frequent droughts in central regions of China and North America and cooler conditions in Europe and other coastal areas. Climate scientists estimate that by the nineties, recurrent droughts, heat waves, and other unusual weather may have increased to the point that ordinary citizens are convinced that their climate is changing.

These changes, however, are mild compared with what is expected in later decades. Between the years 2025 and 2050, when greenhouse gas accumulation is projected to be double preindustrial levels, the global average temperature is expected to be up between 3 and 8 degrees. However, midlatitude regions, such as much of Australia, the United States, and China, may experience higher temperature rises than projected for the world as a whole—ranging as high as 8 to 10 degrees.

By then it is anticipated that Washington, D.C., will have an average of 12 days a year with temperatures over 100 degrees, compared with an average of 1 day a year recently. Ninety-degree days will go from an average of 36 per year to 87. Temperature increases in northern Africa and in the Antarctic could exceed 10 degrees. To suggest how severe the consequences of a seemingly small change can be, the coldest average temperature during the last ice age is estimated at just 10 degrees lower than today's.

If permitted to continue, global warming may soon affect economies and societies worldwide. Indeed, it can be compared to nuclear war for its potential to disrupt a wide range of human and natural systems and thus complicate the task of managing economies and coping with other problems. Water supply systems, settlement patterns, and food production could all be badly disrupted by a rapid warming.

One of the dangers of climate change is that its impacts cannot be fully anticipated. A handful of more-extreme hurricanes could kill millions of people. In much of Africa or on the Indian subcontinent, two or three drought years in a row could leave millions on the brink of starvation. Global circulation models are best at forecasting averages, but in the game of climate change, it is not the averages that kill, it is the extremes.

World agriculture, in particular, is closely tied to current weather patterns. In this decade, recurrent droughts could begin to undermine food producing systems in some areas. The long-term prospect is far gloomier. From the U.S. corn crop to China's rice harvest and Africa's subsistence crops, food production could become erratic and ultimately not sustainable at the high levels needed to support a growing population.

Forests and other forms of natural vegetation may also find it difficult to cope with climate change. Trees are adapted to a narrow range of temperature and moisture levels. A global temperature increase of several degrees could be catastrophic; it would shift climatic zones northward by hundreds of miles. If such a change occurred rapidly, there would be no opportunity for tropical forests to adequately supplant temperate ones. The resulting loss of carbon-rich trees could actually accelerate the warming—a sort of climatic death spiral.

Sea level rise is another threat. As the water in the ocean warms, it will expand. In addition, the warming at the poles will reduce the amount of water trapped in glaciers and ice caps. Studies have found that a temperature rise of 6 degrees would increase sea level about 3 feet. This would hurt most in Asia, where rice is produced on low-lying river deltas and floodplains. Without heavy investments in dikes and seawalls to protect the rice fields from saltwater intrusion, such a rise would markedly reduce harvests. Large areas of wetlands that nourish the world's fisheries would also be destroyed.

A rise in sea level would also affect many coastal cities. A 3-foot rise would threaten New Orleans, Cairo, and Shanghai, to cite a few. In Charleston, South Carolina, for example, it is estimated that the cost of adapting to the sea level rise projected for midcentury could reach $1.5 billion. Protecting the entire East Coast could cost as much as $100 billion. But not all countries can afford such an investment. At some point political leaders will have to decide whether to spend massive amounts of capital on dikes and other structures to prevent inundation or to abandon low-lying areas.

In an impassioned address to the UN General Assembly in October 1987, the president of the Maldives described his country as an "endangered nation." With most of its 1,196 islands barely 6 feet above sea level, little of it may be left by the end of the next century. The president poignantly noted, "We did not contribute to the impending catastrophe to our nation and alone we cannot save ourselves."

THE POLICY CHALLENGE

The world *can* save itself, but to do so will require an unprecedented mobilization of resources and a new attitude on the part of all political leaders. There is already a huge momentum behind global warming—exponential energy and population trends are forcing greenhouse gas concentrations ever upward.

Based simply on the greenhouse gases currently in the atmosphere, we are already committed to perhaps a 3-degree increase above current temperatures. But additional gases are entering the atmosphere each year, and the annual increment itself is in many cases growing. Only the highest level of commitment and far-reaching policy changes can now make a meaningful difference.

The issue is not stopping global warming; this will almost certainly not be possible within most of our lifetimes. Rather, the challenge is to slow the production of greenhouse gases immediately, so as to avoid the most sudden and catastrophic climate changes. If trends continue unabated, only radical, draconian measures would be sufficient to save the climate later on. Chlorofluorocarbons, which account for about 15 percent of the annual increment of gases responsible for global warming, are the emissions easiest to eliminate. Used as refrigerants, solvents, and blowing agents for insulation and other plastic foams, CFCs have in recent years become ubiquitous in industrial societies. In addition to warming the earth, these chemicals are destroying the protective ozone layer. For that reason, many countries are in the process of phasing them out and replacing them with substitute chemicals.

Under the Montreal Protocol of 1987, most industrial countries have agreed to phase out CFC production by 2000. This was a good start, but is not enough to protect either the climate or the ozone layer. Global CFC production has been growing at a rate of 30 percent annually, and even today's CFC levels will not be reflected fully in global temperatures for at least a decade. Additional industrial uses of chlorine are compounding the problem.

Global warming cannot be slowed unless all countries, including developing ones that do not currently produce CFCs, join in a commitment to stop production entirely by the late nineties. In addition, it is important that emissions of CFCs from existing refrigerators and air conditioners during servicing be kept to a minimum and that limits be adopted on the production of other chlorine compounds.

Of the carbon dioxide that is being added to the atmosphere, about one-fifth—equal to 10 percent of the additional greenhouse gases—is coming from deforestation in tropical countries. These figures are imprecise at best, but global warming cannot be controlled without an effective strategy to halt rampant deforestation.

In Brazil, Indonesia, and elsewhere, there are vast economic and social pressures pushing human settlements even further into the remaining forests. Broad-based development strategies combined with an infusion of international funding to protect forests and to reforest cleared areas are essential.

Large-scale planting of trees is a relatively inexpensive means of trapping carbon, and is key to protecting the climate. In addition, uncontrolled development in the tropics has to be restrained and alternative livelihoods found for the millions of desperate people who are now forced into destroying forests.

REDIRECTING ENERGY TRENDS

The most serious challenge in controlling global warming lies in reducing dependence on fossil fuels. Today's energy systems are in large measure run on carbon-based fuels that have been buried in the earth for millions of years. When oil, coal, and natural gas are burned, the carbon that makes up the fuels combines with oxygen to form carbon dioxide. Nearly 6 billion tons of carbon are liberated in this way each year, or more than a ton for each person on the planet. Carbon dioxide contributes 40 percent of the gases now warming the atmosphere, while the nitrous oxide and methane liberated from fossil fuels cause additional warming.

The World Conference on the Changing Atmosphere held in Toronto in June 1988 found a need to cut fossil fuel use by 20 percent by 2005, and national policymakers are now considering similar goals. But cuts of such a magnitude will require extraordinary efforts—probably more than politicians yet realize (see Figure 2). Indeed, without policy changes, recent trends suggest that the world is headed toward an 80 percent increase in carbon emissions in the next two decades.

The one thing that could turn this around is a commitment to improved energy efficiency. While new energy sources such as solar or nuclear power take time to develop

FIGURE 2
Carbon Emissions
from Fossil Fuels,
1950–1987

Million tons
of carbon

Source: Oak Ridge National Laboratory.

on a large scale, efficiency can be improved right away. From 1973 to 1986, energy efficiency in the industrial countries increased at such a pace that by the mid-eighties fossil-fuel use and carbon emissions were about 25 percent lower than projected.

Today, there are a host of improved technologies available that use far less energy than those now in place. Today's cars that get just 25 miles per gallon of gasoline can be replaced by ones that get upward of 60 miles per gallon, and 60-watt light bulbs can be replaced by 13-watt bulbs that give as much light. Since much of the world's electricity is generated with coal and other fossil fuels, using electricity more efficiently is especially important.

Most official energy projections assume that worldwide energy efficiency will continue to increase by between 0.5 and 1.0 percent per year. But carbon dioxide buildup is ongoing and cumulative. Even a 1 percent rate of efficiency improvement would allow an increase in atmospheric carbon dioxide from 349 parts per million in 1988 to about 600 parts per million in 2075.

An alternative energy scenario developed by William Chandler, an energy analyst with Battelle Pacific Northwest Laboratories, demonstrates that a successful effort to improve worldwide efficiency by 2 percent annually would hold carbon dioxide concentrations to 463 parts per million in 2075 and thus substantially slow global warming.

Although many nations have implemented effective programs to improve energy efficiency in the past decade, it is generally agreed that higher energy prices were key to the vast improvements that have been made. Now that prices are down, the efficiency revolution is beginning to peter out. In the United States, for example, energy efficiency has hardly improved since 1986.

Therein lies a challenge: how to improve efficiency in a period of low energy prices. One essential step has to be higher energy taxes designed to ensure that climate change and other environmental costs of fossil-fuel use are reflected in the prices that consumers pay. This can be accomplished by excise taxes on gasoline and other fuels or across the board "carbon taxes" on all fossil fuels. Such taxes would hit coal particularly hard, since it produces more carbon per unit of energy than does either oil or natural gas. Electricity prices would rise, but so would conservation.

Large-scale programs to invest in improved efficiency in buildings are also essential. State and local governments can provide building owners with technical assistance and utility companies can be encouraged to invest in improved building efficiency rather than new plants. Also important are a combination of fuel economy standards and financial incentives to encourage the production of much more efficient automobiles. Just by using technologies available today, new cars could achieve an efficiency of at least 45 miles per gallon by the year 2000.

Even while energy efficiency is being improved, there is a clear need to continue the process of developing alternative energy sources. The outlines of a successful strategy already exist. The development of renewable energy—solar, wind, and geothermal power—has been pursued with notable success by governments and private companies since the mid-seventies. Solar collectors are a major source of hot water in Israel, wind power has taken hold in California, and geothermal energy is a major electricity source in the Philippines. However, a general takeoff in renewable energy development has yet to occur, and future advances are threatened by low energy prices and flagging government commitments.

If these energy forms are to serve as a major substitute for fossil fuels within the next decade or two, a renewed commitment to their development will have to be made almost immediately. Accelerated research and development and new programs for commercialization are particularly important.

The other alternative to fossil fuels is nuclear power. Already used to provide about 15 percent of the world's electricity, nuclear power receives strong support from many national governments, and its expansion could reduce fossil-fuel dependence. Unlike renewable energy, however, nuclear power's problems are growing. It has become increasingly expensive and accident prone in the past decade. And the critical problem of disposing of radioactive wastes remains unresolved.

Nuclear power's key obstacle is public acceptability, particularly on the part of those who live near proposed plants. What is indisputable is that for nuclear power to make a real contribution to slowing global warming, hundreds of additional reactors would be needed. Unless the technology were completely revamped, that scale of expansion would be unacceptable.

REVISING NATIONAL ENERGY POLICIES

It was only a few days after Hansen's disturbing testimony that national debates over the world's energy future reopened. Policy analysts, editorial writers, and politicians were soon calling for fundamental changes in direction.

Unfortunately, advocates for everything from nuclear power to hydrogen energy have used this new threat to buttress their old arguments rather than to rethink their prejudices. Old battlelines first established when high oil prices commanded the nation's attention have in many cases been redrawn.

Nonetheless, many countries have begun to consider the possibility of lowering their dependence on fossil fuels. Australia, Austria, Denmark, Germany, and New Zealand have all agreed to meet or go beyond the Toronto goal of reducing carbon dioxide emissions 20 percent by 2005, citing improved energy efficiency and increasing reliance on renewable energy technologies as key policy tools. The European Community and other industrial nations have committed to freezing these emissions.

But the United States remains noticeably absent from the ever-growing list of industrialized countries taking actions to address global warming. In the National Energy Strategy released early in 1991, President Bush failed even to mention the need to reduce reliance on the fossil fuels responsible for carbon dioxide emissions. In fact, the policy document that is meant to guide America's energy future would actually result in an increase in carbon dioxide emissions of 26 percent between 1990 and 2010.

Other energy legislation currently before the U.S. Congress is more promising. Senator Timothy Wirth (D-CO) introduced the National Energy Efficiency and Development Act of 1991. The bill would improve the nation's energy efficiency by encouraging residential, commercial, and industrial efficiency standards, boost funding for renewable energy technologies, and provide tax incentives for efficiency investments—all measures that would tend to limit carbon emissions.

But as the Administration's energy strategy reveals, energy policymaking is often driven by self-interested industries and unions, and some—such as the oil and coal lobbies—have long pushed for policies that accelerate global warming. Key legislative committees are dominated by representatives of states and provinces that produce fossil fuels; many of the laws and tax breaks that emerge are intended to propel their growth. The tendency is simply to add global warming to a long list of considerations that go into making energy policy.

This is not enough. If the climate is to be preserved, it must become the cornerstone of national energy policymaking. Fortunately, most of the changes needed are in the long-run economical and, so, can promote national economic strength as well. But if energy policymaking continues to be the domain of short-term thinking and narrow political considerations, we should all probably begin packing for Alaska.

What would a serious commitment to slowing global warming look like? It would logically include a worldwide commitment to 50-mile-per-gallon automobile fleets, and an effort to gradually phase out coal-fired power production by improving efficiency and developing renewable energy sources. Worldwide spending on solar energy technologies could be expanded tenfold, with the goal of making it the energy source of choice for villages and suburbs by the end of the century.

A COMMON PROBLEM

In his 1970 essay "The Tragedy of the Commons," Garrett Hardin noted the enormous difficulty that people have in managing resources whose ownership is communal or poorly defined. Like the village commons that is prone to overgrazing, so today are oceans, international rivers, and the atmosphere subject to all forms of abuse. The undermining of the global climate is in some sense the ultimate tragedy of the commons. No individual nation can stop it, and we will all face the tragic consequences of failing to act (see Table 1).

If climate change is to be controlled, international action may have to precede rather than follow national actions. Already, business and political leaders are arguing against stringent national policies on the grounds that by themselves they would hardly make a difference. This is particularly true for small nations that understandably perceive themselves as impotent in the face of global changes caused for the most part by the actions of their larger neighbors.

Country	Carbon	Carbon per Capita	Carbon per Dollar GNP
	(million tons)	(tons)	(grams)
U.S.A.	1,224	2.28	276
U.S.S.R.	1,014	1.62	427
W. Europe	792	.94	178
China	555	.24	1,892
Japan	248	.92	154
India	150	.09	652
Canada	106	1.85	239
World	5,311	1.06	311

TABLE 1
Carbon Emissions from Fossil Fuels, Selected Countries, 1987

Source: Oak Ridge National Laboratory.

The first step in dealing with this issue globally is scientific cooperation. Already, the World Meteorological Organization and the International Council of Scientific Unions have been conducting research and coordinating international discussions on climate change for several years. Climate scientists now meet on a regular basis to assess research results and to consider policy options. At a meeting in Bellagio, Italy, in November 1987, a clear consensus was reached about the looming threat of global climate change and the need to initiate frank policy discussions.

The process of formulating an international policy response began in earnest in June 1988 at the World Conference on the Changing Atmosphere, held in Toronto and sponsored by the Canadian government. Although not a formal conference of governments, the Toronto meeting included the prime ministers of Canada and Norway and the top environmental officials of several other countries. The final statement of the conference concluded with a strong call to international action.

The conference statement went on to recommend more ambitious efforts to phase out CFCs and to reduce global carbon emissions by 20 percent by the year 2005. Half of this reduction is to be achieved via improved energy efficiency and half by the development of new energy sources.

If such goals are to be achieved, they must first be formalized in an international treaty. The Montreal Protocol on ozone protection provides a model for such an effort, as does the United Nations-sponsored Convention on Long-Range Transboundary Air Pollution, agreed to by 34 nations in Eastern and Western Europe and North America in 1979. However, for a global warming treaty to be effective, it must be far broader in scope and include additional nations.

In December 1990 a United Nations General Assembly resolution set in motion a negotiating process that could result in a global warming treaty to be signed at the 1992 United Nations Conference on Environment and Development held in Brazil. The first meeting of the Intergovernmental Negotiating Committee, set up to draft the treaty, took place near Washington, D.C., in February 1991. So far, the complex and contentious discussions involving countries of vastly different economic backgrounds have moved slowly. While European nations argue for a strong detailed treaty, the U.S. government is still playing a game of delay.

Developing countries argue that if they are going to improve efficiency vastly and reforest millions of acres, they will need funding from richer nations. One possible solution would be to create an international fund that invests in energy efficiency and reforestation, paid for by an excise tax on fossil-fuel consumption in the industrial countries.

Although the first negotiating meeting did not tackle the substantive issues of reducing greenhouse gas emissions, a treaty process is now underway. The United States, to date, has consistently opposed binding commitments to carbon reductions. But the Administration must now face growing evidence that carbon reductions are economically feasible: the release in early 1991 of two studies by the National Academy of Sciences and the Congressional Office of Technology Assessment that point out the need to adopt cost-effective steps to reduce greenhouse gas emissions.

Bringing the nations of the world together to redirect their energy policies, to reforest their landscapes, and to spend millions of dollars on protecting the atmosphere may seem impossible. But there really isn't any choice. Global warming is an environmental threat on a new scale. Like the religious notion of original sin, climate change will loom as a continuing threat for humanity to consider and ultimately to manage.

3

Making a Mess

YOU ARE WHAT YOU BREATHE

By Hilary F. French

Asked to name the world's top killers, most people wouldn't put air pollution high on their lists. A nuisance, at best, but not a terribly serious threat to health.

The facts say otherwise. In greater Athens, for example, the number of deaths rises sixfold on heavily polluted days. In Hungary, the government attributes 1 in 17 deaths to air pollution. In Bombay, breathing the air is equivalent to smoking 10 cigarettes a day. And in Beijing, air-pollution-related respiratory distress is so common that it has been dubbed the "Beijing Cough."

Air pollution is truly a global public health emergency. United Nations statistics show that more than one billion people—a fifth of humanity—live in areas where the air is not fit to breathe. Once a local phenomenon primarily affecting city dwellers and people living near factories, air pollution now reaches rural as well as urban dwellers. It's also crossing international borders.

In the United States alone, roughly 150 million people live in areas whose air is considered unhealthy by the Environmental Protection Agency (EPA). According to the American Lung Association, this leads to as many as 120,000 deaths each year.

A century ago, air pollution was caused primarily by the

coal burned to fuel the industrial revolution. Since then, the problem and its causes have become more complex and widespread. In some parts of the world, including much of Eastern Europe and China, coal continues to be the main source of pollution. Elsewhere, automobiles and industries are now the primary cause.

Adding to the miasma, industries are emitting pollutants of frightening toxicity. Millions of tons of carcinogens, mutagens, and poisons pour into the air each year and damage health and habitat near their sources and, via the winds, sometimes thousands of miles away. Many regions that have enjoyed partial success combating pollution are finding their efforts overwhelmed as populations and economies grow and bring in more power plants, home furnaces, factories, and motor vehicles.

Meanwhile, global warming has arisen as the preeminent environmental concern; this sometimes conveys the misleading impression that conventional air pollution is yesterday's problem. But air pollutants and greenhouse gases stem largely from fossil fuels burned in energy, transportation, and industrial systems. Having common roots, the two problems can also have common solutions. Unfortunately, policymakers persist in tackling them separately, which runs the risk of lessening one while exacerbating the other.

Air pollution has proven so intractable a phenomenon that a book could be written about the history of efforts to combat it. Law has followed law. As one problem has largely been solved, a new one has frequently emerged to take its place. Even some of the solutions have become part of the problem: The tall smokestacks built in the 1960s and 1970s to disperse emissions from huge coal-burning power plants became conduits to the upper atmosphere for the pollutants that form acid rain.

Turning the corner on air pollution requires moving beyond patchwork, end-of-the-pipe approaches to confront pollution at its sources. This will mean reorienting energy, transportation, and industrial structures toward prevention.

CHEMICAL SOUP

Although air pollution plagues countries on all continents and at all levels of development, it comes in many different varieties. The burning of fossil fuels—predominantly coal— by power plants, industries, and home furnaces was the first pollution problem recognized as a threat to human health. The sulfur dioxide and particulate emissions associated with coal burning—either alone or in combination—can raise the incidence of respiratory diseases such as coughs and colds, asthma, bronchitis, and emphysema. Particulate matter (a general term for a complex and varying mixture of pollutants in minute solid form) can carry toxic metals deep into the lungs.

Pollution from automobiles forms a second front in the battle for clean air. One of the worst auto-related pollutants is ozone, the principal ingredient in urban smog. Formed when sunlight causes hydrocarbons (a by-product of many industrial processes and engines) to react with nitrogen oxides (produced by cars and power plants), ozone can cause serious respiratory distress. Recent U.S. research suggests that ground-level ozone causes temporary breathing difficulty and long-term lung damage at lower concentrations than previously believed.

Other dangerous pollutants spewed by automobiles include nitrogen dioxide, carbon monoxide, lead, and such toxic hydrocarbons as benzene, toluene, xylene, and ethylene dibromide (see Table 1).

At elevated levels, nitrogen dioxide can cause lung irritation, bronchitis, pneumonia, and increased susceptibility to viral infections such as influenza. Carbon monoxide can interfere with the blood's ability to absorb oxygen; this im-

TABLE 1   Health Effects of Pollutants from Automobiles[1]

Pollutant	Health Effect
Carbon monoxide	Interferes with blood's ability to absorb oxygen impairs perception and thinking; slows reflexes; causes drowsiness; and so can cause unconsciousness and death; if inhaled by pregnant women, may threaten growth and mental development of fetus.
Lead	Affects circulatory, reproductive, nervous, and kidney systems; suspected of causing hyperactivity and lowered learning ability in children; hazardous even after exposure ends.
Nitrogen oxides	Can increase susceptibility to viral infections such as influenza. Can also irritate the lungs and cause bronchitis and pneumonia.
Ozone	Irritates mucous membranes of respiratory system; causes coughing, choking, and impaired lung function; reduces resistance to colds and pneumonia; can aggravate chronic heart disease, asthma, bronchitis, and emphysema.
Toxic emissions	Suspected of causing cancer, reproductive problems, and birth defects. Benzene is a known carcinogen.

[1]Automobiles are a primary source, but not the only source, of these pollutants.
Sources: National Clean Air Coalition and the U.S. Environmental Protection Agency.

pairs perception and thinking, slow reflexes, and causes drowsiness and—in extreme cases—unconsciousness and death. If inhaled by a pregnant woman, carbon monoxide can threaten the fetus's physical and mental development.

Lead affects the circulatory, reproductive, nervous, and kidney systems. It is suspected of causing hyperactivity and lowered learning ability in children. Because it accumulates in bone and tissue, it is hazardous long after exposure ends.

Concern is growing around the world about the health threat posed by less common but extremely harmful airborne toxic chemicals such as benzene, vinyl chloride, and other volatile organic chemicals produced by automobiles and industries. These chemicals can cause a variety of illnesses, such as cancer and genetic and birth defects, yet they have received far less regulatory attention around the world than have "conventional" pollutants.

WHERE THE BREATHING ISN'T EASY

With the aid of pollution control equipment and improvements in energy efficiency, many Western industrialized countries have made significant strides in reducing emissions of sulfur dioxide and particulates. The United States, for example, cut sulfur oxides emissions by 28 percent between 1970 and 1987 and particulates by 62 percent (see Figure 1). In Japan, sulfur dioxide emissions fell by 39 percent from 1973 to 1984.

The same cannot be said for Eastern Europe and the Soviet Union, where hasty industrialization after World War II, powered by abundant high-sulfur brown coal, has led to some of the worst air pollution ever experienced. Pollution control technologies have been virtually nonexistent. And, because of heavily subsidized fuel prices and the absence of market forces governing production, these countries never made the impressive gains in energy efficiency registered in the West after the oil shocks of the 1970s.

Many developing countries also confront appalling air pollution problems. The lack of adequate pollution control technologies and regulations, plus plans to expand energy and industrial production, translates into worsening air quality in many cities. Urbanization in much of the Third World means that increasing numbers of people are exposed to polluted city air.

A 1988 report by the United Nations Environment Pro-

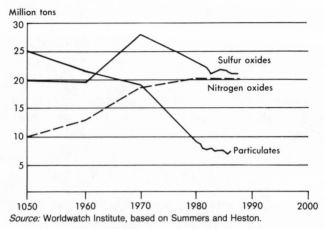

Source: Worldwatch Institute, based on Summers and Heston.

FIGURE 1   Emissions of Selected Pollutants in the United States, 1950–1987.

gram (UNEP) and the World Health Organization (WHO) gives the best picture to date of the global spread of sulfur dioxide and particulate pollution (see Table 2). Of the 54 cities with data available on sulfur dioxide pollution for 1980 to 1984, 27 were on the borderline or in violation of the WHO health standard.

High on the list were Shenyang, Tehran, and Seoul, as well as Milan, Paris, and Madrid; this indicates that sulfur dioxide problems have by no means been cured in industrial countries. Though conditions are gradually improving in most of the cities surveyed, several in the Third World reported a worsening trend.

Suspended particulate matter poses an even more pervasive threat, especially in the developing world, where the appropriate control technologies have not been installed and conditions are frequently dusty. Fully 37 of the 41 cities monitored for particulates averaged either borderline or excessive levels. Annual average concentrations were as much

TABLE 2   Violations of Sulfur Dioxide and Suspended
Particulate Matter Standards, Selected Cities[1]

City	Sulfur Dioxide	Particulates[2]
	(number of days above WHO standard)	
New Delhi	6	294
Xian	71	273
Beijing	68	272
Shenyang	146	219
Tehran	104	174
Bangkok	0	97
Madrid	35	60
Kuala Lampur	0	37
Zagreb	30	34
Sao Paulo	12	31
Paris	46	3
New York	8	0
Milan	66	n.a.
Seoul	87	n.a.

[1]Averages of readings at a variety of monitoring sites from 1980 to 1984.
[2]For Madrid, Sao Paulo, and Paris, the reading is of smoke rather than particulates.
Source: United Nations Environment Program and World Health Organization, *Assessment of Urban Air Quality* (Nairobi: Global Environment Monitoring System, 1988).

as five times the WHO standard in both New Delhi and Beijing.

Ozone pollution, too, has become a seemingly intractable health problem in many parts of the world. In the United States, 1988 ushered in one of the hottest and sunniest years on record, and also one of the worst for ground-level ozone in more than a decade. According to the Natural Resources Defense Council, the air in New York City violated the federal health standard on 34 days—two to three times a week, all summer long. In Los Angeles, ozone levels surged above the federal standard on 172 days. At last count 382 counties, home to more than half of all Americans, were out of compliance with the EPA ozone standard.

Ozone is becoming a problem elsewhere, too. In Mexico City, the relatively lenient government standard of a one-hour ozone peak of 0.11 parts per million not to be exceeded more than once daily is topped more than 300 days a year—nearly twice as often as Los Angeles violates its much stricter standard.

The other automobile-related pollutants also constitute a far-flung health threat. The WHO/UNEP report estimates that 15 to 20 percent of urban residents in North America and Europe are exposed to unacceptably high levels of nitrogen dioxide, 50 percent to unhealthy carbon monoxide concentrations, and a third to excessive lead levels. In a study in Mexico City, lead levels in the blood of 7 out of 10 newborns were found to exceed WHO standards. "The implication for Mexican society, that an entire generation of children will be intellectually stunted, is truly staggering," says Mexican chemist and environmental activist Manuel Guerra.

Airborne toxic chemical emissions present no less of a danger. In the United States, the one country that has begun to tally total emissions, factories reported 1.3 million tons of hazardous emissions in 1987, including 118,000 tons of carcinogens. According to the EPA, these emissions cause about 2,000 cancer deaths a year.

These deaths fall disproportionately on certain communities. For example, in West Virginia's Kanawha Valley—home to a quarter of a million people and 13 major chemical plants—state health department records show that, between 1968 and 1977, the incidence of respiratory cancer was more than 21 percent above the national average. According to EPA statistics, a lifetime of exposure to the airborne concentrations of butadiene, chloroform, and ethylene oxide in this valley could cause cancer in 1 resident in 1,000.

Unfortunately, data are not so extensive for other countries. Wherever uncontrolled polluting industries such as chemical plants, smelters, and paper mills exist, however, emission levels are undoubtedly high. Measurements of lead and cadmium in the soil of the upper Silesian towns of Olkosz and Slawkow in Poland, for instance, are among the highest recorded anywhere in the world.

The health damage inflicted by air pollution comes at great human cost; it also carries an economic price tag. The American Lung Association estimates that air pollution costs the United States $40 billion annually in health care and lost productivity.

CLEARING THE AIR

In the Western industrial world, the last 20 years has been a period of intense political and scientific activity aimed at restoring clean air. The approaches to date, however, have tended to be technological Band-Aids rather than efforts to address the roots of the problem.

Scrubbers, nitrogen-oxides control technologies, and new cleaner-burning coal technologies can all reduce emissions dramatically, but they are not the ultimate solutions. For one, they can create environmental problems of their own, such as the need to dispose of scrubber ash, a hazardous waste. Second, they do little if anything to reduce carbon dioxide emissions, so make no significant contribution to slowing global warming.

For these reasons, technologies of this kind are best viewed as a bridge to the day when energy-efficient societies are the norm and pollution-free sources such as solar, wind, and water power provide the bulk of the world's electricity.

Improving energy efficiency is a clean air priority. Such measures as more-efficient refrigerators and lighting can markedly and cost-effectively reduce electricity consumption; this will in turn reduce emissions. Equally important, the savings that result from not building power plants because demand has been cut by efficiency can more than offset the additional cost of installing scrubbers at existing plants.

Using conservative assumptions, the Washington, D.C.–based American Council for an Energy Efficient Economy concluded that cutting sulfur dioxide emissions steeply with a scrubbers/conservation combination could actually save consumers in the Midwest up to $8 billion.

Similar rethinking can help reduce auto emissions. To date, modifying car engines and installing catalytic converters have been the primary strategies employed to lower harmful emissions. These devices reduce hydrocarbon emissions by an average of 87 percent, carbon monoxide by an average of 85 percent, and nitrogen oxides by 62 percent over the life of a vehicle. Although catalytic converters are sorely needed in countries that don't require them, they alone are not sufficient. Expanding auto fleets are overwhelming the good they do, even in countries that have mandated their use.

Alternative fuels, such as methanol, ethanol, natural gas, hydrogen, and electricity, are being pushed by many governments as the remedy for the air pollution quagmire. Although these fuels may have some role to play eventually, they can by no means be viewed as a panacea.

Reducing air pollution in cities is likely to require a major shift away from automobiles as the cornerstone of urban transportation systems. As congestion slows traffic to a crawl in many cities, driving to work is becoming unattractive anyway. Convenient public transportation, car pooling, and measures that facilitate bicycle commuting are the cheapest, most effective ways for metropolitan areas to proceed.

Driving restrictions already exist in many of the world's cities. For example, Florence has turned its downtown into a pedestrian mall during daylight hours. Budapest bans motor traffic from all but two streets in the downtown area during particularly polluted spells. In Mexico City and Santiago, one-fifth of all vehicles are kept off the streets each weekday based on their license-plate numbers.

As with power plant and auto emissions, efforts to control airborne toxic chemicals will be most successful if they focus on minimizing waste rather than simply on controlling emissions. Such a strategy also prevents waste from being shifted from one form to another. For instance, control technologies such as scrubbers and filters produce hazardous solid wastes that must be disposed on land.

The Congressional Office of Technology Assessment has concluded it is technically and economically feasible for U.S. industries to lower production of toxic wastes and pollutants by up to 50 percent within the next few years. Similar possibilities exist in other countries.

Freedom of environmental information can also be a powerful regulatory tool. In the United States, "right-to-know" legislation requiring industries to release data on their toxic emissions has been instrumental in raising public awareness of the threat and spurring more responsible industrial behavior. The Monsanto Company, a major chemical producer, was so embarrassed by the enormous pollution figures it was required to release in 1989 that it simultaneously announced its intention to cut back emissions 90 percent by 1992.

Few European countries have released information about emissions from industrial plants, although that may change if the European Economic Community (EEC) issues a directive now in draft form on freedom of information regarding environmental matters. The recent political transformation in Eastern Europe and the Soviet Union are gradually improving the environmental data flow, although much progress in this area remains to be made.

SOLUTION FROM SMOG CITY

In most parts of the world, air pollution is now squarely on the public policy agenda. This is a promising sign. Unfortunately, the public's desire for clean air has not yet been matched with the political leadership needed to provide it. Recent developments at the national and international levels, though constituting steps forward, remain inadequate to the task.

In the United States, for example, recent major amendments to the Clean Air Act of 1970 will cut acid rain emissions in half, tighten emissions standards for automobiles significantly, and require much stricter control of toxic air pollutants.

Almost any legislation would be an improvement. Twenty years after the act became law, 487 counties still are not in compliance. But the legislation fails to address the problem at a fundamental level by not encouraging energy efficiency, waste reduction, and a revamping of transportation systems and urban designs.

Los Angeles—with the worst air quality in the United States—is one of the first regions in the world to really understand that lasting change will not come through mere tinkering. Under a bold new air-quality plan embracing the entire region, the city government will discourage automobile use, boost public transportation, and control household and industrial activities that contribute to smog.

For example, paints and solvents will have to be reformulated to produce fewer ozone-forming fumes; gasoline-powered lawn mowers and lighter fluid will be banned; carpooling will be mandated; and the number of cars per family limited. Even though the plan has been approved by all of the relevant state and federal agencies, implementing it at the local level will be a challenge.

Most of Europe, though quicker than the United States

to cut back sharply on the emissions that cause acid rain, has been slower to tackle urban air quality. Non-EEC countries such as Austria, Norway, Sweden, and Switzerland have had strong auto emissions control legislation in place for several years, but until recently the EEC had been unable to agree on its own stringent standards.

This finally changed in June 1989, when the EEC Council of Environmental Ministers ended a nearly four-year debate and approved new standards for small cars. These will be as tough as those now in effect in the United States. To meet them, small cars will have to be equipped with catalytic converters. Although an important step forward, it's somewhat ironic that Europe sees its adoption of U.S. standards as a major victory at the same time the United States realizes these regulations don't go far enough.

In Eastern Europe and the Soviet Union, air pollution emerged as a pressing political issue as *glasnost* and the revolutions of 1989 opened up public debate. Air pollution in much of the region is taking a devastating toll on human health. Fledgling governments in Eastern Europe are under pressure to show some improvements.

A HELPFUL HAND

To make a dent in their pollution, Eastern Europe and the Soviet Union will need Western technologies and a dose of domestic economic and environmental reform. Given current economic conditions in these countries, money for purchasing pollution control, energy efficiency, renewable energy, and waste reduction technologies will have to come in part in the form of environmental aid from the West.

Aid of this kind can be classified as enlightened philanthropy, since stemming pollution in Eastern Europe, where even rudimentary controls are still lacking, can yield a far greater return on the investment than taking further incremental steps at home. To illustrate this point, Sweden receives 89 percent of the sulfur that contributes to the acid rain poisoning its lakes and forests from other countries. Because much of this is of Eastern European origin, anything Sweden does to combat emissions there helps at home.

Air pollution is beginning to emerge on the political agenda in the Third World as well. In Cubatão, Brazil, a notoriously polluted industrial city known as "the Valley of Death," a five-year-old government cleanup campaign is starting to make a dent in the problem. Total emissions of particulates, for instance, were cut from 521,600 pounds a day in 1984 to 156,000 in 1989.

Mexico City, too, is embarking on an ambitious cleanup. With the support of the World Bank, Japan, the United States, and West Germany, the municipal government is introducing a package of measures aimed at cutting automotive pollution dramatically over the next two to three years. As part of the plan, driving will be restricted on certain days. In March 1991, Mexican President Carlos Salinas de Gortari ordered the shutdown of a large oil refinery on the outskirts of Mexico City that has long been a major contributor to the city's pollution problem.

Industrial countries are involved in a variety of efforts to assist developing countries with air pollution problems. The International Environmental Bureau in Switzerland and the World Environment Center in New York City help facilitate transfer of pollution control information and technology to the Third World. The World Bank is exploring ways to step up its air pollution control activities. One proposed project involving the World Bank and the UN Development Program would help Asian governments confront urban air pollution, among other environmental problems.

Legislation passed by the U.S. Congress requires the Agency for International Development to encourage energy efficiency and renewable energy through its programs in the interests of slowing global warming. This step will reduce air pollution at the same time.

While the means are available to clear the air, it will be a difficult task. In the West, powerful businesses such as auto manufacturers and electric utilities will strongly resist measures that appear costly. In Eastern Europe, the Soviet Union, and the developing world, extreme economic problems coupled with shortages of hard currency mean that money for pollution prevention and control is scarce.

Overcoming these barriers will require fundamental modifications of economic systems. As long as air pollution's costs remain external to economic accounting systems, utilities, industries, and individuals will have little incentive to reduce the amount of pollution they generate. Taxes, regulations, and public awareness can all be harnessed to bring the hidden costs of air pollution out into the open.

On the promising side, faced with mounting costs to human health and the environment, people on every continent are beginning to look at pollution prevention through a different economic lens. Rather than a financial burden, they're seeing that it is a sound investment. The old notion that pollution is the price of progress seems finally to be becoming a relic of the past.

Eastern Europe's Clean Break With the Past

By Hilary F. French

As the Iron Curtain opened during the heady months of autumn 1989, it revealed a land laid to waste by industrial pollution—and a citizenry up in arms over the damage. Environmental outrage ran so high that it helped topple governments in several countries. Now that the initial euphoria of freedom has passed, the region's new leaders must grapple with the legacy of past environmental neglect.

The task is daunting. Under the assault of air pollution and acid deposition, Eastern Europe's medieval cities are blackened and crumbling, whole hillsides are deforested, and crop yields are falling. Rivers serve as open sewers, and clean drinking water is in short supply. Life expectancies in the dirtiest parts of the region are as much as five years shorter, and rates of cancer, reproductive problems, and other ailments far higher than in relatively clean areas.

Restoring Eastern Europe's environment will be a massive undertaking; estimates for cleaning up eastern Germany alone run as high as $300 billion. Given the other economic and social challenges the region faces, focusing on the environment will be difficult.

But the environment and the economy in this region—as everywhere—are inextricably joined. Workers cannot be fully productive if they are made ill by the air they breathe and the water they drink, and harvests cannot be maximized if plants are stunted or killed by pollution. For the countries of Eastern Europe to recover and eventually prosper, environmental reconstruction must be viewed as an integral part of political and economic reform.

THE ROOTS OF THE PROBLEM

Eastern Europe's ecological disaster stems from a set of endemic problems—ranging from the peculiarities of its resource base to the legacies of four decades of Communist rule—that complicate any recovery effort. Leaders inside and outside the region must fully understand these limitations if environmental restoration is to succeed.

The first problem is that much of Eastern Europe is burdened by a reliance on lignite, also known as brown or soft coal, to drive its economies. Relative to hard coal, which is common to Western Europe and the United States, lignite is a poor fuel—more of it has to be burned to heat a room or drive a steam turbine. To compound the problem, Eastern European lignite is high in sulfur. Bulgaria, Czechoslovakia, the former East Germany, and Poland each emit at least five times as much sulfur dioxide per unit of economic output as does the United States, and 20 times as much as the former West Germany. The result is air pollution and acid rain that blackens buildings, kills trees, and shortens lives. Before reunification, East Germany relied on brown coal for 72 percent of its energy consumption, and Czechoslovakia today relies on it for 41 percent.

Second, Eastern Europe was handicapped by central planning. High government subsidies and lack of competition meant industries and individuals had no incentive to conserve energy, water, or materials. The extremely inefficient use of energy is a particular problem—the more energy burned, the worse the air pollution and carbon dioxide emissions. The Soviet Union and East European countries generally use 50 to 100 percent more energy than the United States to produce a dollar of gross national product and 100 to 300 percent more than Japan.

Third, the region suffers environmentally from the heavy-industry orientation of its economies. Chemicals, metallurgy, and other polluting industries were built at breakneck speed in the post-World-War-II period, but the region has since failed to modernize its equipment or follow the West in the shift toward a less-polluting service economy. Industry comprises more than 50 percent of the economic base in Eastern Europe; services make up less than a quarter. In Sweden, by contrast, industry makes up only 32 percent of the total and services 65 percent, a pattern repeated in other Western countries.

Fourth, pollution control in the region is in its infancy. In many cases, control technologies such as power plant scrubbers and sewage treatment devices are nonexistent. Those domestically produced technologies that are employed are inferior to Western versions, and hard currency shortages generally preclude imports from the West. Without pollution controls, the region's aging factories produce prodigious quantities of air and water pollution and toxic waste. For example, a chemical plant in Halle, in eastern Germany, discharges as much mercury in one day into nearby rivers as a comparable plant in the western part of the country spews in a year.

Finally, political repression took an environmental toll. Lack of public accountability shielded governments from scrutiny and criticism as they polluted at will. Until recently, independent organizing was strictly illegal throughout the region, and environmental information remained top secret. As recently as November 1987, secret police in East Berlin raided an environmental library set up by the Lutheran Church and confiscated printed material and duplicating equipment.

COSTS AND BENEFITS

With Eastern European economies teetering on the brink of collapse, many people wonder how the countries of the region can afford to clean up. According to the German Institute of Ecological Economic Research, bringing eastern Germany's environment up to the new Germany's standards will be a 10-year, $249- to $308-billion effort. Poland and Czechoslovakia believe they will need to spend more than $20 billion apiece during the next few decades. Raising even these more modest sums will be difficult.

However, the situation is not as bleak as these numbers imply. For one thing, environmental improvements will be an outgrowth of economic changes such as the shift to market-oriented economies and the arrival of Western investment. Under the sway of these forces, new investment in less-polluting service and information industries will eventually lead to the replacement of polluting factories. The need to show a profit will help encourage energy efficiency and waste reduction.

Even direct investment in pollution control and cleanup can have economic rewards. In the United States, for example, the pollution control industry employs nearly 3 million people and generates $98 billion in revenue, according to Management Information Services, Inc., a Washington, D.C.-based economic consulting firm. To reap similar benefits, countries in Eastern Europe will need to establish their own environmental protection industries.

Though cleaning up may be expensive, the costs of inaction are greater—and mounting. Polish economists estimate that pollution-inflicted damage to health, agriculture, forestry, and buildings costs the country some 10 percent of its GNP every year; the Czechoslovakian Environment Ministry says that environmental degradation there exacts an economic penalty equal to 5 to 7 percent of economic output.

Decontaminating Eastern Europe is thus best seen as a pre-condition to economic recovery, not an obstacle.

LESSONS FROM THE WEST

Eastern Europe has a unique opportunity to "leapfrog" the West by implementing only the most successful Western environmental strategies and sidestepping those that didn't work. Additionally, as obsolete factories are closed down, they can be replaced by modern plants that produce a mini-mum of pollution.

One strategy that should be actively pursued is boosting energy efficiency in homes, offices, and factories. The less energy burned, the less pollution produced. The savings from not having to build new power plants can help finance the installation of scrubbers and other pollution control technologies on existing ones.

A degree of improvement in energy efficiency will natu-rally occur as Eastern nations move toward a greater reliance on markets. The profit motive and higher energy prices brought on by the removal of energy subsidies will spur conservation, pushing energy-hungry heavy industries to take aggressive actions to replace outmoded equipment with more efficient technologies and spurring residents to turn down the heat if their apartments are outfitted with thermo-stats. But more than market pricing will be necessary for efficiency to fulfill its promise. The governments of the re-gion will need to reform the way utilities do business so that it's in their interest to save energy. They will also need to set efficiency standards for appliances, automobiles, and other equipment.

In the industrial arena, Western experience has taught that eliminating pollution in the production process is often both environmentally and economically advantageous over trapping it at the end of a pipe or smokestack. The 3M Com-pany of St. Paul, Minnesota, for example, cut its waste generation in half over a 15-year period, saving nearly $300 million in the process. The company's waste reduction program annually prevents the creation of 100,000 tons of air pollution, 275,000 tons of solid wastes and sludges, and more than 1.5 billion gallons of wastewater.

Ironically, leapfrogging in Eastern Europe will in some cases mean holding on to what exists now rather than imitating the West. For example, two decades of choking on automotive pollution and trying to deal with traffic congestion in the United States have led transportation planners to regret abandoning comprehensive public transportation systems.

Eastern Europe still relies primarily on public transportation systems, but there is a risk that this pattern will change as consumers opt for car travel and budget-conscious finance ministries cut subsidies for buses, subways, trolleys, and trains. In Hungary, for example, 58 percent of urban passenger trips are made on public transportation, only 11 percent by automobile. In the United States, in contrast, public transportation accounts for only 3 percent of urban trips, automobiles for 82 percent. Careful public policymaking could prevent this by treating automobiles as one component, rather than the dominant player, in a diversified transportation scheme.

Similarly, the low levels of household and commercial waste now produced in Eastern Europe are a Western city planner's or environmentalist's dream. The throwaway culture was anathema to the Communist regimes, and many of the Eastern European intellectuals who led the recent revolutions are also wary of consumerism. Czechoslovakian President Vaclav Havel, for one, has written of "the omnipresent dictatorship of consumption, production, advertising, commerce, and consumer culture" in the West.

But the majority of the region's people, who sometimes lack even basic goods such as soap, are understandably unenthusiastic about the notion of restraining their consumption—and thus waste generation—especially with the prospect of rising incomes and greater consumer choices.

THE "50-PERCENT SOLUTION"

The leapfrogging notion has not been embraced wholeheartedly. Some interpret it as a call for the use of only the fanciest, most expensive technologies. Given the capital shortages faced by Eastern European countries, some have argued that this is unrealistic. They argue for "appropriate technologies" that, while offering less in the way of reductions at a particular plant, could be applied on a more widespread scale.

Helmut Schreiber of the Institute of European Environmental Policy in Bonn has been a vocal proponent of this compromise between Western standards and Eastern European realities. "To take sulfur as an example," he wrote in a recent article in *The Environmental Forum,* "it is more expensive to go from 95-percent desulfurization to 97 percent, than from 0 to 50 percent. In the heavily polluted environment of Eastern Europe, however, this first 50-percent reduction in emissions would constitute a major breakthrough. Given the wide extent of the problem and the limited capital to combat it, sheer economics argues for such a '50-percent solution.' "

Though such a solution will be called for in many cases, it is not universally applicable. The worst polluters will need to be shut down altogether. As new plants are built to replace them, they might as well be endowed with state-of-the-art environmental controls. Also, over-investing in "50-percent solutions" could be money down the drain if existing plants are to be shut down anyway for economic reasons within a few years.

HELPING HANDS

As Eastern Europe becomes integrated with the West, international policies will have an increasingly important impact on environmental developments in the region. Western aid, trade, and debt policies will all help to determine whether or not the vaunted "common European home" will be a clean one.

Given the dire economic conditions prevailing in the region, Eastern European governments are relying on the West to help finance environmental reconstruction. Self-interest argues for some measure of Western aid for pollution control. Since a significant share of Eastern air and water pollution spills over into Western Europe, investing in pollution control in East European countries can be a cost-effective way for Western European nations to clean up at home.

The region's contribution to global environmental problems is another motivating factor for Western assistance: Eastern Europe and the Soviet Union together account for 26 percent of all carbon dioxide emissions (the primary greenhouse gas) and 17 percent of chlorofluorocarbons (CFCs), which are responsible for the depletion of the ozone layer.

In the last year, environmental aid programs have blossomed. The European Community has so far committed $136 million for environmental programs in Bulgaria, Czechoslovakia, eastern Germany, Hungary, and Poland. The Nordic Environmental Financing Corporation, which is an arm of the Nordic Investment Bank, is soon expected to approve $45 million for joint-venture projects to reduce air and water pollution and improve energy efficiency in the region.

In addition to its commitment to clean up the eastern part of its new nation, Germany has launched a $120-million aid program for Poland, which also expects to receive $60 million from Sweden, $70 million from Denmark, and

$35 million from Finland for pollution control projects, some of which are intended to help clean up the shared Baltic Sea. The United States has already provided Hungary and Poland with $40 million in environmental aid, and recently appropriated an additional $65 million for energy and environmental projects in the region. Also, the World Bank made an $18-million loan to Poland to help improve environmental management practices, and a loan for Hungary is forthcoming. Czechoslovakia and Bulgaria recently became World Bank members, opening the way for loans.

The aid offered so far will help, but the funds set aside for the environment are very small compared with the total economic assistance flowing eastward. Cleaning up the region entails making environmental considerations integral to all aid and trade deliberations.

An opportunity was missed to do this when the U.S. Overseas Private Investment Corporation recently underwrote General Electric's $150-million project to refurbish 13 Hungarian incandescent light bulb factories. Had the lending gone to build factories that produce efficient compact-fluorescent bulbs instead, the energy savings associated with using the new bulbs would have reduced the need for new power plants. According to an analysis by Michael Totten, legislative assistant to ex-Representative Claudine Schneider (R-RI), this would have saved Hungary $10 billion, as well as reduced pollution significantly.

Environmentalists are urging the new European Bank for Reconstruction and Development to avoid just such a piecemeal approach to the region's environmental problems. They've succeeded in placing a mandate in the bank's charter that calls for environmental concerns to be integrated into the full range of activities funded by the new bank's $12-billion portfolio.

Western industries investing in the region would ideally choose the most energy-efficient, least-polluting technologies available. The European Community is planning to establish an environmental code of conduct for investment in Eastern Europe to encourage this and to discourage "ecological colonialism"—the export of environmentally hazardous industrial processes to countries where regulations are lax.

One of the biggest impediments to cleaning up Eastern Europe is the huge debt load carried by most countries—hard currency spent on paying back debts is money unavailable for investments in environmental programs. Poland is saddled with a $42 billion debt that represents 64 percent of its annual GNP, Hungary carries $18 billion in debt (65 percent of GNP), and Czechoslovakia and Bulgaria also have large outstanding bills.

Debt-for-environmental-protection swaps, whereby debt is forgiven in exchange for a commitment to spend the money saved on environmental programs financed with local currency, are one creative way Western countries could help Eastern Europe out of its morass. Two such swaps have been negotiated thus far with Poland. One is by the German government, which will wipe $60 million of debt off the books. The other, by the World Wide Fund for Nature in Gland, Switzerland, will forgive $50,000 in debt to help finance a project to establish a natural park to protect the ecologically valuable Biebrza wetlands in northeastern Poland.

Strength from Within

Though Western aid will help, it is not the ultimate solution to Eastern Europe's environmental woes. Reversing the region's ecological decline will require strong national policies. Environmental reforms need to be instituted now, as economic and political reform proceeds, to lay a strong foundation for an environmentally sound future.

One necessary step is setting up a system of ecological taxation. Although markets offer the environmental benefit of encouraging energy and resource efficiency, they fail miserably at taking environmental costs into account. The costs of the pollution created by industrial processes are generally borne by society as a whole, rather than by the consumer or producer of the manufactured item.

To compensate for this, and thereby create an incentive to minimize pollution production, Eastern European countries could adopt "eco-taxes" similar to those now under consideration in the West. For example, emissions of harmful pollutants or the use of virgin materials could be taxed at a level high enough to discourage the practice. These levies can then replace other taxes if the goal is to keep total revenue unchanged. As new tax systems are put in place in Eastern Europe in the coming years, "green" levies can be incorporated from the beginning.

In some cases, economic incentives will not suffice. Strong regulations such as efficiency standards and prohibitions on carcinogenic pesticides will be essential. These will also steer Western investment in environmentally helpful directions. The adoption of European Community environmental standards would help keep the region from becoming the dumping ground of Europe.

The countries of the region are still not ready to enact these and other farsighted strategies. Environmental ministries are being strengthened, and innovative new policies proposed. But powerful finance and industrial ministries are thwarting environmental efforts for the sake of streamlining budgets or boosting production.

Eastern Germany is a special case, as it is now part of a unified Germany. New factories, power plants, or engines must now comply with the standards of the former West Germany; existing enterprises have until the end of the decade to either conform or close down. Other countries of the region aren't so lucky as to have a "rich uncle." Still, Poland and Czechoslovakia are launching cleanup programs.

Poland's environment ministry has targeted 80 major industrial polluters that will either soon comply with environmental regulations or shut their doors. It has plans to close regulatory loopholes for polluters and overhaul and tighten existing environmental legislation. It also wants to invest extensively in environmental protection, particularly sewage treatment plants, 3,000 of which are to be completed by 1995.

In Czechoslovakia, Minister of the Environment Josef Vavroušek recently spelled out a policy designed to make environmental protection a central element in the country's shift to a market economy. Under his plan, ecological taxes would play a large role. He has sent to parliament draft laws calling for environmental impact assessments, strong laws governing toxic waste dumping, and air pollution regulations. So far, though, resuscitating the nation's economy has dominated the parliamentary debate and Vavrousek's proposals have received short shrift.

Bulgaria, Hungary, and Romania are moving somewhat more slowly. Hungary still has a relatively ineffective environment ministry that, until September of last year, was combined with a public-works-style water development agency. Unfortunately, the environment ministry has now merged with the ministry of construction. Of the arrangement, Hungarian environmentalist János Vargha says, "this could be a new fox in the henhouse."

Bulgarian Prime Minister Andrey Lukanov presented a $1.2-billion plan in March 1990 to combat industrial pollution, but critics question whether the government will be able to come up with the money. In Romania, environmentalists did not waste much time taking advantage of the revolution: a new environment ministry was formed on December 28, 1989, just days after fighting stopped in the streets of Bucharest. But continuing political instability in Romania does not bode well for the environment receiving the attention it needs.

Some grounds for optimism can be found in the green movement that has developed in the region. After helping to topple the old governments, environmental groups are turning their attention to pushing for public participation in environmental policymaking and strong environmental controls as economic reform proceeds. Nongovernmental groups and green parties now exist in each country in the region.

The movement faces considerable challenges as it learns to operate in rapidly changing circumstances. Many groups are struggling with organizational questions, such as how to finance themselves and what their agenda should be. The green parties face an ongoing battle to increase their representation in parliaments. In a major upset, the Green Party of the former West Germany failed to capture any seats in the new German parliament, although a coalition that includes the green party of the former East Germany did win eight seats.

The next few decades are critical for Eastern Europe's environment. Without determined action, the environmental restoration promised by the revolutions of 1989 will not materialize. The key to success will be for all involved to regard environmental reconstruction in Eastern Europe as fundamental to societal transformation, rather than as a sideshow to the main act.

4

A Water-Short World

EMERGING WATER SCARCITIES

By Sandra Postel

Parakrama Bahu the Great, twelfth-century king of Sri Lanka, set the ultimate standard for water engineers. "Let not even a small quantity of water obtained by rain go to the sea, without benefiting man," he decreed.

Eight hundred years later, Parakrama's dictum has largely been carried out in many parts of the world. Engineers have built thousands of dams, reservoirs, and diversion canals to capture water and deliver it where and when needed. Technological feats, such as Egypt's Aswan High Dam and the California Aqueduct, have literally made deserts bloom. Cities and farms have sprung up and flourished in the driest of regions, with the faith that water would be brought to them.

Central to food production, industrial expansion, and urban growth, water development has advanced living standards virtually everywhere. But limits to Parakrama's vision are swiftly coming to light. Exhausted rivers, falling water tables, and shrinking lakes testify to extensive human abuse of the world's water resources. Mounting concern about this environmental damage and the accelerating costs of new supplies have put the brakes on water development, even as demands continue to escalate.

Regional shortages cropping up around the world under-

127

score the stakes when water is used as if from a bottomless well. Although water deficits currently are limited geographically, they are certain to spread if consumption goes unchecked. The question for many areas is not if a crunch will come, but when.

Where scarcity looms, heated competition is brewing between neighboring nations, between regions within nations and, increasingly, between cities and farms. Agriculture's heavy claim on available water is already being eyed longingly by thirsty urban areas facing constraints to their growth. How these various battles play out will shape regional landscapes, economic fortunes, and food production in the decades ahead. One outcome is certain: The struggle for water security will have no winners until societies recognize water's natural limits and begin to bring human numbers and wants into line with them.

HIGH STAKES IN THE MIDDLE EAST

"The next war in our region will be over the waters of the Nile, not politics," says Boutros Ghali, Egypt's minister of state for foreign affairs. The prophecy turns ominous with the echo of Israel's Meir Ben-Meir, a former head of the agriculture ministry: "If the people of the region are not clever enough to discuss a mutual solution to the problem of water scarcity, war is unavoidable."

Nowhere are conflicts over water potentially more combustible than in the water-short Middle East. A look at the geopolitical landscape quickly reveals why. Three river basins form the backbone of water development efforts: the Jordan, the Tigris-Euphrates, and the Nile. Supplies are stretched nearly to the limit in two of the three, and contentious political relations have thwarted efforts to reach water-sharing agreements.

Religious and ethnic tensions greatly exacerbate the region's water problems, but even without them, the specter of shortages would be real and growing. Middle Eastern countries have some of the highest population growth rates in the world, and because of their dry climate, food production depends heavily on irrigation (see Table 1).

Israel, Jordan, and Syria get most of their water from the Jordan River basin. Israel already uses 95 percent of the renewable supplies available to it, largely because of its sixfold expansion in irrigated area since 1948. In little more than a decade, the nation's supplies could fall 30 percent short of demand.

Although Israeli farmers are among the most water-efficient in the world, the government may soon face the politically difficult choice of supplying domestic and industrial needs only by shifting water out of agriculture. Immediate plans are to use more reclaimed wastewater and less

Table 1
Population Growth and Irrigation Dependence, Selected Middle Eastern Countries

Country	Annual Rate of Population Growth	Share of Cropland That Is Irrigated
	(percent)	
Egypt	2.8	100.0
Israel	1.6	65.6
Iran	3.4	38.7
Saudi Arabia	3.4	35.6
Iraq	3.8	32.1
Lebanon	2.1	28.7
Syria	3.8	11.5
Jordan	3.5	10.2
World average	1.8	15.4

Sources: Population Reference Bureau, *1989 World Population Data Sheet* (Washington, D.C.: 1989) and UN Food and Agriculture Organization, *1987 Production Yearbook* (Rome: 1988).

freshwater for irrigation, but it remains to be seen whether this can avert shortages for long.

Jordan projects a 50 percent increase in its water needs by the year 2005. There is already talk of a crisis by the mid-nineties that could require a transfer of water away from farms to meet the domestic needs of a population expanding at 3.6 percent per year, among the fastest growth rates in the world.

Moreover, Joyce Starr, chairman of the Global Water Summit Initiative in Washington, D.C., points out Jordan's plight could worsen if Syria, its upstream neighbor, acts aggressively to augment its own supplies. Syria expects shortages by 2000, even with additional supplies from a joint project with Jordan to dam the Yarmuk River, the only major undeveloped tributary in the basin.

Adding to the tension, Palestinians on the West Bank and in the Gaza Strip must compete with Israelis for dwindling groundwater supplies. Overpumping of the aquifer underlying the Gaza Strip has caused seawater to intrude and partially contaminate this vital source. Much of the water supplying northern and central Israel comes from aquifers that originate on the West Bank and drain westward toward the Mediterranean Sea. John K. Cooley, former Mideast correspondent for the *Christian Science Monitor,* notes that "keeping Tel Aviv, Haifa and the other cities of the Israeli coastal plain from running dry depends on blocking Arab water development in the West Bank that could stop the aquifers' flow westward."

Tensions in the Tigris-Euphrates watershed are heightening, as well. The mountains of eastern Turkey give rise to both rivers, with the Euphrates flowing through Syria and Iraq before reaching the Persian Gulf and the Tigris running directly through Iraq.

Despite a healthy surplus of water in the 430,000-square-mile basin, Syria and Iraq stand to lose from Turkey's massive Anatolia project, which aims to increase hydroelectric power and irrigation. Following completion of the Ataturk Dam, the scheme's centerpiece, Turkey's added use of Euphrates water could foil Syrian and Iraqi plans to draw more for themselves. Some experts estimate that flows into Iraq could drop below the minimum the country claims it will need.

Turkey is studying the idea of two "peace pipelines" that would transport some of its surplus water to thirstier nations downstream. Consultants say the water, which would be used primarily for drinking and other domestic needs, would be competitive in price with desalinated water, an expensive source of last resort. However, with an estimated combined cost of $21 billion, the pipelines could well run into economic and political hang-ups.

EGYPT'S LIFELINE

In Egypt, where it rarely ever rains, the country's 55 million people depend almost entirely on the waters of the Nile—none of which originate within the nation's boundaries. About 80 percent of the flow into Lake Nasser, behind the Aswan High Dam, stems from the Blue Nile, which forms in Ethiopia. The remaining 20 percent comes from the White Nile system, with headwaters at Lake Victoria in Tanzania. Nine countries draw from the basin's runoff, with Egypt last in line.

Under a 1959 agreement with Sudan, where both Niles converge, Egypt is entitled to 55.5 billion cubic meters (bcm) of water per year, about two-thirds of the flow entering at Aswan in an average year. While the Sudan apparently accepts this allocation as a perpetual right, upper-basin countries recognize no obligation to limit their use of Nile waters for the sake of Egypt and the Sudan. Indeed, Ethiopia's development plans could reduce the Blue Nile's flow at the Sudan border by 5.4 bcm and bring drastic consequences downstream.

To make matters worse, the Nile can diminish markedly in dry periods. During the 1984 to 1985 drought, the flow at Aswan dropped to 38 bcm, well below Egypt's allotted share. Since 1983, the country has met its needs by drawing down reserves at Lake Nasser. As of late 1986, storage was down to a precarious 24 bcm, or less than one-fifth of the reservoir's capacity and about a third of Egypt's annual water use. Fortunately, heavy rainfall in the watershed since the fall of 1988 has brought the reservoir nearly back to its predrought level. But, long-term records suggest more trouble ahead. The Nile's runoff pattern exhibits a 100-year cycle that includes low-flow periods at the beginning of each century.

Even under the best of assumptions about supplies, including a nearly 10 percent increase from completion of a joint project with Sudan, Egypt appears headed for crisis. Its population leaps by one million every nine months; this increases both drinking-water and food demands. With virtually no additional sources to tap, Egypt has no choice but to squeeze more out of its existing supplies by upgrading and better managing its irrigation systems. Cutting food imports—running at half or more of the country's needs—also may require removing from production some water-intensive cash crops, such as cotton and sugar cane, to free water to grow more food. That would sacrifice foreign exchange earnings—a difficult move given the nation's $44 billion external debt. The alternative—increasing reliance on foreign food—could threaten Egypt's economic security even more.

A BROKEN WATER CYCLE

Several consecutive years of drought during the mid-eighties brought the realities of water scarcity home to many of India's 835 million people. But the nation's worsening water problems stem as much or more from gross mismanagement of its land and water resources as from nature's fickleness.

Managing water in India is undeniably a monumental challenge. On a per-capita basis, the amount of runoff produced annually by precipitation is just one-fourth the world average. Most rainfall comes during the monsoon season, typically June through September, so the central task is to control flooding and to capture and store enough water for the dry season.

By the late seventies, the government had invested over $12 billion in 1,554 large dams to accomplish that, as well as to generate hydroelectricity. Deforestation, however, has undercut many of the benefits of these engineering works. With the denuding of watersheds, more water now runs off in floods and less percolates into the ground to recharge aquifers. The area prone to flooding has tripled since 1971 and once-perennial streams and rivers now dry up for parts of the year.

According to Jayanto Bandyopadhyay, director of the Research Foundation for Science and Ecology in Dehra Dun, this loss of recharge largely explains why even high-rainfall areas now petition for drought relief. "Water is only a renewable resource if we respect the ecological processes that maintain and give stability to the water cycle," he writes. "This, India has signally failed to do."

Tens of thousands of villages across the subcontinent now live with shortages and their numbers are growing. In many areas dependent on groundwater, competition is intensifying as water tables fall. Heavy pumping in the coastal districts of the western state of Gujarat has caused saltwater to intrude into the aquifer and contaminate village drinking supplies. Even large portions of New Delhi, which gets supplies from the heavily used Tamura and Ganges rivers, now have water for only a few hours a day.

That the capital faces severe problems greatly complicates efforts to resolve lingering disputes with neighboring Bangladesh. The vast majority of low-lying Bangladesh's water supply originates in India. Although the two countries first agreed to share water in 1977, a new agreement has not been reached since the last one expired in mid-1988. Officials in Dacca understandably see their economic prospects and food security held hostage to New Delhi's water decisions. An Indian proposal to augment the Ganges' flow by channeling water from the Brahmaputra River has only heightened Bangladesh's fear of shortages.

North China in the Red

With 21 percent of the world's people but only 8 percent of its renewable freshwater, China faces obvious water constraints. Feeding 1.1 billion people off limited fertile land requires the high and fairly dependable yields that irrigation can offer. Yet, water-short cities are challenging agriculture's heavy claim on scarce supplies. That most cropland and people are concentrated in the eastern third of the country only makes the competition keener.

Already, more than 200 major cities lack sufficient water and a quarter of these face acute shortages. The situation is especially dire in the North China Plain, the location of Beijing, the important commercial city of Tianjin, and millions of acres of flat, fertile farmland. *China Daily* reported in mid-May 1989 that Beijing's two main reservoirs were dropping rapidly, even before the onset of the peak consumption season. Water tables beneath the capital continue to drop by 3 to 6 feet per year. A third of its wells have gone dry and, in another third, groundwater is at half the normal level.

Most of the region's water sources already have been tapped, yet demands are rising rapidly. Planners project Beijing's water needs will increase by 50 percent by the year 2000 if current consumption patterns continue. In Tianjin, where groundwater levels have also been falling precipitously, demand is projected to more than double.

Officials are hoping that completion of a long-awaited diversion of the Yangtze River in central China will help ease the pinch. Even this grandiose scheme will fulfill no more than 10 percent of Beijing's anticipated needs in 2000, though, still leaving a gap.

An all-out effort to boost water efficiency and prevent pollution from diminishing usable supplies will help defuse the impending crisis, but in some areas of the north, shifting water from farm to city use seems the only way to approach a water balance. Projections for Beijing's water budget suggest that farmers in the vicinity could lose 30 to 40 percent of their current supply. Indeed, in dry years, they already lose out; when the levels of Beijing's two major reservoirs fell to a record low in 1985, supplies to all nonvegetable farmers were cut off.

China expert James E. Nickum of the East-West Center in Honolulu, Hawaii, points out that, since the government controls all reservoirs and river flows, there are no legal barriers to its shifting supplies among users. In fact, he says, such reallocations "are often carried out with breathtaking speed." The ultimate question is how much water China can divert from agriculture without jeopardizing its long-term food security.

SHRIVELING UP IN THE SOVIET UNION

Without doubt, the Soviet Union has created the biggest ecological catastrophe from excessive water use anywhere: the shrinking of the Aral Sea. The fate of the Aral also signals a worsening water shortage in Soviet Central Asia that threatens to fuel political tensions and impose a grave economic and social toll.

With its warm, sunny climate, Central Asia is to the Soviet Union what California's Central Valley is to the United States—a rich fruit and vegetable basket. It covers only 7.3 percent of the U.S.S.R.'s territory but yields a third of the country's fruit, a quarter of its vegetables, and two-fifths of its rice. However, cotton is king in the Central Asian republics. Fully 95 percent of the Soviets' cotton harvest is grown there.

Although ideal for heat-loving crops, the dry climate makes irrigation essential. Over time, as agricultural production expanded and larger quantities of water were diverted from the Syr Dar'ya and Amu Dar'ya rivers, the Aral Sea was deprived of its two principal sources of replenishment. By 1980, flows from these two rivers into the sea were reduced to a trickle.

Officials in Moscow face some difficult choices. According to Soviet water expert Philip P. Micklin of Western Michigan University, "If preventive measures are not taken, the Aral will shrink to several residual brine lakes in the next century." Writing off the Aral completely, with the aim of using what water remains to expand irrigation and industries, would wreak ecological havoc and render areas adjacent to the sea uninhabitable. Harvests already are being damaged as winds pick up dried salt from the former seabed and dump up to 48 million tons of it on surrounding cropland each year. Deteriorating health conditions from poor-quality drinking water, and diminishing employment opportunities from the demise of Aral Sea fisheries have forced tens of thousands of people from their homes.

Saving the Aral would entail shifting water out of agriculture, but that poses the problem of meeting food and job security for the basin's rapidly expanding population. Increasing inflow enough to return the Aral to its pre-1960 condition would require slashing irrigated area in the basin by 60 percent, and this would cause agricultural losses of $28 to $31 billion per year. Even preserving the sea at roughly its current level demands a fivefold increase in average annual inflow over that of recent years; this could only be achieved with large cutbacks in agricultural water use.

As in north China, many in Soviet Central Asia hold out hope for a huge river diversion, in this case, from the north-flowing Siberian rivers southwest into the Aral Sea basin.

Although the scheme has been on the drawing board for decades and design work progressed steadily during the early eighties, Soviet officials halted the project in 1986 in response to strong opposition from Soviet environmentalists and President Gorbachev's dismay at its high price tag.

In a decree issued in October 1988, the Communist Party's Central Committee laid out, in some detail, what Central Asia's near-term water future will look like. It reduces the 1991 target for irrigation expansion by 420,000 acres; after that date, no new large irrigation projects can draw water from the Amu or Syr Dar'ya. By 2000 farmers must upgrade irrigation systems to cut water withdrawals by one-quarter. Water fees are to be instituted nationwide within two years. The goal is to raise minimum flows into the Aral tenfold over their current level by 2005. Officials claim this will preserve the sea, albeit in some diminished form.

The plan could easily cost more than $78 billion, an enormous sum given the sad state of the Soviet economy. Some experts, including Micklin, harbor serious doubts about whether both the Aral and the regional economy can survive without the Siberian river diversions, which could cost in the neighborhood of $150 billion and cause ecological damage of their own.

Soviet Central Asia by no means rounds out the list of the world's water problem areas. The Valley of Mexico, much of northern and eastern Africa, the American West, and pockets of Eastern Europe and Latin America would have to be included to complete the picture.

A MARKET SOLUTION?

Common to these tales of shortage is the near-universal failure to value water properly and to treat it like the scarce commodity it is. In the western United States, a region troubled by numerous local and regional shortages, an imperfect but promising remedy to this neglect is catching on in the form of water markets.

As the phrase implies, water marketing involves the transfer of water or water rights between willing buyers and sellers for an agreed-upon price. It can operate where systems of water law and allocation establish clear property rights to this resource.

Water marketing is not a new or isolated phenomenon. Farmers in Spain have traded irrigation water for centuries, and private well owners in India, Pakistan, and Bangladesh frequently sell their water to neighbors. Marketing in the American West was quite common around the turn of the century, but the pace of activity slowed during the era of government water projects. With that era fast coming to an end, purchasing someone else's water becomes an attractive alternative to developing costly new supplies.

Most buyers are cities trying to secure enough water to support continued growth. Most sellers are irrigators, who find they can make more money by selling their water than by applying it to their cropland (see Table 2). Sale prices have varied greatly, with perpetual rights typically going for less than $200 per acre-foot in the Salt Lake City area, but as high as $3,000 to $6,000 per acre-foot in the rapidly urbanizing Colorado Front Range. (One acre-foot equals 325,850 gallons, enough to supply a typical four-person household in the United States for about two years.)

Not all water transfers require shifting water rights permanently out of agriculture. For example, the Metropolitan Water District of Southern California (MWD)—water wholesaler for roughly half the state's 30 million residents—has agreed to finance conservation projects, such as lining canals, in the nearby Imperial Irrigation District in exchange for the estimated 100,000 acre-feet of water those conservation investments will save each year. The cost per acre-foot conserved is estimated at $128, far lower than MWD's best new-supply option. Although water will be transferred to

TABLE 2   A Sampling of Water Rights Sales in the Western
United States, 1988–89

Buyer	Seller	Amount, Acre-Feet per Year[1]	Cost per Acre-Foot	Purpose
Westminster, Colorado	Local irrigators	272	$6,176	Municipal use
Westpac Utilities, Reno, Nevada	Urban home owners on formerly irrigated land	2,000	$2,000	Municipal use
Phoenix, Arizona[2]	McMullen Valley Farm	30,000	$1,017	Projected municipal needs after the year 2000
Albuquerque, New Mexico	Local irrigators	1,360	$1,000	Projected municipal needs after the year 2020
Nevada Waterfowl Association	Truckee-Carson Irrigation District	35	$214	Wetlands and waterfowl protection
Central Utah Water Conservancy District	Local irrigators	85,000	$164	Municipal use in lieu of a previous plan to drain wetlands to increase supplies

Sources: Water Market Update, vols. 2–3 (Santa Fe, N.M.: Shupe & Associates, 1988–1989) and Elizabeth Checchio, *Water Farming: The Promise and Problems of Water Transfers in Arizona* (Tucson, Ariz.: University of Arizona, 1988).

[1] One acre-foot equals 325,850 gallons, enough to supply a four-person household for about two years.

[2] 1986.

city use, no cropland is being taken out of production and no irrigation water rights are actually being sold.

At the other extreme are transactions in Arizona, where Phoenix, Tucson, and other burgeoning cities have taken to "water ranching." Since state law makes it difficult to buy rights to water independent of the land, cities that want the water must acquire the land. More than 575,000 acres of agricultural land in Arizona have been purchased as water farms. In Pima County, where Tucson is located, irrigated agriculture is expected to disappear by 2020.

By helping establish a scarcity price, markets push water toward higher-valued uses. If a farmer can profit more by selling water to a nearby city than by spraying it on cotton, alfalfa, or wheat, shifting that water from farm to city use is economically beneficial. If it prevents the city from damming another river to increase supplies, that transfer also can benefit the environment.

Markets raise some difficult issues, though. Should society protect the economies of rural areas that lose their water to thirsty cities and, if so, how? Who protects freshwater fisheries, recreational white water, and other ecologic and aesthetic values of rivers? Should water rights for these purposes be bought and sold just like those for irrigation or urban use, or are these common interests that the legal and regulatory system should safeguard for the public? Case by case, answers to such questions are being hammered out.

LIVING WITHIN WATER'S LIMITS

Whether or not marketing is put to use, incentives to use water more efficiently—to get more out of each gallon used—are essential. Unfortunately, the policies, laws, and institutions governing water use in most countries discourage efficiency, rather than foster it. Irrigation systems often are built, maintained, and controlled by public agencies that charge next to nothing for these services. Economist Robert Repetto of the World Resources Institute has found that government revenues from irrigation projects in six Asian countries averaged less than 10 percent of the full cost of delivering the water. When undercharging is common practice, governments lack funds to properly maintain and manage their projects and farmers have little incentive to conserve.

The problem is just as severe in the United States. One-quarter of the West's irrigated land—about 11 million acres—gets water from federal projects run by the Bureau of Reclamation. Charged by the 1902 Reclamation Act with helping settle the arid West, the bureau supplies water to farmers under long-term contracts (typically 40 years) at greatly subsidized prices. California farmers benefiting from the federal Central Valley Project (CVP), for example, have repaid only 5 percent of the project's cost over the last 40 years, with the total subsidy exceeding $930 million.

This free ride largely explains why a third of the water supplied by the Bureau of Reclamation goes to low-value forage crops, such as alfalfa for cattle grazing, even while so many other, higher-valued activities need additional water. Even more perverse, the bureau gave farmers at least $200 million in water subsidies in 1986 to grow crops that the Department of Agriculture was paying other farmers *not* to grow because of surpluses. Times may be changing, but slowly. In early 1989, when the 40-year contract for one of the CVP's irrigation districts came up for renewal, the government raised the price of the district's water from $3.50 to $14.94 per acre-foot—a hefty jump, but still only 28 percent of the water's true cost.

When water either is priced more realistically, governments regulate its use, or the cost of extracting it goes up, efficiency increases. Farmers in Israel and the Texas High Plains have shown that irrigation efficiencies can be raised 20 to 30 percent in a matter of years by adopting modern technologies and better management practices. Using lasers to level fields, upgrading sprinklers, recycling used irrigation water, installing water-thrifty drip systems, and irrigating only when crops really need it are just a few of the ways farmers can save.

Since agriculture consumes such a disproportionately large share of water in most water-short areas, freeing even a small percentage can cover enormous growth in urban demands. The 100,000 acre-feet per year expected to be saved through the Southern California transfer described earlier is enough to meet the needs of 800,000 of the state's residents. Through similar investments in efficiency, crises can be prevented, or at least delayed, in rapidly growing cities such as Amman, Beijing, Cairo, and New Delhi.

Although crucial, proper economic incentives alone cannot avert conflicts and shortages where populations are expanding faster than efficiency can release new supplies. Any hope for balancing Egypt's water budget, for example, rests as much on the nation's ability to slow birthrates as it does in modernizing irrigation systems. Indeed, limiting population size appears to be the only way of meeting minimal per-capita needs in the near future for the northern tier of African countries, especially as they attempt to reduce their dependence on food imports.

In degraded areas, such as the Himalayas, joint reforestation efforts may be needed to restore critical watersheds. Where a water source is vital to several nations, lasting and equitable water-sharing agreements will have to be negotiated to minimize potential conflicts. Averting outright water wars in the Middle East will require that Israel, Jordan, Syria, and other neighboring nations begin cooperating to find mutually acceptable solutions to their shared predicament.

No Quick Fixes

It is tempting to assume some technological fix will come along to settle the world's water problems. But seeding clouds to enhance rainfall and towing icebergs from Antarctica are simply not going to do the trick. Technologies to desalinate ocean water—in a sense, the ultimate solution—are well-established and improving, but desalination is an energy- and capital-intensive process that remains far too expensive to make much of a contribution. Two-thirds of the world's installed desalination capacity is on the Arabian Peninsula, where oil-rich countries can afford, at least for the time being, to expend three kilowatt-hours of energy to make one gallon of freshwater.

Conservation, increased efficiency, and more recycling can buy much-needed time. Ultimately, though, emerging scarcities call upon governments and communities to rethink their notions of needs and wants. Does California really need more water if one-seventh of it now goes to raising grass and hay for livestock? Irrigated pasture contributes a tiny amount to the state's economy but consumes as much water as all 30 million Californians. Similarly, does it make sense for Soviet officials to prop up a cotton economy in the parched deserts of Central Asia? And, how much longer can water-short regions ignore the population factor in their water budget equations and still legitimately cry crisis?

Societies can continue to muddle through with another dam here, another well there, but only for so long. Ignoring water's limits will only make the consequences of overstepping them hit home sooner and harsher.

5

The Food
Prospect

FEEDING SIX BILLION

By Lester R. Brown

Nearly two centuries have passed since Malthus published his famous treatise in which he argued that population tends to grow exponentially while food production grows arithmetically. He argued that unless profligate childbearing was checked, preferably through abstinence, famine and hunger would be inevitable.

Malthus was wrong, of course, in the sense that he did not anticipate the enormus potential of advancing technology to raise land productivity. He was writing before Mendel formulated the basic principles of genetics and before Von Leibeg concluded that all the nutrients taken from the soil by plants could be returned in mineral form.

On the other hand, Malthus was correct in anticipating the difficulty in expanding food output as fast as population growth. Today, two centuries later, and with advances in technology that Malthus could not even have dreamed of, we still struggle with the problem of human hunger. And as the nineties begin, the ranks of the hungry are swelling.

THE ENVIRONMENTAL WILD CARD

After a generation of record growth in world food output following World War II, it sometimes seemed that the rapid ascent in food production could continue indefinitely. Between 1950 and 1984, the world grain harvest expanded some 2.6 times, or nearly 3 percent per year, raising per-capita grain production by more than one-third. But between 1984 and 1990, output rose scarcely 1 percent per year. This six-year period is obviously too short to show a trend, but it does suggest an unsettling slowdown in food output, one that is partly attributable to environmental degradation.

Among the environmental trends adversely affecting agriculture, soil erosion tops the list. As the demand for food has risen in recent decades, so have the pressures on the earth's soils. Soil erosion is accelerating as the world's farmers are pressed into plowing highly erodible land, and as traditional rotation systems that maintain soil stability break down.

Some one-third of the world's cropland is losing topsoil at a rate that undermines its future productivity. An estimated 24 billion tons of topsoil washes or blows off the land annually—roughly the amount on Australia's wheatland. Each year, the world's farmers must try to feed 88 million more people with 24 billion fewer tons of topsoil.

This loss is beginning to show up in diminished harvests. Studies undertaken in the U.S. Corn Belt conclude that the loss of 1 inch of topsoil reduces corn yields from 3 to 6 bushels per acre, or an average of 6 percent. Wheat yields follow a similar pattern.

Soil erosion and cropland loss in Third World nations is intimately linked with another form of environmental degradation: deforestation. As firewood becomes scarce, villagers begin to burn crop residues and animal dung for fuel and thus deprive the land of organic matter and nutrients. With less organic matter, the soil's ability to absorb and store moisture decreases and makes the land more vulnerable to drought. Further, loss of organic matter increases runoff and thus reduces the percolation of rainfall into the subsoil and the recharge of aquifers.

Increased runoff, in turn, leads to flooding. This is now strikingly evident in the Indian subcontinent, where deforestation is destroying tree cover in the Himalayan watersheds. The area subject to annual flooding in India expanded from 47 million acres in 1960 to 124 million acres in 1984, an area larger than California. Accelerated runoff as a result of deforestation was evident in early September 1988, when two-thirds of Bangladesh was inundated for several days. That flood, the worst on record, led to extensive crop damage.

Damage to crops from air pollution now is measurable in the automobile-centered societies of Western Europe and the United States and in the coal-burning economies of Eastern Europe and China. A U.S. Environmental Protection Agency study estimates that ground-level ozone spawned by fossil-fuel burning is reducing the U.S. corn, wheat, soybean, and peanut harvests by at least 5 percent. Walter Heck, the U.S. Department of Agriculture representative on the EPA study panel, estimates that cutting ground-level ozone by half would cut crop losses by up to $5 billion.

All plants and animals are affected to some degree by the increased exposure to ultraviolet radiation resulting from depletion of the stratospheric ozone layer. Data gathered from experimental plots by professor Alan Teramura at the University of Maryland indicate that each 1 percent increase in ultraviolet radiation reduces soybean yields by a like amount. This suggests that the worldwide depletion in the ozone layer, roughly 3 percent over the last two decades, now may be reducing the output of soybeans, the world's largest leading protein crop. Unfortunately, no one is monitoring this loss to determine its precise dimensions.

The effect of hotter summers on world food output can be estimated from the computerized projections of global climate change. As global warming progresses, farm output could be cut sharply in North America and Central Asia, the regions of the earth likely to experience the greatest temperature rise. If the summer of 1988, which reduced U.S. grain production below domestic consumption for the first time in modern history, is a glimpse of what summers will be like, then the days of the North American breadbasket could be numbered.

THE POPULATION FACTOR

Even while wrestling with the new uncertainties associated with hotter summers, farmers recently learned that they may have to feed more people than they had reckoned. The United Nations Population Fund announced in 1989 that UN demographers have revised their earlier projections of world population upward, chiefly because of failed family planning efforts. Instead of leveling off at 10 billion, world population will settle at 14 billion. For a world that can't adequately feed 5.3 billion inhabitants today, this comes as sobering news.

The World population increased by some 93 million in 1990. Accelerating sharply during the recovery period after World War II, the annual rate of world population growth peaked at close to 2 percent in 1970. It then slowed gradually, declining to 1.7 percent in the early eighties. During the late eighties, a decade when family planning success stories were rare, it began to climb again, reaching 1.8 percent per year. As a result, world population is projected to expand by 960 million during the nineties, up from the 840 million added in the eighties. (see Table 1).

In many developing countries, soaring population now has a dual effect on food balance: it increases demand as it degrades the agricultural resource base. For instance, crowded cities and villages create a need for firewood that exceeds the sustainable yield of local forests. Deforestation is the outcome, which in turn increases rainfall runoff and soil erosion. Once started, this vicious cycle is hard to stop.

TABLE 1 World Population Growth by Decade, 1950–90, with Projections to 2000	Year	Population	Increase by Decade	Average Annual Increase
		(billions)	(millions)	(millions)
	1950	2.515	n.a.	n.a.
	1960	3.019	504	50
	1970	3.698	679	68
	1980	4.450	752	75
	1990	5.292	842	84
	2000	6.251	959	96

Source: U.N. Department of International Economic and Social Affairs, *World Population Prospects 1988.*

As a result, the agricultural base for hundreds of millions of people is deteriorating on a scale whose consequences are fearful to imagine.

As a result of continuing rapid population growth and slower growth in world grain output, grain production per person fell sharply during the late eighties, interrupting the long-term gradual rise since midcentury. This fall was cushioned by consuming part of the record level of grain stocks on hand when the decline began. But, even after drawing down stocks, per-capita grain consumption fell 2 percent between 1986 and 1990.

Nowhere is the agricultural breakdown more evident than in Africa. With the fastest population growth of any continent on record, a combination of deforestation, overgrazing, soil erosion, and desertification has helped lower per-capita grain production some 28 percent from its peak in the late sixties. This fall has converted the continent into a grain-importing region, fueled the region's mounting external debt, and left millions of Africans hungry and physically weakened, drained of their vitality and productivity.

Sadly, there is nothing in sight to reverse this fall in African living standards. World Bank analysts assessing several scenarios for Africa's future label the one based on a simple extrapolation of recent trends "the nightmare scenario."

Nowhere to Grow

From the beginning of agriculture until midcentury, growth in the world's cultivated area more or less kept pace with that of population. After that point, the growth in cultivated area slowed to a crawl. After falling in the mid-eighties, it recovered somewhat as the United States returned to production cropland previously idled under farm commodity programs.

Each year, millions of acres of cropland are lost, either because the land is so severely eroded that it is not worth plowing anymore or because of its conversion to nonfarm uses, such as construction of new homes, factories, and highways. Losses are most pronounced in the densely populated, rapidly industrializing countries of east Asia, including Japan, South Korea, Taiwan, and China. Beijing, in its near desperate efforts to save cropland, is publicly advocating cremation instead of burial. Despite this effort to reduce competition between the living and dead for precious land, and numerous other land-saving measures, nonfarm uses still claim more than a million acres of cropland per year.

Other densely populated countries that are suffering heavy losses include Egypt, Indonesia, India, and Mexico. Both the Soviet Union and the United States are pulling back from their rapidly eroding land. A combination of abandonment of badly eroded cropland plus an increase in alternate-year fallow has reduced the Soviet grain area some 13 percent since 1977. Fearing a similar fate, the United States adopted a five-year plan beginning in 1986 to plant 40 million acres of rapidly eroding cropland to grass or trees.

Worldwide, the potential for expanding the cultivated

area profitably is limited. A few countries, such as Brazil, will be able to add new cropland, but on balance, gains and losses for the nineties will offset each other, as they have during the eighties. Food for the 960 million people to be added during the nineties will have to come from raising land productivity.

The prospect for expanding the irrigated area is only slightly more promising. After growing slowly during the first half of this century, the irrigated area expanded from 232 million acres in 1950 to 615 million acres in 1980, increasing the irrigated area per person by 56 percent (see Figure 1). Since 1980, however, the growth in world irrigated area has slowed dramatically and fallen behind population growth.

Several countries, including this United States and China, actually are losing irrigated land as water tables fall and as water is diverted to nonfarm uses. With the net gain in irrigated land estimated at only 59 million acres during the eighties, the supply of irrigation water per person has shrunk by close to 8 percent. Although the cropland area per person has been falling steadily for decades, the eighties

FIGURE 1
World Irrigated
Cropland,
1900–1989

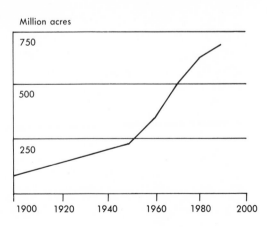

were the first decade in which both cropland area and irrigation water per person declined.

THE NECESSARY INGREDIENT

From midcentury on, the increasing use of fertilizer has been the engine powering the growth in world food output. Between 1950 and 1990, world fertilizer use climbed from a meager 14 million tons to an estimated 145 million tons. If, for whatever reason, fertilizer use were abruptly discontinued, world food output would plummet by an estimated 40 percent.

The contribution of irrigation and high-yielding varieties to food output derives heavily from their ability to boost the effectiveness of fertilizer. Investments in irrigation would yield low returns if not for heavy amounts of fertilizer. Hybrid corn, which was initially developed in the United States and has since spread throughout the world, was a winner because it responded readily to heavy applications of nitrogen fertilizer. Third World farmers were attracted to the high-yielding dwarf wheats and rices that brought the Green Revolution, precisely because they were so responsive to fertilizer. Before these varieties came along, fertilizer use on traditional cereal varieties in the Third World was limited.

Rapid growth in fertilizer use depends on rapid growth in irrigation and in the spread of high-yielding seeds. Like the growth in irrigation, the adoption of high-yielding crop varieties follows an S-shaped trend. Over time, adoption by farmers increases slowly at first as a few innovative farmers plant new varieties and then more rapidly as large numbers of farmers see their advantage. Eventually, adoption slows and levels off as the new strains are planted on all suitable land.

The adoption curve for high-yielding wheats in India, which helped to more than double the country's wheat harvest between 1965 and 1972, illustrates this well (see Figure 2). The spread of these new strains is unlikely to reach all wheatland because much of what's left is semiarid land, where the new varieties do not fare well. Graphing the adoption of high-yielding corn in the United States, high-yielding rices in Indonesia, or high-yielding wheats in Mexico shows the same S-shaped growth curve. Once the new fertilizer-responsive varieties are planted on all suitable land, growth in fertilizer use slows.

Such a trend is now apparent in some major food-producing countries. After multiplying several times over between 1950 and 1980, fertilizer use in the United States leveled off during the eighties. Within the Soviet Union, heavy subsidies have led to the overuse of fertilizer. Recent agricultural reforms, which are keyed to the adoption of world market prices, have actually reduced fertilizer use. Unlike China in the years following its economic reforms of the mid-seventies, the Soviet Union can't anticipate a huge increase in its grain output because the country is already on the upper part of the S-shaped curve for fertilizer responsiveness.

Many developing countries also are experiencing dimin-

FIGURE 2
Share of Wheat
Land Planted to
High-Yielding
Varieties in India,
1965–1983

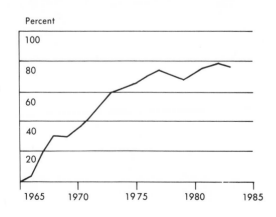

Percent

ishing returns. Analyzing recent crop trends in Indonesia, agricultural economists Duane Chapman and Randy Barker of Cornell University note that "while 1 pound of fertilizer nutrients probably led to a yield increase of 10 pounds of unmilled rice in 1972, this ratio has fallen to about 1 to 5, at present."

Like the growth of any biological process in a finite environment, the rise in grain yield per acre will eventually conform to the S-shaped curve. So, too, will the response to any input contributing to grain yield, such as fertilizer. Not surprisingly, the fertilizer-use curve appears to be conforming in textbook fashion to the S-shaped growth curve so familiar to biologists (see Figure 3). Future fertilizer use will expand as varieties with an even greater yield potential are developed, but the output gains are likely to be modest compared with the quantum jump that came from the initial adoption of the high-yielding varieties.

The ultimate constraints on the rise of crop yields will be imposed by the upper limit of photosynthetic efficiency, a limit set by the basic laws of physics and chemistry. As the genetic potential of high-yielding varieties approaches this

FIGURE 3
World Fertilizer
Use, 1950–1989

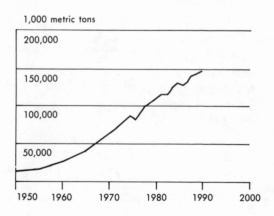

limit, their response to the use of additional fertilizer diminishes. Advances in plant breeding, including those using biotechnology, can hasten the rise of yields toward the photosynthetic limit, but there is little hope of altering the basic mechanics of photosynthesis.

THE SOCIAL FALLOUT

As grain supplies tighten in more and more countries, world prices will rise. A foreshadowing of this development occurred between July 1987 and July 1988, when world grain prices jumped by roughly one-half. They stayed at that level through early 1990. For many heavily indebted Third World countries, rising grain prices are combining with falling personal incomes to pose a policy dilemma. Price hikes are needed to stimulate output and encourage additional investment by farmers, but the world's poor can't cope easily. Perhaps a billion or more of the world's people already spend 70 percent of their income on food. For many in this group, a dramatic rise in the cost of grain is life threatening.

The social effect of rising grain prices is much greater in developing countries than in industrial ones. In the United States, for example, a $1 loaf of bread contains roughly 5 cents worth of wheat. If the price of wheat were to double, the price of the loaf would increase only to $1.05. However, in developing countries, where wheat is purchased in the market and ground into flour at home, a doubling of retail grain prices translates into a doubling of bread prices. A food-price rise that is merely annoying to the world's affluent can drive consumption below the survival level among the poor.

Even before the late-eighties price increases, the social effects of agricultural adversity were becoming evident throughout Africa and Latin America. A World Bank study, using data through 1986, reported that "both the proportion and the total number of Africans with deficient diets have climbed and will continue to rise unless special action is taken."

In Africa, the number of "food-insecure" people, defined by the Bank as those not having enough food for normal health and physical activity, now totals more than 100 million. Some 14.7 million Ethiopians, nearly one-third of the country, are undernourished. Nigeria is close behind, with 13.7 million undernourished people. The Bank summarized the findings of its study by noting that "Africa's food situation is not only serious, it is deteriorating."

Perhaps the most tragic consequence of the deteriorating food situation in Africa and Latin America is the alarming increase in nutrition-related child mortality. In Madagascar, where soil erosion rates exceed even those of Ethiopia and where the deteriorating food situation remarkably parallels that of Africa as a whole, infant deaths climbed by nearly one-fifth in the first six years of the eighties.

Throughout Africa, the increase in malnutrition among children is putting additional pressure on already strained medical facilities. A survey at the Lusaka University Teaching Hospital in Zambia showed that of 433 children admitted in one week in late 1987, more than 100 died, most of them because their malnutrition had reached an irreversible stage.

UNICEF reports that in Nigeria between 120,000 and 150,000 children die each year of malnutrition. In its *State of the World's Children, 1988,* UNICEF declares that "for approximately one-sixth of mankind, the march of human progress has now become a retreat and, in many nations, development is being thrown into reverse. After decades of steady economic advance, large areas of the world are sliding backward into poverty."

In *The Global State of Hunger and Malnutrition, 1988,* the UN's World Food Council reports that the number of malnourished preschoolers in Peru increased from 42 percent to 68 percent between 1980 and 1983. Infant deaths have risen in Brazil during the eighties. The council summarized: "Earlier progress in fighting hunger, malnutrition and poverty has come to a halt or is being reversed in many parts of the world."

AN UNPLEASANT SCENARIO

The world entered the nineties not only with a low level of grain in reserve, but with little confidence that the "carry-over" stocks could be rebuilt quickly. Sketching out the consequences of a poor harvest when stocks are down begins to sound like the social equivalent of science fiction. If the United States were to experience a drought-reduced harvest similar to that of 1988 before stocks are rebuilt, its grain exports would slow to a trickle. By September of that fateful year, the more than 100 countries that import U.S. grain would be competing for meager exportable supplies from Argentina, Australia, and France. Fierce competition among importers could double or triple grain prices and thus drive them far beyond any level previously experienced.

By November, the extent of starvation, food riots, and political instability in the Third World would force governments in affluent industrial societies to consider tapping the only remaining food reserve of any size—the 450 million tons of grain fed to livestock. If they decided to restrict livestock feeding and use the grain saved for food relief, governments would have to devise a mechanism for doing so. Would they impose a meat tax to discourage consumption, or would they ration livestock products, much as meat was rationed in many countries during World War II?

While the most immediate consequences of a disastrous harvest would force millions of the world's poor to the brink of starvation, the international monetary system also would be in jeopardy. Debt-ridden Third World governments desperately trying to import enough high-priced grain to avoid widespread starvation would have little foreign exchange for debt payments. Whether the major international banks could withstand such a wholesale forfeiture of payments is problematic.

Looking at the Future

Projecting future food production trends was once a simple matter, but as yields in many countries approach the upper bend on the S-shaped growth curve, simple linear extrapolations of the recent past become irrelevant. The grain outputs of several countries, including China, Indonesia, Mexico, and the Soviet Union, have shown little or no growth since 1984. In addition, land degradation and hotter summers—the former difficult to measure and the latter impossible to project with precision—will shape future production trends.

In one respect, however, projections are simpler now than in the past. Since cultivated area is not likely to change appreciably during the nineties, assessing the production prospect becomes solely a matter of estimating how fast land productivity will rise. Historically, the rise in world cropland productivity, as measured by grain yield per acre, peaked during the sixties when it climbed 27 percent during the decade. It rose only 21 percent during the seventies and an estimated 19 percent in the eighties. It seems likely, given the emerging constraints outlined earlier, that the growth in world cropland productivity will slow further during the nineties. Perhaps a harbinger of things to come, it increased only 3.4 percent in the last half of the eighties.

Even though projecting food production trends is now a complex undertaking, we do have a model to help us. The recent experience of Japan, where grain yields started rising several decades before those in other countries, offers insight about how rapidly land productivity might rise for the rest of the world. The world grain yield today, taking into account the wide range of growing conditions, appears to be roughly where Japan's grain yield was in 1970. For example, 1989's rice yield in China was 1.5 tons of milled rice per acre, exactly the same as Japan's rice yield in 1970.

Since 1970, Japan's rice yield per acre has risen an average of 0.9 percent per year, scarcely half the 1.8 percent annual growth in world population. If the world can raise grain yields during the nineties at that rate, then grain output will increase by 158 million tons, for an overall gain of 9 percent (see Table 2).

With world population expected to increase by more than 960 million, or 18 percent, per-capita grain production would fall 9 percent during the nineties. If the world cannot do any better in this decade than Japan has over the last two decades, then a steady deterioration of diets for many and starvation for some seems inevitable.

TABLE 2 World Grain Production, 1950–90, with Projections to 2000

	World Grain Production			Per Person	
Year	Total	Change per Decade	Percent	Total	Change per Decade
	(million metric tons)			(kg)	(percent)
1950	631	n.a.	n.a.	251	n.a.
1960	847	216	34	281	12
1970	1,103	256	30	298	6
1980	1,442	339	31	324	9
1990	1,758	316	19	332	3
2000	1,916	158	9	307	−8

Source: USDA, ERS, World Grain Database, unpublished data, 1990, with Worldwatch Institute projection for 2000.

Note: Projection for 2000 assumes no appreciable gains or losses in world grain area and a rate-of-yield increase for world grain between 1990 and 2000 that will equal the increase in Japan's rice yield between 1969–71 and 1986–88.

The key question for the nineties is whether the world will even be able to match the Japanese. Despite the powerful incentive of a domestic price support for their rice pegged at four times the world market, Japanese farmers have run out of agronomic options to achieve major gains in productivity. Farmers in the rest of the world, who are not as skilled, literate, or scientifically oriented as are those in Japan, will find it difficult to do better.

BITING THE BULLET

A deterioration in diet and an increase in hunger for part of humanity is no longer a matter of conjecture. It is a matter of record. Evidence that the world is in trouble on the food front is mounting. In Africa and Latin America, both the absolute number of people and the share of population that is hungry is increasing. Infant mortality, the most sensitive indicator of a society's nutritional state, appears to be rising in dozens of countries.

If the Japanese agricultural record provides a reasonable sense of what the world can expect during the nineties, and if the world continues with business-as-usual policies in agriculture and family planning, a food emergency within a matter of years may be inevitable. Soaring grain prices and ensuing food riots could both destabilize national governments and threaten the integrity of the international monetary system.

Barring any dramatic technological breakthroughs on the food front, the gap between population growth and food production will widen. In all-too-many countries, the opportunity to slow population growth with the time bought on the food front by the Green Revolution has been wasted. To be sure, there will be further gains in output from the Green Revolution, but they are not likely to match the impressive jumps registered from the mid-sixties to the mid-eighties.

The world needs to continue to strengthen agriculture in every way possible. A massive international effort is needed to protect soil, conserve water, and restore the productivity of degraded land. But the Japanese experience suggests that even doing everything feasible on the food side of the food/population equation is not enough.

Avoiding a life-threatening food situation during the nineties may depend on quickly slowing world population growth to bring it in line with food output. The only reasonable goal will be to try and cut it in half by the end of the century, that is, essentially do what Japan did in the fifties and what China did in the seventies.

Reaching that goal will be extraordinarily difficult, perhaps more demanding than anything the international community has ever undertaken. Cutting population growth is not merely a matter of providing family planning services, although this is obviously essential. It depends on raising public understanding of the relationship between family size today and the quality of human existence tomorrow. Unless these goals are given top priority in national capitals, the effort will fail. Braking population growth is unlikely without much greater investment in education, particularly for Third World women, and in health care and other social improvements that facilitate the shift to small families.

Nor is a family planning effort of this magnitude likely to succeed if the international community does not effectively address the issue of Third World debt. The economic and social progress that normally leads to smaller families is now missing in many debt-ridden countries. Unless debt can be reduced to the point where economic progress resumes, the needed decline in fertility may not materialize.

For the United States, the obvious first step is to restore its funding of the United Nations Population Fund and International Planned Parenthood Federation, which was canceled several years ago in response to pressures from the political right. Given the link between population growth and environmental degradation, President George Bush cannot credibly call himself an environmentalist if funding is not resumed. In the process, the United States could reinvigorate the international family planning effort.

Future international political stability and global economic security may depend on reining in population growth more than any other single factor. Since national security depends on global economic security and international political stability, it may need redefinition. Uncontrolled population growth may now be a far greater threat to future political stability in the world than the East-West ideological conflict that has dominated world affairs over the past generation.

The best forum for getting all these issues on the table would be an emergency UN conference of the world's national political leaders. Such a gathering would permit a review of the shifting food and population balance and an examination of the projections so that people everywhere could better understand the consequences of continuing on the current demographic trajectory.

The time may have come for world leaders to issue a call to action. It may now be appropriate for the United Nations' secretary general, the president of the World Bank, and national political leaders to urge couples everywhere to stop at two surviving children. Difficult and harsh though this may seem, bringing population and food into balance by lowering birthrates is surely preferable to doing so inadvertently by allowing death rates to rise.

6

Saving the
Trees

CRADLES OF LIFE

By Alan Durning

M oses Barriga, if he is still alive, recently celebrated his third birthday among the charred remains of a rain forest. In each of the years since he was born, the earth has lost more tropical forest—and more plant and animal species— than during any one of the previous 4.5 billion years. A beautiful, brown-eyed child with a penchant for holding onto people's fingers, Moses represents both the most intractable obstacle *to* and the strongest argument *for* forest protection: poverty.

Moses lives with his 15-year-old mother and 60-year-old great-grandfather in an insect-ridden slash-and-burn plot, six hours by rutted dirt road from Santa Cruz, Bolivia. When I met the family in June 1988, they were rocking the baby in a burlap hammock under the eaves of their hut. We sat together, out of range of the midday sun, and talked about the odyssey that brought them to this spot. Tens of millions of peasants who have gone into the rain forests in hopes of a better future could have told the same sad tale.

Roman Barriga, a good-natured man with a light in his eye, began, "We came from the highlands originally, where the soils are fertile and crops grow like magic—corn, quinoa, barley, potatoes, whatever you want. But 20 years ago the work disappeared. You couldn't find a piece of land to till—

chock-full of peasants. So we came down to Valle Seco, over by the Rio Seco, where the big farms and ranches are."

As he looked down at his bare, leathery feet, some of the music drained from his voice. "I stayed there for 15 years working as a day laborer . . . but we could never get ahead of the debts we owed to the landlords. It just went on and on. Four years ago, I made up my mind to try my luck out here in the forest." His voice quickened. "The first year, I cut the trees and burned them. And the corn grew tall and sweet in the ashes, and we all thought we had finally made it. What a party we had!"

His eyes sinking back to the powder-dry dirt, he paused. "But since then, things have gone bad. The soil gets drier and drier, and it won't grow anything but weeds. I tell you, the weeds here never sleep. And the pests? I've never seen so many kinds. My wife and daughters had to go to the city to look for work . . . as domestics, as washerwomen, because the corn won't grow right. We're just about done for."

For a long moment we looked out over the two-acre lot he had claimed from the jungle. It was like the fields of forest colonists everywhere: charred tree trunks lay where they had fallen, crops and weeds fought for sunlight in between. "I think we'll try somewhere else, maybe farther south. Some part of this great thicket of trees and weeds must be fertile!" Roman's mischievous grin finally returned as he nodded at the newest member of his family. "And now we have this little one. We named him after Moses, who led his people to the promised land. Maybe this little Moses will help us find good soil!"

We laughed together, but inside I knew it would probably never come true—not in the rain forest. For one thing, Moses may not live long enough. Almost one in five Bolivian children dies before his or her fifth birthday. Among poor rural children the ratio is worse. If Moses survives, there still may be no fertile land. According to British forest watcher Norman Myers, less than 5 percent of the

Amazon basin, a great fan that overlays six countries, is suitable for single-crop agriculture; the rest was long ago washed clean of nutrients by the countless centuries of steady rains.

As I rode away on the back of a motorcycle, kidneys jiggling, I considered the matter. Tropical deforestation, above all the burning of the Amazon jungle, has finally captured public attention in the world's temperate regions. Talk of massive debt-for-nature schemes and international monitoring authorities has swept the capitals of the developed world. But an appreciation for the intricate forces that drive forest clearing is largely absent, as is a vision of the future that reconciles the needs of poor farmers with the needs of local and global ecosystems. The problem with all the talk of saving tropical forests is simple: What is to become of Moses?

CRADLES OF LIFE

Rain forests fill the lowland tropics with a luxuriant mantle that rings the globe at the equator, wherever rainfall and temperatures remain high and relatively constant. They include evergreen rain forests (two-thirds of the total), where precipitation is distributed evenly throughout the year, and seasonal forests, where there are at least two dry months.

Although these forests cover just 7 percent of the planet's land area, their importance to the biosphere is disproportionate. With warm, wet conditions nearly year round, growing seasons never stop. Tropical forests serve as a gigantic storehouse for carbon. As whole tracts are cleared and burned, they release it as carbon dioxide into the atmosphere, where it traps heat and adds to global warming. Although ecologists cannot pinpoint the figures, tropical deforestation overall probably contributes between 7 and 31 percent of the carbon dioxide humanity releases each year. Destruction of virgin rain forests probably accounts for nearly half of that, with the remainder mostly coming from the clearing of regrown "secondary" forests and the more widely spaced trees of open woodlands.

The vast scale of the forests masks extraordinary diversity. Botanists from the Smithsonian Tropical Research Institute found 835 species of trees in one 125-acre plot of Malaysian rain forest; an equivalent area of temperate forests might hold two dozen. Many tropical species have evolved to the point of living only in conjunction with one other species—the 900 varieties of fig trees, for instance, are each pollinated by a distinct species of wasp.

Rain forests are home to half of all species on earth, most of which are still undiscovered, unstudied, and unnamed. Biologists do not know whether humans share the earth with 3 million or 30 million living species, nor how many species have been lost already. According to Edward Wilson of Harvard University, 10,000 species may be going extinct each year—about one per hour.

The loss of species, along with its ecological implications, foretells the loss of human lives, since tropical species are common sources of new medicines. One in four drugs, including the treatment for childhood leukemia, comes from tropical forest plants. At least 1,400 tropical forest plants—and perhaps more than 10,000—have some effect against cancer; among them could be several miracle drugs. We may never know.

The current status of rain forests is equally shrouded in uncertainty. Existing assessments are dated and spotty, yet paint a gloomy picture nonetheless. One-third of the world's original tropical rain forests are gone and with them undoubtedly went tens of thousands of species. The remainder, an area just larger than the United States, is going fast (see Table 1). As of the early eighties, according to the United Nations Food and Agriculture Organization, 15 million acres of tropical rain forest were lost annually to the

TABLE 1
Estimated Status
of Tropical Rain
Forests[1]

Region	Area		Annual Loss[2]
	Original	1980	
	(million acres)		
Latin America	1,983	1,509	21.2
Asia	1,074	652	4.0
Africa	894	501	3.0
Total	3,951	2,662	28.2

[1]As throughout the article, tropical rain forests cited here encompass all moist forests in the tropics, which include both evergreen and seasonal forests. They do not include dry forests or open woodlands.

[2]All figures are for 1980, except for Latin America, which includes 1987 data for Brazil. The other regions would undoubtedly be higher if current data were available.

Sources: Adrian Sommer, United Nations Food and Agriculture Organization, World Resources Institute, Brazilian National Space Research Institute.

chain saw and torch, with another 9 million disturbed or degraded by careless logging.

Recent findings prove deforestation is progressing far more rapidly today. According to satellite images analyzed by the Brazilian National Institute of Space Research, 20 million acres of virgin Brazilian forest, an area the size of Maine, went up in smoke in 1987 alone—four times the annual loss previously estimated for Brazil.

KEEPERS OF THE FOREST

The human drama in the rain forests is as complex as the natural one, involving perhaps 100 million people with diverse and often conflicting interests. They include loggers, developers, ranchers, land speculators, peasant colonists like the Barriga family (most numerous by far), and indigenous tribal groups. The latter are pivotal to saving the forests.

When Columbus crossed the Atlantic, between three and six million people sustained themselves on the riches of the Amazon forests by fishing, hunting, and cultivating a wide variety of root, annual, and tree crops. Today, no more than 500,000 of their descendants remain, and the number is falling. On average, one tribe of Amazonian Indians has been lost each year of this century, as the descendants of European colonists subject them to violence, expulsion from their native lands, and exposure to infectious diseases against which they have little resistance.

The same tale could be told of Africa and Asia. The tribal groups that have learned in exquisite detail the uses of rain forest plants and animals are now disappearing as rapidly as the forests themselves. Rain forests' indigenous population worldwide is between 5 and 10 million; the majority live in Asia.

Over millennia, each tribe developed its own pattern of life, until the diversity among rain forest people came to rival the biological diversity of their environment. The African rain forests of the Congo River basin are home to 200 distinct tribes, each with its own dialect. The Amazon basin holds 340 ethno-linguistic groups, and the island of New Guinea has 700. All learned, however, to prosper while depending only on the renewable natural resources around them, developing a profound respect for the balance of ecological systems in the process.

The Lacandon Maya of southern Mexico imitate the natural diversity of their surroundings by raising up to 70 food, fiber, and medicinal plants, along with animals, in 2-acre gardens cleared from the forest. To protect the fragile soil from the leaching rains and drying sun, they interplant trees, vines, shrubs, and annual crops; this enables them to cultivate the same area intensively for seven years. They can then continue harvesting fruit and other tree crops almost indefinitely.

The rice-growing Lua communities of Thailand meticulously follow a 10-year rotation of plots that allows them to stay on one site indefinitely. In Zaire's Ituri rain forest, the Efe pygmies hunt game and collect forest products, like honey, for trade with nearby farmers.

The ecological wisdom of rain forest people dwarfs the scientific knowledge of tropical biologists and botanists. The Kayapo, one of the Amazon's hundreds of endangered Indian tribes, provide a rare, well-documented inventory of indigenous knowledge. American anthropologist Darrell Posey, of the Goeldi Museum in Belem, Brazil, who has spent 15 years studying the 2,500-member group, reports that the tribe makes use of 250 types of wild fruit, hundreds of nut and tuber species, and perhaps thousands of medicinal plants. They cultivate 13 distinct bananas, 11 kinds of manioc (cassava), 16 sweet potato strains, and 17 different yams. Many of these varieties are unknown to non-Indians. The Kayapo herbal pharmacopeia includes, among other things, a drug effective against intestinal parasites and an insect repellent found to reduce bites by 84 percent.

Most important, the Kayapo possess a thorough understanding, much of it encoded in myth, of complex ecological relationships. The most trivial customs can have deep ecological significance. Kayapo women, for instance, mix a few red ants into their face paint for the traditional maize festival. The explanation for this, Posey found, was that "the little red ant is the friend of the manioc," a root that is a mainstay of local diets.

Ecological studies revealed how true that was. Manioc produces a nectar that attracts the ants; the ants, trying to get at the nectar, chew through wandering bean vines that otherwise trap the manioc stems. The beans, in turn, are left to climb the neighboring corn stalks, which can easily support them. And the corn benefits from the nitrogen that the beans add to the soil. Thus, ants boost yields of three staple crops—manioc, beans, and corn—all of which are cultivated by the women.

Few of the world's hundreds of jungle groups have been studied as intensively as the Kayapo, but there is no reason to think they are unusual. Ghillean Prance and his colleagues at the New York Botanical Gardens' Institute for Economic Botany studied four widely scattered Indian tribes and found two used almost 80 percent of local tree species for one thing or another, a third used 60 percent, and the fourth 50 percent. Multiplying the breadth of this knowledge by the hundreds of rain forest groups suggests the enormous wealth of opportunities rain forests hold for bettering human life. "With the extinction of each indigenous group," writes Posey, "the world loses millennia of accumulated knowledge about life in, and adaptation to, tropical ecosystems."

In the Amazon basin, two relatively new groups of inhabitants have also developed effective—though less sophisticated—strategies for living within the means of the forest. *Ribereños,* a culturally mixed group numbering in the tens of thousands, take their living from fishing, intensive farming, and gathering dozens of natural products on the banks of the Amazon River and its 1,000 tributaries. In addition, 300,000 rubber tappers, a guild of workers who trace their roots and their residence in the forests to the cyclical rubber booms of the late-nineteenth and early-twentieth centuries, earn their keep by harvesting latex from the rubber trees spread liberally throughout the region. They also gather Brazil nuts, fruits, and fibers in the woods and cultivate small plots near their homes.

In the long run, indigenous knowledge will be the key to sustainable human use of the forests, assuming, of course, that the keepers of the forests and the forests themselves make it in the long run.

AGENTS OF DESTRUCTION

The causes and details of destruction of rain forests vary from one country to the next, yet almost everywhere it is migrant farmers who fell the trees. The critical question is what drives them, for there are almost always deeper forces at work.

Most directly, large-scale commodity booms are behind the process. Rubber and palm oil plantations have replaced much of the original forests in peninsular Malaysia. Industrial charcoal production in the eastern Amazon has escalated with the opening of pig iron plants. Mining projects directly degrade large areas and in many places make virgin forests accessible to migrants. Brazilian prospectors poison rivers with mercury as they process their gold. In desperately impoverished Peru and Bolivia, the U.S. cocaine habit plays itself out by sending millions of peasants scurrying into remote jungle regions to grow the coca plant.

The biggest, most sustained commodity booms, though, are in timber and cattle. Logging itself rarely clears an area completely, but, particularly in Asia and Africa, the careless methods commonly used injure dozens of trees for each tree harvested and open remote areas to colonization by migrants. They finish off the job already started.

In Latin America, the cattle rancher is king. Ranching, primarily for export beef, has indirectly leveled half of Central America's forests since 1960. Small farmers do the ranchers' dirty work. Denied access to land in the fertile Pacific lowlands and encouraged by their governments, Costa Rican, Nicaraguan, and Honduran peasants clear plots on the forest frontier, farm them for a year, and move on. Ranchers bring up the rear. In Brazil, the massive cattle-ranching business is driven by land speculation.

Beneath these proximate causes, however, lies the sheer pressure of human population growth. Brazil, Indonesia, and Zaire, which between them contain half the world's remaining tropical rain forests, must feed, clothe, and care for an additional seven million people each year. Some of them, dreaming of independence and security, inevitably make their way to the forests to carve out plots of their own.

Grossly inequitable distribution of farmland magnifies the impact of population growth in Latin America and the Philippines. While only 7 percent of Latin American landowners control 93 percent of arable land, an estimated 20 million peasant families lack plots large enough for subsistence. Much of the private farmland, meanwhile, stands idle, because its owners are more interested in speculation in land values than in producing crops. The ranks of the dispossessed are the source of most newcomers to the Amazon.

Based on this analysis of the causes of deforestation, a viable strategy to save the tropical rain forests can be sketched. A complex challenge, it requires simultaneous progress on three fronts: Forest people's own grass-roots organizations must continue to grow and gain influence; policies at the national and international levels, including land tenure and family planning, will need to be reoriented to promote forest conservation; and sustainable methods of crop production—many of them long used by indigenous populations—must be rapidly taught to forest migrants.

Rain Forest Rebellion

"The only ones who know how to defend the forest are we who have lived here for a hundred years or more—the rubber tappers and the Indians." These words, spoken to me by an old rubber tapper in a dusty cafe near Brazil's border with Bolivia, distill a critical lesson about rain forest politics: Local people are leading the struggle to harmonize humanity's relationship with the forests.

The bullet that killed Francisco "Chico" Mendes in the Brazilian jungle in December 1988 proved that the Amazon's rubber tappers are willing to put their lives on the line to save the forests. But they are not alone. From the Congo to Kalimantan, rain forest people have begun defending their homes.

Mendes's story is illustrative. In the late seventies, he began organizing a union among the 30,000 rubber tappers in the Brazilian state of Acre. He urged them to draw the line against the cattle ranchers and land speculators who were razing the forests.

When I visited Acre in 1988, Mendes's cousin, Raimundo Mendes de Barros, told me about the early days. "In those times, we didn't know what the 'natural environment' was. The forest was our life—our survival." Their tactics were simple and direct at first. Where the chain saws were working, men, women, and children would peacefully occupy the forest: they would put their bodies in the path of destruction. This nonviolent strategy has, since the beginning, been met with violent reprisals from local land barons.

A week before my visit, a landlord's hired assassins had gunned down a peasant politician allied with the rubber tappers; a month later, a rubber-tapper leader was shot. Then, continuing the cruel history of bloodshed in the rain forest, two gunmen ambushed Chico Mendes behind his simple, three-room house and killed him instantly.

The price has been high, but the rubber tappers have made modest gains. Bolstered by an unprecedented alliance with indigenous tribes and the scattered beginnings of a nationwide rubber-tappers movement, Acre's union has demanded an end to the destruction of their lands—and an end to violence against their members. They have helped reshape World Bank and Inter-American Development Bank lending policies by showing that, over the long run, natural rubber production is more profitable and creates more employment per acre than cattle ranching or farming.

With help from international environmental groups, the union has called on the Brazilian government to set aside large "extractive reserves" where tappers can carry on their way of life in perpetuity. And, among the rubber trees of Acre, they have built community schools and health posts. In other parts of the Brazilian Amazon and across the border in Bolivia, rubber tappers inspired by their peers in Acre have begun organizing themselves to safeguard the forest. In Peru, *ribereños* are now following a similar course.

Less noticed but somewhat older has been the struggle of indigenous forest people. From a slow start in the mid-sixties, the Indian rights movements of Latin America have swelled and spread.

By 1982, Brazilian Indians had formed the Union of Indian Nations and thus unified their disparate efforts to gain land rights; more recently a pan-Amazonian network was established to coordinate indigenous peoples' efforts in different countries. Philippine tribal groups have also formed a powerful land rights movement, embodied in the Cordillera People's Alliance, which incorporates 120 tribes. The fundamental objective of all Indian movements is to achieve legal recognition, demarcation, and protection of native people's traditional land base and effective local control of it.

Despite the best efforts of indigenous people, history continues to move inexorably against them. On the border of Venezuela and Brazil, the Amazon's largest surviving tribe, the Yanomamo, long isolated from the influences of white society by vast expanses of forest, now battle for their lands against gold miners who have invaded since 1985. As in the times of the conquistadors, disease kills off hundreds of natives. In 1985 alone, 50 percent of one group of Yanomamo were killed by measles, according to Kenneth Taylor, Washington representative of the indigenous rights monitoring group Survival International.

Across the Pacific, Borneo's Dayak tribe has been similarly victimized. The island's dense forests are a foundation of Malaysia's foreign exchange strategy: they provide the country with most of its $1 billion hardwood trade. The

Dayaks, however, want it cut only on a sustainable basis and have battled timber contractors by constructing roadblocks and appealing to European consumers to boycott Malaysian hardwoods. To date, government intransigence has stymied their efforts.

More than 100 Malaysian indigenous people were imprisoned between November 1988 and March 1989 under a state law that makes interfering with logging operations a criminal offense. Although all were subsequently released, timber extraction continues apace. Most poignant has been the plight of the Penan, the last nomadic tribe of hunter-gatherers in Borneo, who could face starvation as their forests shrink. The official attitude is summed up by state Minister of the Environment Datuk James Wong, himself a timber tycoon: "There is too much sympathy for the Dayaks. Their swidden [slash and burn] lifestyle must be stamped out."

The 50,000 well-organized Kuna Indians of Panama, on the other hand, have been able to establish their homelands as a biological reserve and put it off limits to the settlers and cattle ranchers who, predictably, are encroaching along a new access road. Deftly building alliances with international aid donors and environmental organizations in the early eighties, the Kuna now use their leverage to keep illegal settlers out of their lands. As well, they regularly host representatives of indigenous people from across Latin America to share strategies for protecting traditional lands.

The struggle of forest people to save their homelands has, so far, been a rearguard action. With support from grass-roots groups around the world that see their interest in preserving rain forests, indigenous movements could become major centers of influence, setting the tone of international opinion and thereby the agenda for political action.

There is no doubt they have the personal courage to carry it off. A month after Chico Mendes's death, Raimundo Mendes, in Washington, D.C., for his cousin's memorial service, reflected the unflagging commitment of forest movements worldwide when he told reporters at a press conference: "We are not going to stop the struggle . . . . Our cause is just. Perhaps I will be the next to die, but we will never abandon the fight."

THE LAW AND THE JUNGLE

A thick tangle of national and international policies channels millions of peasant colonists into the forests and sucks forest resources out wastefully. Untangling these policies is a precondition to sustainable development in the forests (see Table 2).

TABLE 2   Saving Rain Forests: Priorities for Action

At the international level
- Support sustainable development programs that attack root causes of poverty, including maldistribution of farmland.
- Support family planning programs in poor nations.
- Reduce international debt, in exchange for forest protection policies.

At the national level
- Recognize and defend indigenous people's rights, including the right to exercise effective control over traditional lands and natural resources.
- Launch aggressive family planning and land reform programs, step up participatory poverty alleviation programs.
- Reform land tenure, credit, subsidy, and tax policies to eliminate antiforest bias.
- Carry out thorough land use planning based on ecological capacities of soils and biological diversity, to demarcate and enforce biological reserves, extractive reserves, sustainable forestry areas, and agricultural land.
- Develop and disseminate tree-garden techniques based on indigenous models.

International debt is an unyielding vise on several tropical nations, particularly in Latin America. It leaves them few alternatives to selling off their resource base to pay foreign creditors. A possible cure? Debt reduction could be granted in exchange for reversing national policies antithetical to sustaining rain forests.

Within many nations, tackling the strife-ridden issues of population policy and land reform is unavoidable if forests are to be protected. Indonesia's most densely populated island, Java, continues to grow at an annual rate of 1.8 percent, and so adds two million future workers each year, despite a relatively strong family planning effort. Land ownership on the island is fairly evenly distributed, but the sheer numbers of farming families means that two-thirds of the farms are scarcely an acre in size. The result is a steady stream of migrants to the sparsely populated outer islands of the archipelago, where forests now recede before the advancing agricultural frontier. Under current policies, the World Bank projects that Indonesia's population will not stabilize until it has grown from the mid-1988 figure of 177 million to 335 million in the next century. Slowing the migration to the jungles hinges on implementing a more aggressive family planning program.

In Brazil, 2 percent of landowners hold 60 percent of the arable land, while close to 70 percent of rural households have little or none; the 350 largest properties alone cover an area larger than California. Efforts to redistribute idle land have been repeatedly thwarted by landowners who make ready use of violence—1,000 peasants and their allies were killed in land disputes in the eighties, according to Amnesty International. Without real rural reform, the long road to the Amazon will lure millions more of these dispossessed peasants.

Beside digging up these root causes of environmental destruction, great gains in forest protection could be made by picking out the many incentives for deforestation that are hidden in the fine grain of national policies. From rural credit schemes to timber concession procedures, most tropical nations manifest a pervasive and insidious antiforest bias.

The bias may be unintended, even unnoticed, but its impact is none the weaker. A perverse twist in Latin American land rights laws, for example, virtually dooms forests: Where titles are in dispute—as in most frontier regions— preference goes to whoever has "improved" the property or had it in "productive use." In practical terms, that translates to clear-cutting for cattle or row crops, since natural forest is considered all but useless. Land taxes that put lower rates on agricultural land than forested areas, ostensibly to encourage food production, similarly encourage deforestation.

Tropical rain forests are often, in fact, more lucrative when left standing than when leveled. Over the long term, as anthropologist Stephan Schwartzman of the Environmental Defense Fund has shown, economic returns and employment per acre are higher for natural forest products than for either cattle ranching or single-crop farming (see Figure 1). Rewriting land tenure laws and tax codes to recognize this inherent productivity would save millions of acres of forest.

Well-executed land titling programs that define productive land to include forests would give rich and poor migrants alike assurance that the land they work will remain their own indefinitely and encourage them to tend it well. Farmers who are not sure if property is theirs are unlikely to be serious about long-term planning and investment.

Land speculation is an explosive catalyst to deforestation. Well-heeled investors buy up enormous tracts, protect their tenure by clearing it and putting a few cattle out to graze, and resell it for up to 10 times the original price once roads reach the area. Where inflation rates are high, as in much of Latin America, fixed assets such as land retain their value; this makes land speculation all the more enticing. Low

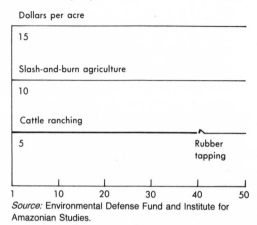

FIGURE 1
Estimated
Economic Return
of Alternative
Land Uses in
Acre, Brazil, as of
early 1980s

taxes—and piecemeal tax collection—on the profits specula-tors make as land values appreciate allow the practice to go unchecked in many countries.

To these sins of omission can be added direct govern-ment subsidies for deforestation; the sad fact is that much of the world's tropical forest land is cleared at taxpayers' ex-pense. In Southeast Asia, as economist Robert Repetto of the Washington, D.C.-based World Resources Institute has demonstrated, timber concessions are sold for a fraction of their market value. The Indonesian treasury saw only 38 percent of the economic "rent"—the market value of the timber minus the total costs of harvesting, transporting, and processing it—from public lands logged between 1979 and 1982; the Philippines got only 16 percent during the same period. It's not unusual for African governments to offer logging companies decade-long tax holidays.

Such policies lead to timber booms, during which com-panies buy enormous concessions and harvest a few mahog-any, teak, or other high-price species, while they carelessly disturb much of the surrounding forest. Within weeks after loggers have bulldozed roads into virgin rain forest, landless peasants begin streaming in to clear what remains standing.

In Brazil, as U.C.L.A. geographer Susanna Hecht and her colleagues reported, cattle ranching in the Amazon is demonstrably unprofitable. Ranches only stay in the black because of generous government tax breaks and subsidized credit, along with revenues from land speculation.

Around the world, similar subsidies promote mining, industrial projects, and the large-scale migration programs that virtually every rain forest nation has tried at one time or another, often to avoid dealing with inequitable distribution of fertile lands elsewhere. It is almost always easier to export an underclass to the frontier than to redivide estates in the heartland.

Much deforestation, in other words, is caused not by the greed of wealthy capitalists nor the desperation of starving peasants but by the failure of national authorities to protect the public interest. Ecologically, it is catastrophic; economically, it is just plain foolish.

GARDENS AMONG THE TREES

Rain forest people's own movements may one day succeed in winning them full and effective rights to their lands. Deep reforms at the national level could slow the tide of migrants and ill-planned investments. But an intractable part of the problem will persist: attending to Moses.

The momentum of population growth is too great, poverty holds too many in its grip, and the lure of the frontier is too enticing for continued colonization of the rain forests to be avoided completely. Far from an inevitable evil, it is only right that forests' biological riches should be tapped to help alleviate human poverty. The salient question, then, is how tens of millions of people can prosper in the forests without diminishing them.

A detailed plan for sustainable rain forest development cannot yet be prepared, but the general principles can be laid out.

Of course, no single model of development can work throughout the rain forests. Rather, a rich tapestry of models, all of them built on the basic form and structure of the natural forest, will have to emerge. The ecological constraints on intensive cultivation are severe, including thin soils and voracious pests, so careful planning of land uses will be necessary. As mentioned above, less than 5 percent of the Amazon basin can sustain single-crop agriculture, perhaps another 15 percent could support mixed tree cropping, and the remainder can produce a variety of forest goods, such as medicinal plants, rubber, timber, fruits, nuts, and fibers. With the help of forest people, these zones can be carefully mapped to guide development planning.

The simplest method of economic activity is gathering the natural products of the forest. Rubber tappers, who follow this strategy, are studying ways to increase the number of rubber trees in the forest while collecting additional forest products so that human population density can rise. Currently, a typical rubber-tapper family requires almost 500 acres to survive.

Tree-garden cultivation is a yet more intensive use of land. Exemplified by the system of the Lacandon Maya described earlier, tree gardens are multilayer farms that mix tall and short trees, shrubs, vines, roots, and annual cereals to create what is truly an agriculturally productive ecosystem. The hundred-odd plant species of a mature tree garden protect soils, recycle nutrients, filter the sun's rays, and prevent sudden pest outbreaks that can wipe out an entire crop under monoculture.

Indigenous subsistence methods are paradigms of sustainability, but it would be naive to think they can be widely replicated without alteration. Their shortcoming is in cash crops, for in the modern world, few are content with subsistence. Colonists—and now indigenous people who have been exposed to the flood of modern consumer goods—aspire to higher material living standards.

To boost cash earnings, exotic new products might be integrated into traditional techniques. In Panama, pilot projects for iguana ranching in the jungles have shown commercial promise; in Papua New Guinea, butterfly farms have started to spring up to meet demand from overseas collectors.

Alternatively, traditional cash crops might be worked into tree gardening systems. One promising starting point can be found in the farms of Japanese immigrants in the eastern Amazon. These farms, recently studied by Christopher Uhl of Pennsylvania State University, are among the few examples of profitable, decades-old commercial agriculture in the Amazon.

Japanese rain forest farmers succeed in the same way the Indians do: by identifying soil types where agriculture is viable and by planting diverse mixtures of crops in a long-term rotation that goes from annuals, to vines like pepper and passion fruit, to short-lived trees like papaya, to forest patriarchs like rubber and mango. While improvements in the methods used on Japanese farms could boost their sustainability, their mere existence proves that, given careful stewardship, profitable agricultural techniques can be developed for rain forest regions.

WASTELAND OR PROMISED LAND?

The biblical Moses spent 40 years in the desert. By the time Moses Barriga has spent 40 years in the jungle, it too may be a desert. The alternatives are stark: Either Moses and his people will have turned the rain forest from a land of milk and honey into a wasteland, or they will have learned to prosper within its natural bounty and follow in the tracks of the keepers of the forests.

Yet the choice is largely out of their hands; Roman Barriga, after all, must feed his family. Ultimately, responsibility for the forests falls to those of us whose bellies are full.

SUSTAINABLE FORESTRY

By John C. Ryan

The earth shakes as the forest giant crashes down, its crown landing hundreds of feet from the massive stump left behind. The product of countless seasons of clean air, stable climate, and freedom from human disturbance, the centuries-old tree represents a windfall profit to its sawyers, one never to be realized again.

Whether it was a western hemlock or a Philippine mahogany, the tree's fall also symbolizes one of the most widespread, and visibly shocking, forms of environmental degradation: deforestation. Few images breed concern for the planet like the denuded moonscape of an Oregon clear-cut or the plot of scorched earth that was once rain forest.

Images can only partially capture the legacy of logging and the world's insatiable demand for wood products, however. Fragmented ecosystems in British Columbia, threatened native cultures in Malaysia, collapsed timber industries in western Africa, and diminished biological diversity from Germany to Java attest to the fact that forest destruction is a global phenomenon.

In the tropics, the timber trade is a supporting player in a drama that sees the richest ecosystems on the planet grossly disrupted and then eliminated as forests shrink before cattle ranchers and desperate peasants. In Europe and North

America, where the area under tree cover is fairly stable, foresters have overseen the conversion of diverse natural systems into uniform tree farms, as different from their predecessors as a corn field is from a prairie.

It is clear that the time for a new forestry—one that seeks to use and maintain the complexity of forests, rather than eliminate it—is now. Although it's hard to imagine a timber industry that treads lightly on the land, it should be possible, since wood, in theory at least, is a renewable resource. As human numbers and demands continue to rise, and as forests continue to dwindle, it is urgent that we learn to tap forests' varied riches without impoverishing their source. As the timber industry confronts the exhaustion of both woodlands and the public's tolerance of its practices, it faces the inevitable choice of living up to this challenge, or following its resource base into rapid decline.

Fortunately, in places as disparate as Peru's Palcazu Valley and Oregon's Cascade Range, small bands of researchers and activists are piecing together the beginnings of a sustainable forestry.

MINING OUR HERITAGE

Reeling from a barrage of threats, forests in many regions of the world have a dim future. If rain-forest loss is not slowed, according to British forest watcher Norman Myers, "by early next century there will be little left of tropical forests except for a few large blocks in New Guinea, the Zaire basin, western Amazonia in Brazil and the Guyana highlands." Tropical logging degrades about 11 million acres annually and, especially in Southeast Asia and central Africa, contributes to complete deforestation—now estimated to total 42 million acres annually (an area the size of the state of Washington)—by making entire regions more susceptible to fire and accessible to peasants and ranchers.

In the temperate zones, which provide most of the

world's timber (see Table 1), logging, farming, and human settlements have spread to such an extent that, outside of remote northern regions, little primary forest remains. The coastal rain forest of British Columbia is given 15 years before it is wiped out from logging, and the less than 5 percent of the United States' ancient groves that still exist face rapid fragmentation and extinction.

The timber trade's attraction to primeval stands appears to be unquenchable. Much like the loggers of Siberia who set up temporary camps, cut all the usable timber from the

TABLE 1   World's Top 15 Timber Producers, 1988[1]

Country	Volume	Share of Total
	(million cubic meters)	(percent)
U.S.A.	417	25
U.S.S.R.	305	18
Canada	173	10
China	98	6
Brazil	67	4
Sweden	48	3
Finland	46	3
Indonesia	40	2
Malaysia	36	2
France	32	2
W. Germany	31	2
Japan	28	2
India	24	2
Poland	20	1
Australia	18	1
Others	281	17
World total	1,664	100

[1]Includes all wood products except fuel wood and charcoal.
Source: FAO, *Forest Products Yearbook 1988* (Rome: 1990).

area, and move on, the international timber industry mines one source then seeks out another. Canadian and Soviet foresters are now looking to their remote, and less lucrative, northern forests, while several U.S. companies have relocated operations from the Northwest to the pine plantations of the Southeast.

The focus of the tropical timber trade shifted in the 1960s from Africa, where overcutting has brought forests and forest industries crashing down, to Southeast Asia, where similar depletion is now occurring. According to an analysis done for the International Tropical Timber Organization (ITTO), a 48-nation trade group based in Yokohama, Japan, timber exporters Ivory Coast and Ghana will likely become net importers before the end of this decade. They follow the trail blazed by Nigeria in the 1970s.

The quality and availability of wood from Southeast Asia have declined, and several nations have responded with bans on log exports or on logging altogether. As one Japanese importer declared in *Nikkan Mokuzai Shimbun* (Daily Timber News) in 1988: "The depletion of tropical timber resources in Southeast Asia has become a matter of reality today, so we have to look to Brazil for a new supply. . . ."

THE ROAD TO RUIN

Even if timber is managed on a "sustained yield" basis (which considers only the yield of wood, and not any of the other benefits of forests), logging can still devastate forests. Timber harvesting typically begins with a network of roads, which themselves deforest large areas and, especially in the steeper regions now being cut, can greatly increase soil erosion and sediment buildup in streams and rivers. Approximately 8 percent of logging areas in the Pacific Northwest are cleared for road building; as much as 14 percent is cleared in Southeast Asia. Myers reports that for every tree cut for timber in certain areas of Zaire, 25 are cleared making roads to get to it. In Idaho, and in northern Palawan in the Philippines, logging roads have caused erosion more than 200 times greater than on undisturbed sites.

Roads expose forests to miners, hunters, and especially poor farmers; they also allow nonhuman invaders access to once-deep forest. Logging roads have accelerated the spread of destructive pests in the U.S. Northwest, including Port Orford cedar root rot, a fatal disease spreading rapidly into the remaining upland groves of the cedar, the region's most prized timber tree. As roads, logging, and forest clearance spread, large areas of habitat are turned into islands in a sea of degraded lands. Research in both tropical and temperate forests has shown that such fragmented landscapes are unable to support the biological diversity present in continuous forest. Recent studies of isolated patches of Amazonian forest, for example, confirm that edges of forest "islands" deteriorate rapidly from exposure to damaging winds, exotic species, and dramatic changes in temperature, humidity, and light levels.

Some of the long-term degradation that follows from loss of tree cover, such as increased soil erosion and water runoff, can be minimized by reforestation after logging. But young stands cannot provide the wildlife habitat or high-quality, fine-grained wood of ancient forest. Industrial-style "reforestation"—the planting of rows of identical trees accompanied by slash burning, soil plowing, and the use of fertilizers or herbicides—provides even fewer environmental benefits than natural regrowth.

All told, these and other impacts add up to a global failure to sustain forests. A 1989 study for ITTO found that less than 0.1 percent of tropical logging was being done sustainably. Former U.S. Bureau of Land Management biologist Chris Maser argues that sustainable forestry isn't practiced outside the tropics either. "Liquidating old-growth is not forestry," he writes, "it is simply spending our inheritance."

THE ECONOMICS OF DESTRUCTION

As the world's greatest storehouses of life, forests are valuable for much more than their timber. When these riches are sacrificed to wood production, logging often becomes difficult to justify on economic grounds.

Damage to fisheries and coral reefs caused by logging-induced sedimentation has been documented around the world. The harvesting of timber worth $14 million from the drainage of the South Fork of the Salmon River in central Idaho in the mid-1960s, for instance, caused an estimated $100 million in damage to the river's chinook salmon fishery. That industry has still not recovered. Fisheries in Bacuit Bay near Palawan in the Philippines were depleted after logging commenced in 1985 on surrounding hillsides. Sediment rushing into the bay killed up to half of the living coral that supported the fishery and thus deprived local villagers of their source of protein.

The costs of logging have usually fallen on those who depend on intact forest—forest dwellers, downstream communities, tourism-based economies, among others. But as the area of untouched forest shrinks, it is becoming clear that the timber industry is also putting itself out of business. Tropical hardwood exports, worth $8 billion in 1980, have fallen to $6 billion, and are projected to shrink to $2 billion by the end of this decade.

When diverse populations of trees are replaced with genetically uniform stands, there is a double loss to future timber harvests. Plantations can relieve pressure on natural forests by producing wood quickly, but because the natural system of checks and balances has been stripped to maximize tree growth, monocultures are prone to unravel. Widespread disease and pest outbreaks—common throughout the conifer plantations of the United States, central Europe and China, and a chronic problem in tropical plantations—can decimate entire forests, rather than localized groups of trees.

In western Germany, where forests have been logged, grazed, and raked for centuries, single-species plantations have spread to such an extent that 97 percent of forest land is covered by just three tree species. Scientists speculate (since there is virtually no natural forest left for comparison, it is impossible to prove) that the lasting damage caused by intensive forestry may have helped speed Germany's woodlands down the road to *Waldsterben:* the widespread "forest death" linked to air pollution and acid rain.

When native forests are lost, industry also loses its reservoirs of genetic variety and its scientific laboratories for uncovering the many hidden relationships that make timber growth possible. For instance, according to work done by Oregon State University entomologist Tim Schowalter and others, intact stands of natural forest are valuable as physical barriers and as sources of insect predators to stop the spread of pest outbreaks on adjacent plantations. As long as wilderness is left to tap and study, then foresters have the opportunity to learn from their mistakes. But, as industry converts native stands to plantations—putting all its eggs in the monoculture basket—its options keep narrowing.

Toward a New Forestry

How can timber be harvested without destroying forests? The answer to this question is being discovered in some very unlikely places: in a chunk of rotting wood on a forest floor, amid a buzz of insects hundreds of feet up a Douglas fir, in the fecal pellets of a flying squirrel. In these and untold other places lie the essentials of forest productivity that foresters ignore to the detriment of forests and timber production.

A small group of researchers and forest managers based at the H. J. Andrews Experimental Forest in western Oregon have been studying the lessons of natural forests and have started applying them in an attempt to reconcile the seemingly unsolvable conflict between logging and forests. The "New Forestry," as their ideas are being called, represents a fundamental change, a revolution, even, for the forestry profession, which has traditionally focused narrowly on timber production.

Perpetuation of diverse forest ecosystems has to become the focus of forestry if the forest products industry is to survive, states Jerry Franklin, an ecologist with the University of Washington and the U.S. Forest Service, and the leading proponent of New Forestry. "Already we are learning that parts of forests that we have never considered seriously are proving significant, even essential, to ecosystem functioning," he says.

One part of the forest overlooked until recently is the array of underground organisms that help keep soils fertile. Among the most important of these are the "mycorrhizal" fungi that attach to the roots of 90 percent of the world's plant species and whose vast threadlike networks literally form the base of forests in the Pacific Northwest. Eaten and dispersed by small mammals, the fungi enable trees to absorb nutrients and water from the soil and fix nitrogen. After clear-cutting, when all "host" plants and ground cover for mammals are removed, many of the fungus species are eliminated, and thus the land is robbed of its ability to grow more timber.

These and many other hidden linkages discovered within forest communities demonstrate the importance of maintaining intact as many of the prelogging conditions as possible throughout the timber cutting cycle. Similarly, foresters are starting to recognize dead trees and logs on the forest floor as essential parts of a healthy forest, not a form of waste to be burned off or shredded. Beside providing important wildlife habitat, woody debris maintains soil fertility by returning organic matter and nutrients to the soil and helping to control erosion.

On a handful of sites on the Willamette and Siskiyou

national forests in Oregon, U.S. Forest Service managers are beginning to actively apply these principles to their work. They leave behind live and dead trees, corridors of trees along stream banks, and small and large woody debris. The goal is to maintain the land's productivity and its diversity. They have also begun to lump timber cutting areas together to minimize fragmentation and road building.

Every Day, Every Acre

New Forestry is no substitute for protecting natural areas: no forester can create 1,000-year-old ecosystems or bring back species driven to extinction. Environmentalists are rightly suspicious of anyone trying to sell new types of logging as the solution to deforestation. Especially in places such as the United States, where the amount of wilderness left is small, preservation is still the top priority.

Nonetheless, given that logging of primary forest is not going to stop tomorrow, New Forestry promises to minimize the damage to areas that will be lumbered. The New Forestry has been researched and applied almost exclusively in the ancient forests of the Pacific Northwest, but, as David Perry, a forest ecologist at Oregon State University, notes, although particular techniques will vary greatly, "there are certain ecological principles translatable virtually anywhere in the world." The philosophical core of the New Forestry—the goal of working with the complexity of natural systems, rather than eliminating it—can apply as well to farmland and oceans as it does to forests.

Reducing the risk of future pest outbreaks and ensuring that soil is not robbed of its nutrients makes sense whether wood is harvested from a pristine rain forest, a logged-over woodland, or an intensively cropped tree farm. As evidence builds that the intensive forestry practices used today often fail to sustain timber productivity over time, timber managers may see the wisdom of restoring natural resilience and diversity to their lands.

Since most of the world's forests are already logged over or cleared, and many of the remaining areas are severely fragmented, any attempt to protect biological diversity will have to address the lands that humans use intensively. "We could never hope to protect biological diversity solely through preservation," says Franklin, "since so much diversity occurs on commodity landscapes. . . . Protection of diversity must be incorporated into everything we do every day on *every* acre, whether preserve or commodity land."

TROPICAL TROUBLES

In primary rain forest, still the predominant resource for the tropical timber trade, the social, political, and biological complexities of forest use raise doubts whether sustainable timbering is even possible. Removing too much wood from these forests, in which nutrients are found mostly in the plant life itself, not in the soil, leaves behind a nutritionally impoverished system that may take hundreds of years to rebound. Even selective logging is typically very destructive because of the tremendous diversity of tree species: loggers inevitably trample wide areas as they "cream" the forest—taking only a handful of desired species.

Third World governments, saddled with debt and swelling populations, typically see their rain forests as quick sources of foreign exchange or as safety valves for an expanding underclass. Unstable conditions outside the forest make long-term policy inside—such as enforcing minimum lengths of logging rotations or preventing illegal entry in logged-over areas—difficult to enforce. The sheer number of people looking to tropical moist forests as sources of sustenance and profit may already overwhelm their carrying capacity.

Despite the numerous obstacles, a handful of projects show how sustainable tropical logging might work. The Yanesha Forestry Cooperative, the first Indian forestry cooperative in Amazonia, has been operating since 1985 in Peru's Palcazu Valley. Local people own and process the forest products; timber cutting is designed with protection of diversity in mind. By clear-cutting in narrow strips, leaving most of the forest intact, the Palcazu project seeks to mimic small-scale natural disturbances. Creating gaps in the forest canopy allows the shade-intolerant seedlings of hundreds of different species from the uncut areas to colonize the strips. Bark and branches are left in place, rather than burned off, to maintain soil fertility.

Portico S.A., a Costa Rican door manufacturer, may be the only timber company in the world researching natural forest management. Recognizing that its resource base of *caobilla,* a type of mahogany, was endangered by deforestation, Portico has been buying up forest land and trying different harvest techniques and rotations since 1988 to assure itself a steady supply of wood. Because *caobilla* cannot be grown outside its natural, swampy habitat, the company is buying from local farmers marginal farmland where the tree is found and hiring them as part-time guardians against illegal loggers. Portico's logging in important wildlife areas, and its inflated claims of environmental purity, have alienated some local environmentalists. But most agree that its operations are a big step in the right direction.

These projects are both so new that it is not possible to call them successful yet. It would take decades of steady production and biological monitoring to do that; unfortunately, few nations have the luxury of that much time. New approaches to logging that incorporate rather than ignore natural linkages and local people can, at the very least, prolong the useful life of logging areas, and buy time for other solutions to deforestation to be worked out.

ENDING THE TIMBER BIAS

If the conflict between timber and forests is to be resolved, a two-prong strategy is needed: protection of large, viable areas of natural forest and new forestry practices on areas to be logged. Probably the greatest obstacle to achieving these goals is the commonly held view of forests primarily as timber factories. It is this timber bias, prevalent among foresters and policymakers the world over, that has already sent much of the world's natural heritage to the mill.

Most nations have laws and regulations proclaiming their commitment to sustained-yield or multiple-use forestry, but almost nowhere does this translate into a balanced approach to forest use. Economist Robert Repetto of the World Resources Institute (WRI) in Washington, D.C., has documented the worldwide occurrence of government subsidies that encourage destructive logging at taxpayers' and forests' expense.

The much-heralded Tropical Forestry Action Plan, an international strategy launched in 1985 by the Food and Agriculture Organization, the United Nations Development Program, the World Bank, and WRI, is expected to accelerate deforestation because of its reliance on increased logging as a means of saving forests. The Peruvian Forestry Action Plan, for example, advocates an expansion of the road network and a four- to sixfold increase in logging, even though it recognizes that Peru's forests "are exploited in the same way as the mines of the Sierra" and describes present management as "chaos."

The timber focus also ignores the root causes of deforestation—including maldistribution of farmland, international debt, and population growth. Shifting control of forests away from exploitative users—such as timber cutters and cattle ranchers—and toward sustainable users of forests, especially the millions of forest dwellers who have lived within the forests' limits for ages, can do much to halt forest loss. Colombia's decision in February 1990 to recognize Indian rights to half of its Amazon forests is a landmark achievement in both forest policy and social justice.

PROTECTING FORESTS, PROTECTING JOBS

While the crush of human demands ensures that most forests will be used in one way or another, turning natural areas of global significance into pulp—as is happening in Alaska's Tongass rain forest and Southeast Asia's last large area of coastal mangroves in Bintuni Bay, Indonesia—is a travesty considering that pulpwood can be obtained with much less impact from second-growth forests and plantations. Ending subsidies for conversion of primary forests and putting in place incentives for better management on less valuable lands could help increase sustainable timber supplies.

But new supplies will take time to develop; forests will continue to be pushed beyond their limits until the world begins to curb its spiraling appetite for wood products. Because sustainable forestry will often yield less wood per acre in the near term than timber mining, and because increased recognition of the nonwood values of forest will mean fewer acres available for timber harvest, reducing the demand for wood is an inevitable part of the sustainability equation.

Many opportunities exist to reduce wasteful use of wood products—from the 50 percent of raw wood turned to chips and dust in a typical sawmill to the 20 billion disposable chopsticks consumed annually in Japan. Less than one-third of the paper used in the United States, the world's most gluttonous consumer of paper (see Table 2), is recycled; one-half of the total is consumed as packaging.

Wherever forests are cut down, governments can act to get the most out of each tree. In the Pacific Northwest, the timber industry blames the loss of jobs upon environmentalists, yet one out of every four trees harvested in 1989 was

TABLE 2
Per-Capita Paper
Use, Selected
Countries and
Regions, 1988

Country/ Region	Pounds per Year	Percent Recycled[1]
U.S.A.	699	29
Sweden	685	40
Canada	543	20
Japan	450	50
Norway	333	27
U.S.S.R.	78	19
Latin America	55	32
China	27	21
Africa	12	17
India	5	26

[1]Amount of waste paper recycled compared with total paper consumption; 1987 figures.
Source: The Greenpeace Guide to Paper (Vancouver: Greenpeace, 1990).

sent abroad as raw logs, untouched by mill workers. Timber-related employment in Oregon declined by 15 percent in the 1980s, even as timber harvests reached record levels. A ban on the export of raw logs would provide four times more wood for local mills as would be set aside under a federal plan to protect ancient forests in which the rare spotted owl lives.

Policymakers can reduce damage to lands that are logged by enforcing forestry regulations, which on paper are often quite sound, and by emphasizing the long-term health of forests, rather than quick profits for logging companies. As WRI's Repetto has noted, economic tools such as pricing reforms can encourage loggers not to waste the forests they are granted access to.

But economics can only accomplish so much. Ultimately, it's essential that widespread recognition of the ethical responsibility not to trade present yields for future degradation take hold. The introduction of codes of conduct among

European tropical timber importers and the growth of the Association of Forest Service Employees for Environmental Ethics in the United States are two hopeful signs in this area. Jobs and profits based on ecological destruction simply cannot last. If societies can come to grips with this fact, perhaps we can make the transition to sustainability while there are still ecosystems left worth protecting.

7

A New Energy
Strategy

THE CASE AGAINST REVIVING
NUCLEAR POWER

By Christopher Flavin

At 1:00 on the morning of May 26th, 1988, the Long Island Lighting Company and the State of New York reached an extraordinary settlement. The utility agreed to sell its completed but never operated nuclear plant at Shoreham to the state for one dollar, while the state promised to permanently close the $5.3 billion facility and grant the utility a series of rate increases intended to save it from imminent bankruptcy.

To one not familiar with the current status of nuclear power, the Shoreham saga has an Alice-in-Wonderland quality. How, might one wonder, could nuclear planners have sited a plant in a densely populated part of Long Island, and then pushed the project forward despite overwhelming local opposition?

How could the original construction schedule have been missed by more than a decade and the budget by more than $4 billion? How could a private company have tied its very survival to the completion of a single power plant whose cost exceeded the value of all of its other assets?

And how could the Nuclear Regulatory Commission have allowed a utility to load radioactive fuel into a plant unlikely to ever get a full operating license, an act that will add hundreds of millions of dollars to New York's expense for decommissioning Shoreham?

The Shoreham case is extreme, but it is symbolic of the problems currently facing nuclear power. It includes colossal mismanagement, cost overruns that would make the Pentagon blanch, and fierce political battles that pit citizens and local officials against government bureaucracies committed to expanding nuclear power.

Five years after the Chernobyl accident, the political and economic tide around the world is running strongly against nuclear power—pushed by many of the same forces that did in Shoreham. Nuclear power has become expensive, its growth has been mismanaged, and an increasing number of citizens are rejecting it. The daunting problems of nuclear waste disposal and nuclear materials proliferation grow ever more indomitable as governments fail to come up with solutions and the materials themselves accumulate.

Despite the lack of such solutions, some officials are now calling for a revival of nuclear power. The new impetus: global warming and other environmental threats caused by the world's reliance on fossil fuels. Once a scientific theory, human-induced climate change is now an accepted reality. The world's current energy trends are beginning to undermine the health of environmental systems crucial for humanity's survival.

As governments and international agencies look for alternatives to oil and coal, nuclear power is once again presented as a candidate. Societies are now in danger of banking on a new generation of nuclear reactors without fully understanding the enormity of the problems that ruined the last generation.

A DECADE OF SETBACKS

When disaster struck the Three Mile Island nuclear plant in March of 1979, the global nuclear industry was running at full throttle. New plants were being built at a record pace, governments were almost universally in favor of nuclear power, and public acceptance of these plans was unquestioned. Three Mile Island, however, was the first in what would be a series of setbacks for nuclear power. Now, 12 years later, the nuclear programs of nearly every country have been touched by the ripple of doubt set off by that accident and the one at Chernobyl.

At first glance, it would seem that nuclear power has continued to flourish in the past decade. Generating capacity, for example, has risen more than fourfold to 312,000 megawatts. But beneath this veneer of progress is a sick industry that is getting few new orders and in many countries is clearly winding down.

In the United States, Three Mile Island was a pivotal event. As the pioneering nuclear nation, the U.S. had by far and away the world's most ambitious nuclear program in 1979. Yet, not a single nuclear plant has been ordered in the United States since, and 108 have been canceled, including all of those ordered after 1974. The U.S. business magazine *Forbes* has called the failure of the U.S. nuclear power program "the largest managerial disaster in U.S. business history," involving perhaps $100 billion in wasted investments, cost overruns, and unnecessarily high electricity costs.

The U.S. nuclear construction industry has for the most part disappeared, and the pipeline of new projects is nearly empty, sustained only by a handful of plants that are a decade behind schedule on average. It now appears that the nuclear share of U.S. electricity production has peaked in the early nineties—at about 20 percent—and will soon begin a slow decline as older plants are retired.

Country	Before Chernobyl	After Chernobyl	TABLE 1
	(percent)		Public Opposition in Selected Countries to Building Additional Nuclear Power Plants[1]
United Kingdom	65	83	
West Germany	46	83	
Italy	—	79	
United States	67	78	
Yugoslavia	40	74	
Canada	60	70	
Finland	33	64	
France	—	52	

[1]Wording and polling techniques varied, but data are broadly comparable. Pre-Chernobyl figures are from polls taken between 1982 and 1986.

Source: Worldwatch Institute, based on Gallup and other polls.

It was economic more than political or technological failure that doomed nuclear power in the United States. As with the Shoreham plant, most U.S. nuclear facilities completed in the eighties are grossly uneconomical; they provide power that is five times as costly as that from plants completed a decade ago.

Hundreds of changes introduced to make nuclear power safer have added billions of dollars to costs. The industry attempted to blame regulators for requiring expensive changes, but it is clear in retrospect that the changes were needed to help avert accidents that would have caused the nuclear industry even greater damage.

EUROPE AFTER CHERNOBYL

Advocates of nuclear power often argue that the U.S. nuclear program is beset by problems of little relevance to the rest of the world. The supposed strength of nuclear power throughout Europe and much of the rest of the world is often held out as evidence that if nuclear managers and regulators would simply clean up their acts, the problems would soon be resolved.

As attractive as this argument may seem, it is belied by the declining fortunes of nuclear power across a wide spectrum of countries—from the Western democracies to the Soviet Union and the developing world. A process of gradual attrition during the early eighties has mushroomed into a massive rejection of nuclear power since Chernobyl—more for political reasons than for technological or economic ones.

In Europe, several countries have made formal commitments to shut down their nuclear programs in the wake of Chernobyl. Months after the Soviet disaster, Austria abandoned its only nuclear plant, at Zwentendorf—a plant that like the one at Shoreham had never been operated. Greece decided at about the same time to scrap plans to build its first nuclear plant.

After a protracted political debate that contributed to the collapse of two governments, Italian voters decided in March 1988 to block the expansion of the country's already stalled nuclear program. Two months later, under intense political pressure, the Italian government decided to stop work on the country's only remaining nuclear construction project, at Montalto di Castro; this leaves three completed reactors operating intermittently. Though not quite officially dead, Italy's nuclear program shows few remaining vital signs.

Early in 1988, the government of Belgium, which is already heavily nuclearized, decided to postpone expansion plans indefinitely. The Netherlands, which has no large reactors, has also canceled its plans. Switzerland, which has not completed a nuclear plant since 1980, decided in 1988 to cancel 22-year-old plans to build the country's sixth nuclear facility at Kaiseraugst.

Scandinavia's nuclear programs have also been moving

in reverse. Finland, with a substantial nuclear capacity, indefinitely postponed expansion plans after Chernobyl. Sweden decided in a 1978 referendum to phase out nuclear power by 2010, despite the fact that nuclear plants supply 40 percent of the country's electricity. The Chernobyl accident forced the government to firm up these plans by scheduling the shutdown of the first two plants in 1995 and 1996. Denmark and Norway, meanwhile, have reaffirmed their vows never to develop nuclear power.

Europe's second and third largest nuclear power programs remain in a state of limbo. Nuclear opposition has flourished in West Germany since Chernobyl; this has further weakened the already remote possibility of the country's building additional nuclear plants. Several state governments and the major opposition party in the federal parliament are vehemently opposed to nuclear power, but the Christian-Democratic government continues to support it.

In Great Britain, the Thatcher government got to work on a nuclear plant at Sizewell after it concluded an eight-year debate in 1987. But since then, the government has decided to forego any further construction, largely due to the objections of the country's financial community.

France, meanwhile, remains Europe's pronuclear holdout. Four more plants were completed in 1987; this gives the country a nuclear capacity second only to that of the United States. Nuclear power now supplies 75 percent of the country's electricity.

But even France's nuclear program is plagued by a growing number of technical malfunctions. In the spring of 1988, one plant at Flamanville lost its cooling capacity twice, a plant at Nogent-sur-Seine released radioactive steam, and several other plants were shut down due to radiation leaks. France has so far avoided a Three Mile Island or Chernobyl-style debacle, and it is uncertain whether the pronuclear consensus would survive such an event.

The more obvious problem in France is too much nuclear capacity. The country has been forced to sell electricity to neighboring countries at bargain prices and to run its plants at partial capacity. This gap will grow larger as more plants come on-line in the next few years. France's nuclear expansion has been slowed from one plant per year to several over the next decade, a level intended just barely to support the government-owned nuclear manufacturing industry.

The French state utility has built up an enormous debt of $37 billion, which continues to grow as high-cost nuclear electricity is subsidized so as to encourage greater consumption and justify the investment. Nuclear power has helped reduce the country's oil import bill, but it has also tended to starve other parts of the French economy of investment capital. Now, the economy is not growing nearly fast enough to support the country's large nuclear program.

SECOND THOUGHTS IN THE SOVIET UNION

Prior to Chernobyl, the Soviet nuclear program—third largest in the world—was generally thought to have avoided the morass of political problems that derailed programs in the West. The Soviet government maintained a firm commitment to nuclear power in building an industry that supplies 11 percent of the country's electricity.

Since Chernobyl, the Soviet nuclear consensus has clearly broken down. Top Soviet officials regularly contradict one another about the status of nuclear power, and local citizens groups and public officials have openly dissented from the national program.

The Chernobyl catastrophe and its aftermath have sowed seeds of doubt about nuclear power and the capacity of Soviet industry to manage it. The cleanup at Chernobyl has not gone well, and the total cost of the accident is now projected to reach $360 billion.

Meanwhile, rumors of radiation-related sickness continue to circulate in the Ukraine, and citizens report a general sense of fearfulness and unease five years after the accident. Public confidence has been further undermined by reports of subsequent mismanagement at the remaining Chernobyl reactors, breaches serious enough to require disciplinary action against key officials.

Such stories have fueled an outburst of antinuclear protests throughout the Soviet Union. Indeed, Soviet press reports indicate that all of the country's operating nuclear plants face local opposition, as do most of those being built. Even in the era of *glasnost,* such protests betray a remarkable degree of disquiet with government policy.

The most vociferous protests, not surprisingly, emanate from the Ukraine, where Chernobyl is located. Both the Ukraine Writers' Union and the Ukrainian Academy of Sciences have drafted a "manifesto" condemning the policies of the Ministry of Atomic Energy. Antinuclear petitions demanding a change of course have circulated at Moscow State University and at the Crimean Agricultural Institute.

Soviet nuclear officials have stuck to their pre-Chernobyl plans; they have agreed only to phase out production of the reactor design used at Chernobyl. Nuclear capacity in the last five-year plan was scheduled to advance by a substantial 40,000 megawatts toward the goal of supplying 21 percent of Soviet electricity by 1990. This target, however, was missed by a huge margin as Soviet nuclear capacity increased by just 6,000 megawatts since the accident.

In May 1987, it was announced that the two additional units planned at Chernobyl would not be built. This was the beginning of a long string of plants cancelled or construction halted in the face of growing public protest. Last year the Ukrainian Republic's ruling body declared it would build no new atomic power plants. This move was followed by a similar decree signed by Russian Republic President Boris Yeltsin.

It is impossible to read this litany of setbacks without

suspecting that the Soviet nuclear program is in the process of coming seriously unglued. The growing cost of safety measures in the aftermath of Chernobyl will likely cast further doubt on the efficacy of nuclear investments. Portions of the Soviet scientific community now seriously question the nuclear program, and an important faction of scientists and economic planners favor an alternative approach to energy policy—in the direction of efficiency, renewable resources, and decentralized power generation.

THE SHIFTING CASE FOR NUCLEAR POWER

As nuclear power programs continue to slip into oblivion, the question remains whether countries can afford *not* to have nuclear power. Many key officials think not. Valeri Ligasov, who headed the Soviet commission that investigated the Chernobyl accident, has stated that "the future of civilization is unthinkable without the peaceful use of atomic energy."

This line is nothing new from the pronuclear camp. Although they've remained stalwart in their conviction of the necessity for atomic power, many nuclear advocates have justified it by repeatedly shifting among various arguments. In the sixties, nuclear power was pressed as an inevitable next step in the technology of energy systems. Few problems were seen as beyond the reach of scientists, and it was assumed that nuclear power would be inexpensive if not actually "too cheap to meter."

In the seventies, nuclear power was seen as an essential alternative to dwindling oil supplies, not without its own problems, but essential to stave off economic collapse. In the late eighties, with oil prices down and nuclear power programs in disarray, nuclear advocates became environmentalists, urgently arguing that only nuclear power can ease acid rain, global warming, and other threats posed by heavy use of fossil fuels.

The "technological inevitability" argument was the first to go. Since the late seventies it has become clear that the evolution of energy technology does not necessarily have to take a nuclear path. High energy prices encouraged dramatic improvements in hundreds of energy technologies, ranging from more-efficient oil refineries to less-expensive solar power.

During the past 15 years, for example, improved energy efficiency has saved far more oil than has nuclear power. Many countries now pursue the long-term development of hydroelectric and wind power, solar, energy, and biological (biomass) fuels as alternatives both to oil and nuclear power. Whatever the arguments for its development, nuclear power must now be fairly weighed against its alternatives.

Using nuclear power to fuel the economy on a large scale is possible only if it is affordable. And the best evidence available indicates that investing in nuclear power has become a risky proposition. In the United States, where financial reporting requirements are strictest, the latest generation of nuclear plants has proven to be decidedly uneconomical. These plants cost more than three times as much to build as equivalent fossil-fuel plants, and significantly more than a number of renewable energy facilities, including wind, geothermal, and biomass-fired power plants. As other power generating technologies evolve, nuclear power's financial disadvantage only widens.

Operating costs—an area in which nuclear power has traditionally enjoyed an economic advantage—are also growing malignantly. The equipment must be repaired or replaced far more frequently than was supposed. Recent surveys in the United States indicate that real operating costs have gone up almost fourfold since 1974 and that it now costs more just to operate the average nuclear plant than it does to operate a coal plant—including the cost of coal. A study by the U.S. Department of Energy suggests that some plants have become so costly to operate that it

Source and Year of Projection	Projection for			TABLE 2
	1980	1990	2000	Projections of Worldwide Nuclear Power Generating Capacity
	(thousand megawatts)			
International Atomic Energy Agency				
1972	315	1,300	3,500	
1974	235	1,600	4,450	
1976	225	1,150	2,300	
1978	170	585	1,400	
1980	137	458	910	
1982	—	386	833	
1984	—	382	605	
1986	—	372	505	
Worldwatch Institute				
1991	—	312	375	

Sources: International Atomic Energy Agency, *Annual Reports* (Vienna: 1972–80); IAEA, *Reference Data Series No. 1,* (Vienna, September 1982); IAEA, *Nuclear Power: Status and Trends* (Vienna: 1984–86); and Worldwatch Institute.

may be more economical to retire them early than to continue operations. Even writing off the $5.3 billion Shoreham plant may in the end turn out to have been a wise business decision.

At the root of these enormous cost escalations is a technology whose complexity defies human management and leads to continuing, unpredictable changes in equipment and operating procedures. Even in countries where regulatory pressures have not been as intense or public opposition as vehement, cost overruns have become endemic.

When planning a nuclear plant today, it is impossible to know how much it will cost to build, how much it will cost to operate, how long it will last, or what it will cost to decommission. This is the kind of investment that only a government or utility would make, and even they are now generally investing elsewhere.

As an alternative to oil, nuclear power's potential is also severely constrained. While nuclear power generation did substitute for oil-fired generation in Europe and Japan during the late seventies and early eighties, the power sector's use of oil is now extremely low, offering little potential for further displacement.

Throughout the world, the major claimants on the world oil supply are automobiles, trucks, buses, and industrial plants. Improved efficiency offers by far the most effective means of displacing oil in these areas.

FALSE HOPE FOR THE WORLD'S CLIMATE

The environmental argument for further nuclear expansion is at first glance more compelling than the other two. Continuing expansion of fossil fuel combustion is now causing ecological havoc around the world. Air quality in most of the world's cities continues to deteriorate, particularly in developing countries, and air pollution carried over long distances has damaged at least 22 percent of Europe's forests.

As serious as these problems are, the ultimate limit to future energy growth may lie with the earth's climate. Scientists now believe that the nearly 6 billion tons of carbon being added to the earth's atmosphere each year from the combustion of fossil fuels is contributing to irreversible climate change. Average global temperatures have already increased by about 1 degree Fahrenheit during the past century, according to a U.S. government-sponsored study published in the spring of 1988.

Global warming has begun, according to the best available scientific evidence, and climate models suggest a 9-degree rise by the middle of the next century—a faster warming than the earth has ever experienced. This would be sufficient to upset weather patterns, damage agricultural output, raise sea levels, and expose humanity to wrenching change. With population expanding rapidly and the world food system already stretched tight, societies would probably find it impossible to adapt to such sudden change.

New scientific evidence along with severe droughts and heat waves in several countries recently have lent a new urgency to the problem of global warming. In this light, many policymakers around the world are reassessing nuclear power. An international conference of scientists and public officials, meeting in Toronto in 1988, called for a worldwide effort to cut fossil-fuel use by 20 percent by 2005. Nuclear power was one of the energy sources the conferees suggested reevaluating for its potential to combat global warming.

Some argue that a few Chernobyls would be a small price to pay to head off global warming. Unfortunately, this is the kind of thinking that has misled nuclear planners in the past. Nuclear power is beset by problems that go well beyond its propensity for occasional accidents. Technologically, economically, and politically, nuclear power faces a series of obstacles that will prevent it from coming close to displacing enough fossil fuels to delay global warming significantly.

Analysts at the Rocky Mountain Institute, a nonprofit research organization in Colorado, have developed a nuclear scenario that reduces global warming by 20 to 30 percent by the middle of the next century through the substitution of nuclear plants for all coal-fired power plants. They found that this would require the completion of one nuclear plant every one to three days during the next 40 years. Many countries would be almost blanketed by nuclear plants, and the total cost would run to as much as $9 trillion.

A nuclear power program of this scale would require not just a reversal of a worldwide trend, but a program of nuclear construction that is ten times as large as any the world has seen. Such an effort is unthinkable, both economically and politically. Indeed, a democratic government that tried it would most likely soon be voted out of office.

Most nuclear technologists agree that a new generation of "inherently safe" reactors will have to be developed before nuclear power expands, even modestly. If governments were to throw their support into research and development programs large enough to accomplish this, it would be after the turn of the century before the first of the commercial reactors could possibly be installed.

Were such a program carried out, it would contribute virtually nothing to the 2005 goal of the Toronto conference, and would contribute only a small part of what is needed by 2050. One problem is that power generation is only part of the reason for global warming, and displacing a substantial part of even this use of fossil fuels would require an impossibly large investment in nuclear power.

TOWARD A VIABLE ENERGY STRATEGY

As the world faces the problem of global warming, it is important to come to grips with the timing of the problem. The earth now appears to be warming at a rate of about 1 degree Fahrenheit per decade, and because of time lags in the process, we are already committed to a significant increase of 3 to 4 degrees. Therefore, immediate action is needed to head off a catastrophic warming during the next several decades.

Nuclear power is clearly incapable of making a meaningful contribution during this period. The global climate would be undermined before an improved technology could even be tested—a fact that many nuclear advocates seem to be unwilling to confront.

Improved energy efficiency, however, does have the potential to reduce the projected warming in 2050 by up to half. Such a scenario requires that energy efficiency be improved by 2 percent per year beginning immediately. The technologies needed to accomplish this are at hand, and they can be economically installed. However, policy reforms are needed if we are to continue the enormous efficiency improvements made during the past decade.

In the long run, of course, societies will have to develop energy sources that replace the fossil fuels on which we rely so heavily. There are really only two alternatives: nuclear power or renewable energy sources such as solar, wind, and biomass. Since the seventies, energy policymakers and analysts have been debating the question of which path to follow. The global warming problem adds new urgency to this debate but does not make the answers any easier to come by.

Renewable energy technologies have advanced rapidly during the past 18 years of research funding, and many are being used commercially on a fairly large scale. They have a long way to go before being ready to provide the predominant share of world energy, but it is quite possible that before improved energy efficiency begins to reach technological limits in the middle of the next century, a diverse mixture of geothermal power, wind power, biomass, and solar energy will have picked up the slack.

Nuclear advocates believe that a new generation of nuclear technologies will be ready for mass deployment as well. This is certainly an arguable point. Technological evolution is notoriously difficult to predict. However, societies are likely to find that nuclear power continues to fall short of its proponents' dreams and that it in the end faces technological, economic, and political limits that are far more intractable than those confronting renewables.

Nuclear power requires increasingly centralized energy systems and intense safety measures and security systems. Renewables are by nature diversified, decentralized, and based on relatively safe technologies. Although renewables will cost large sums to develop, they have the advantage of being more politically palatable, according to public opinion polls.

Most major governments have managed to skirt this central question by funding development of both nuclear power and renewables. The broad trend has been away from nuclear power and toward renewables, though the latter still receive a smaller share of most budgets.

The question now is whether to continue the current approach or to attempt to accelerate the development of either nuclear or renewables. There is no simple answer to this question, but if the lessons of the past decade and a half mean anything for the future, attempts to resuscitate the nuclear option will yield political friction, economic waste, and serious accidents, not a solution to the global warming problem.

HARVESTING THE WIND

By Cynthia Pollock Shea

They may not know it, but office workers in San Francisco, villagers in the Canadian Arctic, and nomadic tribespeople on the Mongolian Plain hold something in common: They are starting to power their lights and appliances with electricity generated by the wind.

Industrial and developing countries alike are turning to wind power, one of the fastest-growing and most adaptable sources of electricity, to complement their existing power sources or to bring electricity to remote regions.

Although using a relatively new technology, wind-powered turbines produced more than 5 percent of the electricity that California-based Pacific Gas and Electric Company sold to its customers at times during the summer of 1987. According to a recent assessment conducted by the utility, one of the nation's largest, there's room for even more growth—less than half of the easily developable wind resources in its service territory have been tapped.

Unexploited, even unsurveyed, potential characterizes the wind power industry. More wind prospecting has been done on some continents than others, but only a few regions have prepared the detailed wind atlases required to assess the resource's full value. It's conceivable that wind meteorologists may become as sought after in the coming decade as petroleum geologists were in the seventies.

Wind speeds generally are highest and most consistent in mountain passes and along coastlines. Of the continents, Europe has the greatest coastal wind resources. The winds that now make offshore oil drilling so difficult may someday supplant, and certainly will outlast, diminishing North Sea oil reserves as an energy source.

It's estimated that sufficient wind energy is available in the United States to provide more than one trillion kilowatt hours of electricity annually, approximately one-fourth of the projected electricity demand at the turn of the century. On energy-short islands in the Caribbean and the South Pacific, tropical tradewinds may soon be harnessed to electrify villages now without power.

Clusters of wind turbines, known as windfarms, are being promoted in much of Europe and Asia and in scattered locations from the tropics to the poles. Denmark, the Netherlands, China, and India are especially interested in fostering the development of domestic wind industries. Electricity-producing wind turbines, distinct from windmills used for mechanical energy, now operate in 95 countries.

BIRTH OF AN INDUSTRY

Wind-driven electric generators were first developed in the 1890s by P. LaCour of Denmark. Several hundred small units were built in that country prior to 1910, and soon Danish industry was obtaining one-quarter of its energy from 150 to 200 megawatts of wind capacity. This would be enough to supply a modern American city of 35,000 households.

By the twenties and thirties, the technology to create electricity from wind was employed by thousands of U.S. farm households. As cheap oil and gas became available and rural electrification expanded, these early generators gradually were abandoned. Wind turbine use languished until its renaissance in the eighties.

The oil price jolts of the seventies breathed new life into the business of generating electricity from wind. Governments concerned about the future availability and price of oil began to offer attractive incentives to developers of alternative energy sources. In the United States, investment, energy, and solar tax credits, along with accelerated depreciation schedules, turned windfarming into a profitable pursuit.

Wind investments became even more attractive when legislative and regulatory changes were enacted to open utility markets for wind-generated electricity. The monopolistic electric utility industry was directed to purchase power from independent generators for the same rate it would cost the utility to produce the electricity. Washington got further involved by offering funds for research and development.

By the early eighties, the stimulated U.S. wind power market was running ahead of U.S. manufacturing capacity. Although the first U.S. windfarm, erected in New Hampshire in late 1980, was built by an American turbine manufacturer, U.S. suppliers had neither the expertise nor the production capacity to launch a new industry independently. Soon, U.S. wind power investors were looking overseas for help from the more advanced wind turbine industry in Denmark.

TECHNOLOGY TRANSFER

For an expanding and improving Danish wind power industry, the timing of the U.S. wind power surge was perfect. Although wind turbines had long been installed on Danish farms, the oil price hikes of the seventies prompted the Danish government to encourage greater use of this technology.

Accordingly, the government introduced a subsidy in 1979 that reimbursed homeowners for 30 percent of the purchase price of their wind turbines plus part of the siting cost. Though the subsidy has since been scaled back to ease the wind power industry's dependence on it, Danes still get a break if they buy their own wind machines.

In wind power circles, "Made in Denmark" has come to be associated with the best-quality wind generating equipment because Danish wind turbines must be approved for safety and reliability to qualify for the subsidy. At Risoe National Laboratories, where the testing takes place, engineers research and develop new wind power technologies and help turbine manufacturers improve their designs.

The hardy Danish turbines, weighing five to seven times more than the latest American models, are sometimes scorned by American manufacturers. While lightweight composite materials someday may improve turbine performance, the more cumbersome Danish units have suffered fewer design problems and have proven to be more mechanically reliable. Less shut-down time means the Danish turbines are "on-line" more; this makes them a less expensive source of power.

Denmark dominates the international market for intermediate-size turbines, with 7 of the world's top 10 manufacturers. Intermediate-size turbines, those that range from 50 to several hundred kilowatts of capacity, are the type most widely used in industrial countries.

There's no doubt that Danish firms have profited from government assistance, but the investment appears to be paying off. Danish turbine sales reached $250 million in 1985, some 42 times greater than the $6 million subsidy provided by the government that year. The Danish Ministry of Energy's share of operating the Risoe testing station has cost only $4 million so far, with the remainder paid by fees charged to the turbine makers.

As more countries move to develop their wind resources, Danish exports and joint-venture opportunities are sure to grow. Nominal but well-conceived government subsidies have catapulted a small national industry into the leading international turbine supplier.

CALIFORNIA WIND RUSH

The American wind power industry got off to a bumpier start. Because American turbine manufacturers were not required to obtain certification for their products, many new and inexperienced developers built inadequately tested machines in attempts to cash in on the heavily subsidized California market.

Inoperative turbines, multiple repairs, and major system overhauls soon bankrupted many of these firms and tarnished the wind power industry's reputation. Today, the companies that remain have created sturdy, proven wind turbines that combine new materials and technologies and operate 80 to 98 percent of the time the wind is blowing.

Despite the excesses of some tax shelterers-cum-windfarm developers, the short history of wind power in California has been impressive. The industry was launched in 1981 with the erection of 144 relatively small turbines capable of generating a combined total of 7 megawatts of electricity (see Table 1).

In little over a year, the number of turbines and their cumulative generating capacity had increased 10-fold. By 1986, they had multiplied 100-fold. At the end of 1987, the state had 16,661 turbines capable of turning out 1,437 megawatts' worth of electricity. In 1987, California produced enough wind-generated electricity to meet 15 percent of San Francisco's electrical demand.

The rapid growth of windfarming in California, which exceeded most expectations, began to slow by 1986 because of the convergence of several factors. Crude oil prices took a nose dive and made oil and natural gas low-cost fuel sources once again.

Concern over the growing federal budget deficit and a

TABLE 1
California
Windfarms,
1981–87

Year	Turbines Installed	Capacity Installed	Cumulative Capacity
	(number)	(megawatts)	
1981	144	7	7
1982	1,145	64	71
1983	2,493	172	243
1984	4,687	366	609
1985	3,922	398	1,007
1986	2,878	276	1,283
1987	1,392	154	1,437

Sources: Paul Gipe, American Wind Energy Association, and Sam Rashkin, California Energy Commission.

lingering suspicion regarding the economic merits of investing in wind turbines resulted in an abrupt end to federal tax credits in late 1985. California's state tax credits expired a year later.

Finally, the unanticipated boom in California's independent power industry during the early 1980s caught up with the state's electric utilities, which responded by suspending new contracts until recent events could be assessed.

Growth in turbine installation consequently slowed but did not stop. Generating capacity increased by 27 percent in 1986 and 12 percent in 1987. And, efforts to improve turbine reliability and performance boosted output.

From 1985 to 1986, sales of wind-generated electricity rose from $40 to $70 million. Over the same period, the amount of electricity produced per kilowatt of installed generating capacity increased by 48 percent. Productivity continues to rise.

Not surprisingly, turbine manufacturers, equipment suppliers, and windfarm developers have been hit hard by the slowdown in orders. Reverberations from the United States' abandonment of renewable energy tax credits have been felt by wind turbine suppliers worldwide.

Outside the United States, the impact has been greatest in Denmark, which had been supplying California with about half of its turbines. In 1985, Danish manufacturers shipped more than 2,500 wind units to North America. By 1986, sales of wind turbines, one of the country's most valuable exports, were off 50 percent.

INTERCROPPING ELECTRICITY AND CATTLE

California hosts most of the intermediate-size wind turbines in use around the world in three mountain passes—Altamont, San Gorgonio, and Tehachapi. Quirks in seasonal wind patterns in Altamont and San Gorgonio make them particularly advantageous for windfarming: Windspeeds are highest in the summer, when utilities' power needs are greatest.

These windy California passes have been the domain of sheep and cattle ranchers for a century now. But many ranchers are finding that they can boost their incomes by leasing land to windfarm developers.

Enough ranchers have seen the wisdom in this that windfarms now cover about 29 square miles of Altamont Pass, with an average of one turbine for every 3 acres of land. For access to the wind that sweeps their hillsides, landowners receive a set fee for each turbine installed and a percentage of the price paid for any electricity generated.

As a consequence, land values in the pass have shot upward. "In 1980, just before the beginning of the windfarm developments, the land [in Altamont Pass] was worth about $400 per acre," says Don Smith, a utility consultant in California. "Land with wind resource potential is now worth about $2,000 per acre. This increased worth reflects the royalties of about $50 to $100 per acre per year."

There's still enough income left over for windfarm developers to turn a handsome profit. Annual gross electricity sales per acre typically reach $6,000—a per-acre return some 15 times greater than the $400-per-acre gross of an Iowa corn farmer and easily 100 times that of a Texas rancher. Because wind and cattle can be farmed on the same land at the same time, the earning potential per acre can increase dramatically.

THE INDUSTRY GROWS UP

Improved turbine design over the years has permitted the size and, therefore, electrical output of California's machines to increase. Potential power output is proportional to the area swept by each revolution of the turbine's blade, or rotor. Doubling the area doubles the energy produced.

In 1984, the average rotor diameter of California's turbines reached 56 feet; this resulted in a 50 percent increase in potential power output compared with that of the 1982 turbine models.

Up to a point, larger rotors effectively lower the capital costs of wind turbines because more electricity can be produced with fewer machines. The average capacity of turbines installed in California increased from 49 kilowatts in 1981 to 111 kilowatts in 1987. Many of the newest models have capacities of between 150 and 750 kilowatts.

The average installation cost for an intermediate-size wind turbine has fallen by almost two-thirds since 1981, to some $800 to $1,200 per kilowatt. Part of the drop is due to the use of larger turbines and part to more economical manufacturing.

In many markets, these turbines now cost less to install per unit of capacity than either coal or nuclear facilities. Costs are likely to be reduced further as more manufacturers start to mass-produce turbines.

Once up and running, the cost comparison more strongly favors wind turbines since there is no need to buy fuel.

Because wind turbines are much smaller than either coal or nuclear plants, they provide greater adaptability in responding to unpredictable growth in power demand. Smith notes, "When the turbines were available, windfarms have been built in Altamont Pass in less than 90 days from surveying to operation." Coal and nuclear plants, on the other hand, frequently take a decade to plan and construct.

Generating electricity with wind also offers many environmental advantages. Windfarms do not emit climate-altering carbon dioxide, acid-rain-forming pollutants, or respiratory irritants. The latter of these is of special concern in areas of California plagued with poor air quality. Nor do windfarms produce radioactive waste.

Since windfarms don't require water to operate, they are especially well-suited for semiarid and arid regions. About the only drawbacks to windfarms are the whirring noise they make and the questionable aesthetics of turbines clustered in scenic mountain passes and along shorelines.

Windfarming offers the added benefits of reducing soil loss on land prone to wind erosion. Turbines effectively capture the wind and decrease its potential for downwind destruction while creating a valuable product. It's possible that the same winds that stirred up the Dust Bowl in the Great Plains may someday be harnessed to provide electricity for distant cities.

A TURBINE FOR EVERY NEED

Another advantage to wind power is that turbines can be tailored for specific locations and power uses. They can be built small (to recharge batteries and provide essential services in Third World villages) or large (to provide electricity to some 1,000 utility customers). Or, as in the case of Denmark, they can fall somewhere in between. Early wind power development in Denmark relied almost exclusively on intermediate-size, 55-kilowatt farm units that fed electricity into the central power grid. Future plans call for clusters of 200-kilowatt turbines.

Other countries have based their wind power development on turbines that fall at either end of the size range. During the decade following the 1973 oil embargo, more than 10,000 wind machines were installed worldwide. Many of these units were quite small, sometimes portable, and used either to charge batteries or to produce minuscule amounts of electricity.

The Chinese market has a proven appetite for these small turbines: 1,282 units were purchased in 1982 and almost 11,000 in 1986. The demand was created largely by the advent of nationwide television reception. Since much of China has no electricity, the small turbines have allowed some Chinese to tune into their favorite shows.

According to a 1987 worldwide survey of turbine shipments conducted by Thomas Jaras of the U.S.-based Wind Data Center, 5 of the world's 10 largest manufacturers of small wind turbines are Chinese. Besides lighting up televisions, these small turbines power communication systems, navigation aids, and military equipment.

Many governments around the world have concentrated their wind power efforts on promoting turbines at the other end of the size range: these multimegawatt turbines produce 10 times the output of the average California model. Eleven wind machines rated at 1 megawatt or higher had been built as of 1985—seven in the United States, two in Sweden, and one each in Denmark and West Germany.

Despite the dismal operating record of some large units, Canada, Denmark, the Netherlands, Sweden, the United Kingdom, and Germany are building new multimegawatt machines. Partly because of space constraints, these governments have made large turbines the centerpiece of research and development activity.

INTERNATIONAL PROSPECTUS

Because California possesses so much of the world's wind power generating capacity, when it experienced slower growth, the international market slowed as well. Annual international turbine sales peaked in 1985 at 567 megawatts, a 17-fold increase from 1981. By 1986, cumulative worldwide turbine sales had reached $2.5 billion.

According to Jaras, turbine sales figures are unlikely to return to the 1985 level until sometime in the nineties. Despite the slow growth in the California market, interest in wind energy is growing rapidly in other areas of the world. Jaras expects the North American share of the world market to decrease gradually to about half of the total by the early nineties as wind power development accelerates elsewhere.

At that point, Europe is likely to account for one-fourth or more of the world market for wind turbines as it will purchase at least 100 megawatts' worth annually. Denmark figures to be in the forefront of the European market. As well as being the leading international supplier of intermediate-size wind turbines, the country has a bustling domestic market. By mid-1987, its installed wind power capacity totaled 100 megawatts, enough to service a city of 30,000 people.

Elkraft and Elsam, Denmark's two utility power pools, expect to install a total of 100 megawatts' worth of turbines by 1991. Private investors will install additional units. The government's goal is for wind to provide 10 percent of the nation's electricity by 2000.

The total number of Danish turbines is growing while improved designs and production techniques are raising the energy produced per turbine. Denmark now produces 16 percent of the world's wind-generated electricity and can claim the world's first offshore windfarm.

The Chinese government is calling for windfarms with a

total capacity of at least 100 megawatts to be built between 1990 and 1996. In the Netherlands, a five-year plan is under way with the goal of installing 150 megawatts of capacity by 1992. By the end of the century, the government hopes to have 1,000 megawatts of capacity on line.

Spain plans 45 megawatts by 1993 and Greece expects to install 80 megawatts' worth on its islands. Also, smaller windfarms are either installed or planned in Australia, Belgium, Israel, Italy, the Soviet Union, the United Kingdom, and Germany.

By far the most ambitious wind energy program belongs to the Ministry of Energy in India. The agency is pushing to have both public and private developers install 5,000 megawatts of capacity by the year 2000. This would be enough electricity to service more than five million customers.

Though it had virtually no wind turbines until 1985, India now boasts as much installed capacity as California had in 1981. It could soon become the world's most rapidly growing market. If the government's plans are successful, wind may supply more electricity than the country's nuclear program.

The growth in wind power use during the eighties was explosive. For the momentum to continue, governments and private industry need to cooperate in reinvigorating their research and development programs, in phasing out subsidies that unfairly favor fossil fuels, and in opening up electric power markets to greater competition.

Low oil prices have engendered a sense of complacency, but the nuclear accident at Chernobyl, coupled with increased evidence of global environmental damage caused by fossil-fuel combustion, is prompting energy planners to look at alternatives once again. Wind power is one of the least expensive, cleanest, and most widely distributed of those alternatives.

8

Rethinking Transport Options

ROCKY ROAD AHEAD FOR THE AUTOMOBILE

By Michael G. Renner

The third quarter of this century was unquestionably the golden age of the automobile. Mass means of production, a growing network of roads and highways, inexpensive gasoline, and higher household incomes made car ownership a popular and convenient form of transportation.

The allure of the automobile was reflected in growing production. Thirty million cars rolled off the world's assembly lines in 1973—almost four times as many vehicles as in 1950.

Optimism about the automobile's future carried into the 1970s. A multimillion dollar study completed for the world auto industry in 1978 showed that the world fleet would expand from just under 300 million vehicles at the time to some 700 million by the year 2000, a density of one car for every eight people.

This implied an astounding production level of 65 to 70 million vehicles per year by the late 1980s. At that rate, the prospect of a car in every garage was not far off.

The oil shocks of 1973 and 1979, with their effects on fuel costs and global economic health, teamed with escalating Third World debt to change all that. Car production in 1987 at 31 million was only slightly higher than in 1973. Overall automobile ownership rates have slowed from an annual average of nearly 7 percent between 1950 and 1973 to 4 percent between 1974 and 1985.

Expectations for the global automobile fleet have been pared back accordingly. The Organization for Economic Co-operation and Development (OECD) estimates that the global car fleet at the end of the century is unlikely to be much larger than 530 million vehicles.

Still, the condition of the automobile is anything but feeble. Because the oil and debt crises affected national economies in different ways and at different times, the world automobile industry has managed to cope. For example, just as higher oil prices choked off the rapid increase in automobile ownership in oil-importing Brazil, they fueled a tripling of total auto registrations in oil-exporting Saudi Arabia.

Also, as the oil price shocks threw American car manufacturers into turmoil, Japanese producers grabbed larger market shares with fuel-efficient models. Indeed, the global automobile industry has proven resilient enough to set sales volume records for the 1985 and 1986 model years.

The long-term trends that are undermining the industry's vitality, though, are real: a new oil crisis is widely expected for the midnineties; the unresolved debt crises of many Third World countries limit their ability to pay for imported fuel and dry up the growth of affluence that is essential for increased car ownership; and the major car-owning societies are approaching market saturation.

A NEW OIL CRISIS?

Because the world's cars run almost exclusively on petroleum-based fuels, the auto industry is extremely sensitive to changes in the price and availability of oil. As a means of transportation, the automobile is, after all, only as reliable as its fuel supplies.

That point was driven home when the oil price shocks of the seventies sent gasoline prices shooting upward. As oil absorbed a larger share of world import bills, car sales dropped. Global car production fell by about five million vehicles, or almost one-fifth, after the first oil price surge in 1973 and slightly less in the wake of the second crisis in 1979 (see Figure 1).

With oil prices up, oil importers around the globe scrambled to lighten their burden of costly oil imports through greater self-sufficiency. As the oil crises unfolded, they reinforced the message that a transportation system centered on the private passenger car imposes tremendous costs on society, whether in the form of escalating fuel import bills or huge expenditures of capital and resources to tap domestic fuel sources.

Brazil's recent history demonstrates the link between oil prices and car production. The country's oil import bill skyrocketed from $280 million in 1970 to $10 billion in 1979. The result? Brazilian car production leveled off in the mid-1970s and slumped by almost 40 percent in 1980 to 1981.

FIGURE 1   World Passenger-Car Production

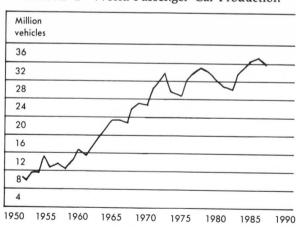

1987 = estimate
Source: The Motor Vehicle Manufacturers Association.

Higher domestic oil production and a controversial alcohol fuel program allowed Brazil to cut its dependence on imported oil by 60 percent between 1979 and 1986. Yet, providing the fuel from domestic sources had its own cost, requiring large-scale investment and a hefty government subsidy. The Brazilian government has spent more than $8 billion to get the country's ethanol industry off the ground.

ROLLER COASTER PRICES

Oil prices on the world market have taken the automobile on an unprecedented roller coaster ride over the past two decades. The dark clouds cast over the auto's future by two oil shocks in the seventies seemed to recede in the eighties when prices eroded and finally collapsed. As concern over oil prices and supplies faded away, car sales and fuel consumption resumed growth. Edging upward again since 1983, global gasoline consumption reached a new peak in 1986 (see Figure 2).

FIGURE 2   World Gasoline Consumption

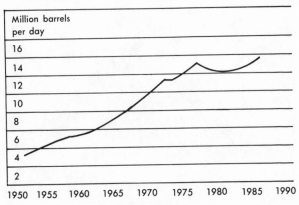

1986 = estimate

Source: United Nations Energy Statistics Yearbook.

Because the opportunities for discovering large new oil deposits or developing alternative fuels in sufficient quantity were limited, the industrialized countries answered dire predictions of continued oil shortages by applying a technical fix: they simply used advanced refining processes to extract more gasoline from each barrel of crude oil. Member states of the OECD report that gasoline accounted for 33 percent of oil products consumed in 1986, up from 28 percent in 1976.

At the same time, energy demand outside the transportation sector has shifted away from oil use—energy from nuclear, coal, and hydroelectric plants completed since 1972 now displace some 12 million barrels per day of potential global oil demand.

Perhaps most important of all, the viability of the automobile as a means of transport was enhanced by improvements in fuel economy. Had average fleet fuel efficiency in the United States remained at the dismal 1973 level of 13 miles per gallon (mpg), the country's gasoline consumption would have grown by one-third. Instead, fuel economy rose to 20.5 mpg in 1989 and held consumption in check.

Falling oil prices and ample supplies have noticeably diminished the urgency to make automobiles more fuel-efficient. Since 1982, gains in car fuel economy in the United States and most other OECD member states have fallen short of the impressive advances made between 1974 and 1981.

In the United States, for example, the Reagan administration reduced the federally mandated fuel economy standards for the 1986 model year from 27.5 to 26 mpg, and attempted to abolish them altogether. The growing popularity of less fuel-efficient light trucks over cars limits future gains.

Because the technical opportunities are far from exhausted, improving fuel efficiency still offers the single best hope to prevent or minimize the impact of a new oil crisis in the coming decade. Raising fuel efficiency of American cars alone to the technically achievable level of 50 mpg would eventually cut global gasoline consumption by almost one-fourth (assuming no growth in the total fleet).

LIFE IN THE SLOW LANE

The Third World debt crisis of the eighties posed a new threat to the car industry. Coming on the heels of the oil price hike of 1979, the debt crisis impeded debtor nations' ability to pay for fuel imports and other goods. Governments were compelled to slash investment spending and create large trade surpluses and in doing so precipitated major recessions.

Between 1980 and 1986, per-capita incomes contracted in virtually all of Latin America, with the exception of Brazil, which reversed a downward trend after 1984. Falling real wages—by 28 percent in Brazil (1981 to 1984) and by 50 percent in Mexico (1982 to 1986)—eroded purchasing power and shrank the already limited ranks of potential car buyers.

By sending the South American economies into a tailspin, the debt crisis shattered predictions that the bulk of future growth in automobile use would occur in the so-called newly industrializing countries of Latin America and Southeast Asia.

From 1970 to 1981, the average annual growth rate of total car registrations in Brazil, Mexico, and Argentina—the three largest markets outside the industrial countries—was among the world's highest. Brazilian car production expanded by an astounding 21 percent a year between 1970 and 1974, or double the rate of its overall industrial growth; this made the country the world's ninth largest producer.

Yet under the strains of the debt crisis, Latin American auto expansion sputtered to a virtual halt. Car demand in Brazil, Mexico, and Argentina was cut in half between 1975 and 1985, and car production in the region, which peaked in

1980, fell and then rebounded by 1985 before collapsing again in 1987.

Uneven income distribution patterns are a significant deterrent to car-ownership growth in the Third World. In Brazil, for example, the top 10 percent of the population earned 51 percent of the national income, but the bottom 60 percent earned only 16 percent. A highly skewed income distribution fosters a small privileged class with ample purchasing power for buying cars but effectively limits the number of potential car owners.

By 1985, only a little more than 1 percent of the Third World's population owned a car, compared with 40 percent of the Western industrial countries', and 8 percent of the world's.

The huge potential market in developing countries measured in people does not translate into an equally large volume of demand because the degree of affluence required to purchase and maintain a car is simply beyond the reach of most Third World people.

To illustrate, a Mexican-assembled 1984 Ford Topaz carried a base price equivalent to 265 weeks of pay for the average Mexican worker; the same car cost a U.S. worker the equivalent of just 27 weeks' wages. In the same year, the least expensive Brazilian car, a Volkswagen Beetle, cost some 284 weeks' pay.

Just as car ownership is beyond the means of most Third World residents, the capital-intensive infrastructure needed to support an automobile-based transportation system has proven to be beyond the means of many Third World nations.

Building and maintaining an elaborate system of roads, highways, bridges, and tunnels demands an extraordinary commitment of a nation's resources. Numerous African countries, for example, abandoned ambitious plans for road expansion early in their automotive history.

Limited land and environmental factors are also beginning to set the parameters for future growth of automobile ownership. In densely populated countries such as China or Bangladesh, agricultural needs often compete for land with the sprawling car infrastructure.

In industrialized nations, concern for the environment grows as the contribution of vehicle emissions to smog, acid rain, and the "greenhouse effect" becomes more evident. Vehicle emission standards raise the cost of purchasing and operating a car, while decisions by municipalities to restrict or prohibit car use in city centers diminish the attraction of car ownership.

PRODUCTION SHIFTS TO EXPORTS

To finance their debt repayments and to maintain their auto industries in the face of the domestic sales slump, Brazil and Mexico have sought to gain a foothold in the lucrative, established car markets of industrialized nations.

The share of Mexican car production sold abroad grew from under 5 percent in 1982, when the debt crisis first broke out, to 20 percent in 1985. In the long run, Mexican auto manufacturers are planning to export roughly three-quarters of their output. Car exports have already become Mexico's largest nonoil revenue earner.

The Brazilian government first started to encourage exports in 1972 to pay for the country's ballooning oil import bills. Now foreign sales, which account for 20 to 25 percent of production, are meant to help finance the country's escalating foreign debt.

In 1987, domestic car sales sank to their lowest level in 15 years as the Brazilian economy encountered new calamities. Meanwhile, car exports soared to 40 percent of Brazilian production.

Whether these export strategies will succeed is problematic. A world car market characterized by slow growth, overcapacities, and the threat of rising protectionism seems unlikely to accommodate a growing number of exporters. South Korea, Yugoslavia, Malaysia, India, and the Soviet Union have joined the car-exporting ranks or are planning to do so.

At the same time that these manufacturers expose themselves to the car market's growing volatility, the low wage rates on which their export strategies hinge inhibit the emergence of a viable domestic market.

South Korea typifies this paradox. The country's auto industry has been geared to penetrate the established markets of the industrialized nations. Indeed, while the Seoul government encouraged the emergence of an indigenous export-oriented auto industry through favorable tax, credit, and export assistance policies, it hobbled car ownership at home through high taxes on car purchase, registration, and gasoline.

Even though Korean domestic car sales are growing rapidly, auto density in 1989 stood at 40 people per car as compared to Argentina's 8, Brazil's 13 and Mexico's 16. Industrial wages are a crucial barometer of Korea's future in the world automobile market: higher labor costs may curb its export drive but at the same time assure the growth of a middle class that can afford to own a car.

MAO, MARX, AND MARKET SATURATION

Economic reform in China and the Soviet Union raises the prospect for the opening of major new markets for automobiles. China is an immense, untapped reservoir of potential car owners. The number of cars there has risen tenfold, to half a million, in only five years, and the economic reforms espoused by the leadership in Beijing will likely spur more growth. Still, there are more than 2,000 people for every car in the country.

The Soviet Union is an industrial society by many measures, but not by levels of car density. The country has relied primarily on trains and buses for transportation and given manufacturing priority to trucks over cars. President Mikhail Gorbachev's attempts at *perestroika,* or the restructuring of the Soviet economy, may lead to a stronger emphasis on consumer goods, with the automobile certainly near the top of the list.

While the emergence of Chinese and Soviet markets is speculative, the traditional auto markets in North America, and increasingly in Western Europe and Japan, are characterized by a high degree of saturation. In 1985, there were two people per car in the United States, three in the four major Western European markets (West Germany, Italy, France, and the United Kingdom), and four in Japan.

Growth of car ownership in the United States has declined from an average of 4 percent per year between 1950 and 1973 to 2 percent between 1974 and 1985. Although growth rates in Europe and Japan have been somewhat higher, the same pattern of gradual decline is discernible. These countries are likely to reach a saturation point at a lower ownership rate than the United States because their extensive public transportation networks, compact urban structures, and lack of space discourage excessive reliance on private automobiles.

The worldwide growth of cars in use has slowed as additions to the existing fleet peaked in 1973 in both the United States and Japan, and even earlier in some European countries. The saturation level fluctuates, then, with oil prices and economic health.

The portion of new car sales in the world's major automobile-owning societies that goes toward replacing older automobiles is now well above two-thirds of the total (with the exception of the United Kingdom). Even though car purchases gathered some momentum after the 1982 downturn, the steep rise in the number of weeks of median family income needed to purchase a new car in the United States— from 18 in 1979 to 23 in 1986—suggests that consumers' purchasing power may not be commensurate with the level required for a strong market.

American sales have increased in recent years primarily owing to unprecedented financial incentives. Analysts agree that these incentives will eat into future sales and possibly deepen an anticipated sales slump: Car purchases in the United States in 1989 declined to 9.9 million from 11.5 million in 1986.

Without a speedy solution to the debt and oil problems, auto production is not likely to rebound to the high levels once forecast. It could even decline.

The Road to Uncertainty

Doubts about the future viability of the private passenger car have hardly diminished its allure. The automobile is still considered a cornerstone of industrial development and a powerful symbol of status.

But a growing reliance on the automobile can actually stifle rather than advance societies. Instead of facilitating individual mobility, cars have become a source of congestion in industrial nations, where their necessity makes them numerous, and in developing countries because there is not enough money to build sufficient roads.

Third World government policies that favor private car ownership by an affluent minority in essence squander resources that could more appropriately be used to develop efficient forms of transport that serve the entire population.

Today's oil glut should not be heralded as a new era of bountiful and cheap supplies, but rather as a reprieve from higher oil prices. It's a break automobile-owning countries should use to make more fuel-efficient cars and to consider alternative forms of transport. If this opportunity is missed, a new oil crisis will impose the same choices, only under considerably less favorable circumstances.

PEDALING INTO THE FUTURE

By Marcia D. Lowe

Traffic noise in Beijing means the whirring of bicycle wheels and tinkling of bells. The streets of New Delhi come alive with thousands of bicycle commuters each day. Office workers in New York City depend on bicycle messengers to cruise past bumper-to-bumper traffic and deliver parcels on time. And police officers in Seattle often find bicycles better than squad cars for apprehending criminals on gridlocked downtown streets.

Outside the city, bicycles also play a vital role. Kenyan dairy farmers cycle through remote regions with milk deliveries, and Nicaraguan health workers on bikes now reach four times as many rural patients as they did on foot.

Whether a cycle rickshaw in Jakarta or a ten-speed in Boston, pedal power plays a key role in transportation. The bicycle is fast becoming the only way to move quickly through congested urban traffic and the only affordable personal transport in the developing world—where an automobile may cost more than a worker earns in a decade.

Despite its demonstrated utility, the bicycle has been formally neglected by transit planners in almost every country on the globe. Only China and a few Western European nations collect transportation data that count bicycles among forms of transport. In the case of the U.S. Department of Commerce, neglect might be a promotion in status for the bicycle; the department refers inquiries on bicycle trade to its Division of Toys and Games.

The World Bank, the main source of urban transit investment in the developing world, published a 1985 study on the Chinese transport sector that does not even mention the word bicycle, although the overwhelming majority of trips in China's cities are made by bike. This is sadly typical of a policy environment in which only motor vehicles are taken seriously.

High Price for Mobility

The automobile has long been considered the vehicle of the future. Indeed, it has brought industrial society into the modern age with a degree of individual mobility and convenience not known before. But overreliance on the car is backfiring as too many cars clutter city streets and highways, bringing rush-hour traffic to a standstill. The side effects of massive oil use show up not only in economy-draining import bills but in deadly air pollution in cities, acid rain in dying lakes and forests, and hastened global warming.

In their enthusiasm for engine power, transit planners have overlooked the value of human power. With congestion, pollution, and debt threatening both the industrial and developing worlds, the vehicle of the future clearly rides on two wheels rather than four.

The bicycle's ascent would not eliminate automobiles, or any other vehicle, but would instead integrate bicycles with cars and mass transit. A well-balanced, diverse transport system could help save precious oil and other resources, reduce pollutants, and provide mobility to people with few or no alternatives to walking. Before this can happen, though, a shift in attitudes must take place.

More Bikers than Drivers

Bicycles already outnumber cars worldwide by two to one, with most of the 800-million-strong bicycle fleet concentrated in the Third World, particularly China and India. In the United States, where one of every two people owns an automobile, bicycles are mainly used for recreation or, at best, supplementary transportation. At the other extreme is China, with one privately owned car for every 75,000 people. Chinese commuters have little choice but to make the most of their bikes.

By bicycle standards, China is in a class by itself with some 270 million bicycles, or roughly one for every four people. In urban areas, half the residents have bicycles. Traffic monitors at an intersection in the northern industrial city of Tianjin once counted more than 50,000 bicycles pass in an hour.

The bicycle fleet in China has nearly tripled since 1979, largely as a result of rising incomes. Domestic bike sales in 1987 reached 35 million units; this actually exceeds total worldwide automobile sales. Bicycles are popular in China because, like cars in industrial countries, they offer the luxury of individual mobility and independence, and door-to-door travel without detours or extra stops for other passengers. When the same trip would take equal time by bicycle or mass transit, Chinese prefer to bike.

Bikes are also popular because Chinese transportation planners in the sixties and seventies used subsidies—paying commuters a monthly fee for biking to work—to relieve the pressure on crowded buses and to postpone public transit investment. This policy, however, failed to foresee the bicycle boom of the eighties.

Now Chinese cities face a phenomenon in which people's appetite for individual mobility is becoming an obstacle to mass mobility. Like car commuters in the industrial

countries, bicycle commuters are now officially encouraged
to use the expanded fleet of public buses for longer trips.

Bicycles transport more people in Asia alone than do automobiles in all other countries combined. Throughout the
continent ingeniously rigged two- and three-wheelers accomplish much of what automobiles do elsewhere. With the
help of trailers, baskets and load platforms, pedal power
hauls everything from sacks of rice to piles of bricks. Cycle
rickshaws are the taxis of Southeast Asia, while sturdy tricy-
cles are the light trucks that haul loads of up to half a ton. In
Bangladesh, cycle rickshaws transport more tonnage than all
motor vehicles combined.

In urban areas, bicycles are the primary means of commuting. In the countryside, they help peasants drastically
cut down on the time needed to transport water and fuel
wood. In many Asian cities, two-thirds of the vehicles on
the road during rush hours are bicycles.

SHUNNED, FEARED, AND NEGLECTED

The rest of the developing world lags far behind Asia in
using bicycles. Particularly in Latin America, the prestige
and power of auto ownership has hypnotized governments
into ignoring pedal power and led citizens to scorn the bicycle as a vehicle for the poor.

African farmers depend heavily on bicycles, but relatively few urban residents do. The few who are able to buy a
bicycle are discouraged by official disdain or even bans on
their use. In some African countries it is taboo for women—
the main haulers of food, water, fuel, and children—to ride
bicycles.

Several heavily polluted Eastern European countries are
taking modest steps to expand the bicycle's role in easing the
burden on the environment. In Poland, a plan for a bicycle
system in the city of Poznan called for a 124-mile network of
bicycle paths by 1990. Bicycle production in Poland has

more than doubled in the last two decades, and demand still exceeds supply. In 1979, the Lithuanian city of Siauliai launched a comprehensive program to encourage cycling, the Soviet Union's first, which included a bicycle-path system and extensive parking facilities.

A surprising share of the world's bicycles is found in developed countries—surprising only because of the small number found on typical city streets. In several European countries—among them Denmark, Germany, and the Netherlands—there are more bike owners than nonowners. The United States had some 95 million bicycles in 1985—second only to China.

Bicycle ownership in the industrial world does not necessarily mean bicycle use. One in four Britons has a bicycle, yet only 1 transport trip out of 33 is made by bike. Only 1 out of 50 bikes in the United States is used for commuting; most of the rest are ridden by children and sports enthusiasts, or are collecting dust in the basement.

A comparison of bicycle and automobile ownership by country shows the relative dependence on the bicycle (see Table 1). The United States, for example, has more than twice as many bicycles as India, but only a fraction of American bicycles get as much use. India's growing middle class of office and factory workers is more likely to get to work by bicycle than any other form of transport.

PLANNING MAKES A DIFFERENCE

Like the United States, most other industrial countries have all but abandoned the bicycle for the automobile. Suburbanization has sprawled jobs, homes, and services over such long distances that automobiles are less a convenience than a necessity. Several North American cities have extensive bike paths, but many cities have become nearly bicycleproof: their roadways and parking facilities are designed with only motor vehicles in mind.

TABLE 1
Bicycles and
Automobiles in
Selected
Countries, circa
1985

Country	Bicycles	Autos	Cycle/ Auto Ratio
	(millions)		
China	270.0	0.5	540.0
India	45.0	1.5	30.0
South Korea	6.0	0.3	20.0
Egypt	1.5	0.5	3.0
Mexico	12.0	4.8	2.5
Netherlands	11.0	4.9	2.2
Japan	58.0	27.8	2.1
West Germany	45.0	26.0	1.7
Argentina	4.5	3.4	1.3
Brazil	12.0	10.0	1.2
Tanzania	0.5	0.5	1.0
United States	95.0	132.1	0.7

Sources: Bicycle Federation of America, Motor Vehicle Manufacturers Association, and International Trade Centre UNCTAD/GATT.

Three outstanding models of nationwide bicycle planning are the Netherlands, West Germany, and Japan. Local governments in these countries—spurred by traffic jams and air pollution—are demonstrating how public policy can be used to make cycling a safe and convenient alternative to the car.

The Netherlands has more than 9,000 miles of bicycle paths, more than any other country. In some Dutch cities, half of all trips are made by bike. The German town of Erlangen has completed a network of paths covering 100 miles, about half the length of the city's streets. Bicycle use has more than doubled as a result.

Bicycle-oriented cities in Europe and Japan have boosted both bicycle and public transit ridership with facilities for carrying bicycles on buses and trains, and for parking them safely at stations. So many Japanese commuters take advantage of this bike-to-rail option that train stations need parking towers. The city of Kasukabe now has a twelve-story structure that uses cranes to park more than 1,500 bicycles.

MOST-EFFICIENT VEHICLE EVER BUILT

Renewable fuels are a hot topic in transportation circles today, with deepening concern over dependence on scarce and expensive oil. In the rush to run engines on gasoline alternatives such as corn-based ethanol, transportation planners have overlooked a technology that converts food directly into fuel. A biker can ride three and a half miles on the calories found in an ear of corn—and there is no distilling or refining involved.

Bicycles consume less energy per passenger mile than any other form of transport, including walking (see Table 2). A 10-mile, round-trip commute by bicycle requires 350 calories of energy, or three-quarters of a cup of macaroni. The same trip in the average American car uses more than half a gallon of gasoline.

A look at national fuel bills makes a strong case for using bicycles. In 1987, U.S. oil imports cost $43 billion, or nearly a quarter of the country's $171 billion trade deficit. Of the country's total annual oil consumption, nearly two-thirds is burned up in transportation. A country's car dependence heightens its vulnerability to oil price hikes and instability in the Middle East, where most of the world's proven oil reserves are.

The debt-ridden Third World is especially burdened by foreign oil dependence. Several developing countries already spend one-third to one-half of their export earnings on imported petroleum, on average about half of it going to the transport sector. By shifting to nonmotorized transport

TABLE 2
Energy Intensity
of Selected
Transport Modes,
U.S., 1984

Mode	Calories/Passenger Mile
Bicycling	35
Walking	100
Transit rail	885
Transit bus	920
Automobile, single occupant	1,860

Sources: President's Council on Physical Fitness and Sports, Washington, D.C., private communication, June 23, 1988; Mary C. Holcomb et al., *Transportation Energy Data Book: Edition 9* (Oak Ridge, Tenn.: Oak Ridge National Laboratory, 1987).

where possible, debtor nations could free their financial resources for other investments.

In 1986, a national campaign in the Netherlands encouraged drivers to switch to bicycles for trips within a 3-mile radius of home. Policymakers figured this would save each motorist at least $400 a year in fuel costs. A 1980 study in Great Britain calculated that if just 10 percent of car trips under 10 miles were made by bicycle, the country would save 14 million barrels of oil a year.

A 1983 study of American commuters revealed that just getting to public transit by bicycle instead of car would save each commuter roughly 150 gallons of gasoline a year. When a motorist who otherwise drives all the way to work switches to this bike-and-ride method, his or her annual gasoline use drops by some 400 gallons, half the amount consumed by the typical car in a year. If 10 percent of the Americans who commute by car switched to bike-and-ride, more than $1.3 billion could be shaved off the U.S. oil import bill.

URBAN BANE

In 1983, a unique experiment began to unfold in the streets of Bogotá, Colombia. Every Sunday morning 37 miles of arterial roads were closed to motor traffic and half a million city dwellers took to the streets to bicycle, roller skate, and stroll. Now in its sixth year, the weekly ritual transforms a cityscape dominated by smog and honking cars into a tranquil, clean environment.

The world's automobile-bound cities, though, are a far cry from Bogotá on Sunday. Dependence on the car exacts a toll on human health, environment, and quality of life in urban areas.

Industrial-world cities typically relinquish at least one-third of their land—two-thirds in Los Angeles—to roads and parking lots. In the United States, this totals 38.4 million acres—more area than the entire state of Georgia. That, say researchers George Work and Lawrence Malone, is more than necessary. According to their calculations, for a bridge of a given size to accommodate 40,000 people in one hour would require 12 lanes for cars, 4 lanes for buses, 2 for trains, and 1 for bicycles.

With mounting pressures on Third World countries to house and feed their swelling populations, they have little room to spare for roads and parking lots. Where people and good cropland are concentrated in a relatively small area of a country, as in China, choices are narrow. If China paved over as much land per capita as the United States has (about 0.15 acres), it would have to give up a total of 158 million acres—equivalent to more than 40 percent of the country's cropland.

The automobile is very much the victim of its own success: it jams urban centers and suburbs alike. Traffic congestion is eroding the quality of life in urban areas, and the amount of time wasted in traffic continues to expand in the world's cities. London rush-hour traffic crawls at an average of 8 miles an hour. In Los Angeles, motorists waste 100,000 hours a day in traffic jams. Traffic engineers estimate that by the turn of the century Californians will lose almost two million hours daily.

Urban residents from Sao Paulo to London face eye, nose, and throat irritation, asthma, headaches, and chest discomfort brought on by car-produced smog. Emissions from gasoline and diesel fuel use are annually linked to as many as 30,000 deaths in the United States alone.

It is short automobile trips—precisely the ones bike-riding could replace—that create the most pollution, because a cold engine does not fire effectively and releases unburnt hydrocarbons into the air. In the United States, where an estimated 40 percent of urban commuters drive less than 4 miles, pedaling to work would have a dramatic effect on air quality.

Both city and country dwellers are endangered in other ways by the automobile. Some 100,000 people in North America, Western Europe, Japan, and Australia died in traffic accidents in 1985. Developing countries—with fewer automobiles but more pedestrian traffic and no provisions for separating the two—have fatality rates as much as 20 times higher than industrial countries.

Bicycle riding is not without its risks. Bicycle accidents do account for many traffic injuries, particularly in Asia, but are unlikely to kill people unless motor vehicles are involved. That is small consolation for would-be bicyclists who are intimidated off the road. Latin America has its urban cyclists—including young boys delivering newspapers and craftspeople hauling goods—but many potential riders are deterred by dangerous traffic conditions. Some Nairobi streets that once were full of bicycles now are only safe for cars.

Where it can be done safely, cycling improves public health. The popularity of stationary exercise bikes is proof that people enjoy cycling to keep fit; the irony is that so many people drive to the health club in order to ride them. Cyclists are less vulnerable to heart attacks or coronary disease than sedentary commuters, and they arrive at work more alert and less stressed by rush-hour traffic.

AN EQUITABLE TECHNOLOGY

Bicycles have a hard time getting the respect they deserve, even in countries where they give crucial mobility and employment to millions. The city of Jakarta, Indonesia, for example, has confiscated more than 20,000 cycle rickshaws over the past several years and dumped them into the sea—ostensibly to reduce traffic congestion.

Public buses are the main mode of transport in most developing countries and often the only one poor people can afford. But transport systems have proved incapable of keeping pace with explosive urban growth rates.

Even where mass transit systems are adequate, they do not serve certain crucial needs. A passenger bus cannot necessarily haul a Ghanaian farmer's produce to market, or carry a Colombo street vendor's hot lunches to a factory. Nor can it help rural people who live a day's walk from the nearest road. With bicycles, the poor and unemployed can earn a living by getting homemade crafts to urban markets, vending wares in the streets, or taking passengers for hire.

A bicycle demands a tiny fraction of the capital necessary to own and operate an automobile. In Brazil, the least expensive domestic car costs an average worker roughly six years' wages, while a bicycle requires only six weeks' pay.

Though many of those who would most benefit from a bicycle are too poor to own one, the bicycle is still the cheapest mode of transport outside urban cores. Governments could encompass rural areas in their transport planning by subsidizing bike purchases—a much less costly approach than extending roads and bus lines. In addition, bicycle production is a low-risk venture for developing countries that have little or no industrial base. A small assembly plant and repair shop can run on about $200 worth of tools. One hundred bicycles can be manufactured with the materials it takes to build a medium-sized car.

India has demonstrated how a nearly self-sufficient bicycle industry can be created by first assembling bicycles with imported parts, then producing frames in local workshops, and gradually establishing small factories to produce parts domestically. From a modest beginning five decades ago, India has become a major world producer. It directs more than 90 percent of its bicycle exports to other developing countries, and through joint-venture and license agreements is sharing its small-scale, labor-intensive techniques with countries throughout Asia, Africa, and the Caribbean.

SUBSIDIZED AUTO DEPENDENCY

The economic and environmental consequences of automobile overdependence may eventually necessitate bicycle use, even without government help. But for now, public policies that ignore bicycles perpetuate private attitudes against using them. Thus, the transport planner's office seems the best place for the philosophical reordering to start.

A major barrier to bicycling is the fact that drivers are in effect paid to use automobiles. Drivers in the United States may receive as much as $300 billion in subsidies each year in the form of public funds for road repair and construction, police and fire services, and health care.

In the private sector, free parking provided by many employers in effect pays the gasoline costs of commuting. The U.S. Environmental Protection Agency has concluded that if employees were directly handed this subsidy, public transit ridership and bicycle use would go up, while auto traffic would decline by 25 percent.

Several cities have made motorists pay for the privilege

of driving automobiles. Singapore charges private cars carrying fewer than four occupants "congestion fees" for entering the downtown area during rush hours, a decade-old scheme that has raised downtown traffic speeds by 20 percent and reduced traffic accidents by 25 percent.

Inconvenience—a general absence of safe parking and locker room facilities—keeps many commuters from bicycling to work, but there are precedents for dealing with this. In China, bicycle parking lots are guarded against theft by attendants. Palo Alto, California, has passed a number of innovative regulations requiring builders of large offices to provide showers and bicycle parking.

All that aside, commuters are still not likely to choose bicycling when it means taking their lives into their hands on busy city streets. Effective bicycle promotion calls for bike paths separate from roads and space on regular roadways devoted to bicycles. Perhaps even more important, cars and bikes should be treated equally in enforcing traffic laws. Along with bicycle safety campaigns, these steps can elevate bicycling to the status of real transportation in the public's mind.

PEDALING INTO THE FUTURE

In terms of sheer number of vehicles, the world is well-equipped to let bicycles take on a larger share of the transportation burden. Around the world, nearly 100 million bicycles are made each year—three times the number of automobiles. The big bicycle producers, especially in Asia, are sure to keep upping their capacities.

With or without bike-oriented planning, financial imperatives may force a shift to the bicycle. For starters, most people in the world will never be able to buy an automobile, and public transit systems in many cities cannot keep pace with explosive population growth. When the next oil crunch hits, even those who can now afford to drive will be looking for alternatives. With relatively modest public investment in parking and road space for bicycles, transportation choices would multiply quickly.

Environmental degradation may also change planners' thinking. The by-products of fossil-fuel combustion—deadly urban air pollution, acid rain on lakes and forests, and global warming—as well as the paving of valuable land, point to the need for an alternative to engines. The bicycle is the only vehicle that can help address all of these problems and still provide convenient and affordable personal transportation.

While transport planners remain fixated on the auto, congestion and commuting costs are already spurring people to switch to bicycling. The number of bicycle commuters in the United States reached 1.8 million in 1985, which is still less than 2 percent of all commuters, but represents a quadrupling in one decade. This happened with virtually no public policy push, and this suggests that official encouragement could inspire a more dramatic changeover.

Just how rapidly the bicycle will expand transport options, check environmental damage, and restore urban quality of life depends on how quickly its use moves from individual preference onto the public agenda.

9

Our Expanding Numbers

CHINA'S BABY BUDGET

By Jodi L. Jacobson

F ew things in China are done on a small scale. The world's most populous nation has a tradition of combining its abundant labor with intensive public education to mount immense attempts at improving living standards and meeting other social and economic goals. Although history has proven that some Chinese campaigns, such as the catastrophic Great Leap Forward of the fifties, were ill-conceived, others, such as the ones to improve health and reduce illiteracy in the sixties, catapulted China far ahead of other poor countries on basic social indicators.

In a series of "patriotic public-health campaigns" conducted in the early fifties, for example, the Chinese people successfully eradicated typhus, wiped out opium addiction, and controlled venereal diseases within a few years. Later in that decade, the government mobilized millions of its citizens to move earth, if not heaven, by manually draining and dredging waterways to destroy the snails that carry schistosomiasis.

Beginning in the mid-sixties, China forced down high rates of death and chronic illness by deploying an army of "barefoot doctors" throughout the countryside. Trained in preventive and curative medicine, and backed by county and regional clinics and hospitals, these villagers provided the grass-roots contact points to what is considered the most extensive primary health-care network in the developing world. This effort also laid the groundwork for another capstone in China's development: family planning.

China's most recent experiment in social engineering—reducing population growth by promoting one-child families—is nothing less than an unprecedented attempt to change the reproductive behavior of an entire nation. Taking to population planning with characteristic zeal, the revolutionary government has strongly encouraged couples to limit themselves to one child. However, achieving the goal of zero population growth by early in the next century is proving to be a Herculean task, even for the Chinese.

In strictly demographic terms, China already is a family planning success story. Sharp reductions in fertility since the sixties have put the country farther down the road toward a stable population size than most other Third World nations. Today, however, due to the legacy of past growth, the share of people of reproductive age in China is large and growing. This indicates that the population will continue to expand for at least three decades. Even at its current low level of fertility, China's population will exceed 1.5 billion by 2020.

The one-child policy, without a doubt the most hotly debated family planning strategy in the world, has been criticized on a number of grounds. First, it is (at least on some levels) a compulsory program in a world where even voluntary family planning remains controversial. Second, with one-child families, the next generation of elderly will have far fewer laborers to support it; this raises questions about how China will provide old-age security. Third, the policy's immediate economic benefits to the largely rural populace remain unclear.

Although alternatives to the one-child program that might meet China's population goals and lessen the growing opposition to current policy have not been universally adopted, there is some evidence that new, more lenient approaches to population planning are being tried in a majority of provinces. Nevertheless, over the next several years China will face a choice between allowing a slightly higher rate of population growth (and, perhaps, the addition of another 100 million to its population) or resorting to more stringent and compulsory measures to restrain fertility.

HITTING A GREAT WALL

At the close of the thirteenth century, when the New World was as yet unexplored and all of Europe contained only 75 million people, Chinese subjects of the Sung Dynasty already numbered 100 million. For several hundred years, sporadic increases in cultivated land and agricultural productivity underwrote population growth; the population reached a total of about 540 million in 1949.

Soon after the half-billion benchmark was reached, China scholar John King Fairbank observed that "the Chinese people's basic problem of livelihood is readily visible from the air: the brown eroded hills, the flood plains of muddy rivers, the crowded green fields . . . all the overcrowding of too many people upon too little land, and the attendant exhaustion of the land resources and of human ingenuity and fortitude in the effort to maintain life." Now that China's population has doubled, these thoughts are an even more apt description of the conflict between population and resources.

Today, China's leaders follow the population's upward climb with the nervous air of an expectant father. Their apprehensions are justifiable. With 1.1 billion people and counting, China may already have reached its environmental limits.

The threat that population growth will unravel past gains and halt further development understandably preoccupies the Chinese. Life for the average Chinese person has improved markedly since the birth of the People's Republic in 1949, at least in terms of health, nutrition, and life expectancy. As in most developing nations, though, population pressures in China threaten to undermine hard-won advances in meeting social needs. And resources—forests, land, and water—are already stretched thin.

Judging quality of life on the basis of per-capita income alone, China appears to be at the same level of development as India, its closest demographic cousin, with a population of 835 million. In both countries, annual income per person in 1989 was about $300. A look behind these figures, though, reveals some startling facts: China far outranks India and even Brazil on basic quality-of-life measures, although per-capita income in the latter was above $2,000.

In India, the infant-mortality rate—a key indicator of development—was a relatively high 96 deaths per 1,000 births (see Table 1). China's infant mortality rate was less than half that—around 44 per 1,000. Indian life expectancy at birth was 58 years, a level close to that of the poorest countries in sub-Saharan Africa. China's life expectancy of 66 years at birth ranks the nation close to the United States and Japan, which have far greater income levels. These achievements are part of the legacy of China's commitment to primary health care.

Yet, although resources are distributed more equitably in China than in many other nations, there are still acute short-

Country	Infant Mortality Rate	Life Expectancy	Per Capita Income
India	96	58	$300
China	44	66	$300
Brazil	63	65	$2,020
United States	10	75	$18,430
Japan	5	78	$15,770

TABLE 1
Basic Indicators, 1989

ages in education, housing, and health care. Additional population growth increases the competition for available resources and reduces the little surplus available to invest in boosting living standards.

Gains in food production also are at risk. With more than one-fifth of the world's population, China has only about 7 percent of its arable land. Until the mid-seventies, grain production in China barely kept pace with population growth; a history of recurrent famine is etched hard upon the collective Chinese memory. Since 1978, though, China has made great strides in raising food output.

In 1950, grain production in China hovered around 361 pounds per person, below the 397 pounds accepted as the subsistence level (see Figure 1). Production rose slowly until 1978, the year agricultural reforms were put in place. Per-capita output since then has increased substantially, to exceed the subsistence standard by a solid margin. Between 1978 and 1984, China's per-capita grain production increased 33 percent to 667 pounds per person, although it did drop back to 600 pounds during 1988's severe drought.

Comparing China with India on this count underscores

FIGURE 1
India and China:
Grain Production
per Capita,
1950–89

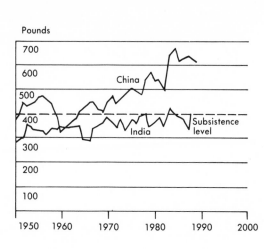

the extent of its achievement. Only four times since 1950 has India managed to reach even the subsistence level, although the country has more land devoted to grain production per person than does China. In fact, each acre of productive Chinese soil must now feed 4.5 people; this leaves little margin for error.

Not only the Chinese are concerned about the size of their population, for, as demographer Ping-ti Ho has noted, "China's population is a world problem."

The global environment is one point of contention. With the world's largest coal supplies and pressures to raise living standards, China has opted so far for an energy strategy based mostly on coal consumption. Air pollution and acid rain have emerged as serious environmental problems, since 85 percent of the country's coal is burned without controls.

China is beginning to weigh in heavily as a contributor to the mounting concentration of greenhouse gases; the country is responsible for 10 percent of the carbon dioxide added to the atmosphere each year, a share that is rising quickly. Its potential contribution to ozone depletion and other global problems also raises serious concerns, not least because the Chinese government has been slow to act on international treaties, such as those limiting production and use of ozone-depleting chemicals.

Population pressures often force a choice between development strategies that bring rapid gains in the short run and those that are economically and environmentally sustainable over time. China finds itself in this bind. Rising household demands and rapid economic growth have left the country in the throes of its worst energy shortage in at least two decades. Shifting to a more sustainable energy path, one based on energy efficiency, conservation, and renewable sources, will become more difficult as population growth creates ever higher demands.

ONE IS BEST

Prior to 1970, official support for family planning was sporadic at best. In the early seventies, with the Chinese population well on its way to one billion, the government recognized the need to reduce fertility and slow growth to reduce pressure on natural resources. The state family planning agency began to promote a policy known as *wan-xi-shao,* literally "later-longer-fewer." The policy encouraged Chinese couples to marry later than the average age of 20, to lengthen the amount of time between first and subsequent births, and to have fewer children overall.

The Chinese are fond of using slogans to communicate a message, and the family planning program certainly has its share. "One is not too few, two is good, three is too many" became a national refrain under *wan-xi-shao.* The central government, recognizing the cultural and economic differences between city and farm, set separate targets for age at marriage and family size. The policy encouraged urban couples to delay marriage until ages 28 for men and 25 for women, 25 and 23 for rural couples. Originally, urban couples were limited to two children, while rural couples could have three.

In 1977, the government began to promote the two-child family universally. Although fertility had declined significantly, Chinese officials began to realize that population growth would not fall quickly to the desired rate of 1 percent per year, owing mostly to the millions of teenagers entering their childbearing years. Projections showed a baby boom ahead, a disturbing demographic echo of the period of high fertility that followed the Great Leap Forward in the early sixties.

Arguing that continued growth would defeat plans to raise living standards, the government adopted a package of economic incentives and disincentives. In 1979, a new slogan, "one is best, at most two, never a third," subtly reflected yet another change in the country's demographic goals—the shift to a policy advocating one child. To this day, couples "pledging" to have only one child receive a package of benefits from the government. The original policy neither levied sanctions on nor offered benefits to couples having two children, but promised that "those who give birth to three or more will suffer economic sanctions."

The national policy sets out the following guidelines: In urban areas, the rewards allocated to couples who sign the one-child certificate include monthly cash payments for 14 years and preference in housing allocations and job assignments; single children receive priority in free medical care and schooling, and jobs at graduation. According to the original policy, rural couples pledging to have one child were promised extra work points (the "currency" earned by farmers working communal land that determined their share of a commune's income) for 14 years, generous allocations of private land, and larger grain rations.

Couples that don't comply, and give birth to a third child, have their salaries reduced for the 14-year period, don't receive additional housing space, and have to bear the full costs of that child's birth, medical care, and schooling. Rural couples could count on reductions in workpoints, land allocations, and grain rations, in addition to paying their own health costs out of pocket. In rural areas, the mix of incentives and disincentives has changed significantly since agricultural reform got under way and communes have virtually disappeared.

BAREFOOT AND NOT PREGNANT

The Chinese exude an urgency about and a willingness to commit funds to family planning not seen in any other country. Not surprisingly, the Chinese program has been wildly successful by virtually any standard over the past two decades. This success is due to a combination of policies and strategies, including persistent efforts to develop new contraceptive technologies and disseminate them through the barefoot-doctor network. The Marriage Law of 1980, which proclaims it the responsibility of every husband and wife to practice family planning, has also been effective.

Childbearing trends, most clearly represented by total fertility rates, bear this out. Between 1960 and the mid-eighties, the total fertility rate in China fell by a remarkable 60 percent, from 6.0 to 2.4 children per woman (see Table 2). India and Indonesia, the next two largest countries in the table, reduced their total fertility rates by only 31 and 38 percent, respectively. In fact, the rate in India has not fallen at all since the late seventies.

While India's effort languishes, the Chinese have built the world's most comprehensive family planning network, one that operates on the same principle of decentralization that made the barefoot doctor famous the world over. At its best, the network has been the prime conduit for educating

TABLE 2   Fertility Declines in Selected Countries, 1960–89

Country	Population 1989	Total Fertility Rates		Change
		1960	1989	
	(millions)	(average number of children per woman)		(percent)
China	1,104	6.0	2.4	−60
Mexico	87	7.2	3.8	−47
Brazil	147	6.2	3.4	−45
Indonesia	185	5.6	3.5	−38
India	835	6.2	4.3	−31

millions of Chinese on the economic, environmental, and health benefits of family planning. At its worst, it has become a tool of coercion.

One result of the Chinese commitment to family planning is that more than 73 percent of couples of reproductive age use a modern form of contraception, a rate that exceeds even the United States' at 68 percent. Moreover, the Chinese populace is highly educated about the benefits to maternal and infant health derived from lower fertility, birth-spacing, and contraceptive use.

In fact, the level of education among Chinese people about one subject—the impact of population on natural resources—probably is higher than anywhere else in the world. By decentralizing and politicizing environmental issues such as deforestation, water shortages, and soil erosion the Chinese government has succeeded, to a remarkable extent, in elevating people's awareness of the impact of their reproductive behavior on the world around them. It has attempted to change a couple's usual question of "How many children do I want?" to "How many children per family can this society afford?" These efforts notwithstanding, there are stirrings of discontent with the one-child policy. Surveys show a considerable share of Chinese couples prefer more than one child, especially if their first is a girl.

Despite the seemingly specific nature of the guidelines outlined above, the national policy has been treated only as a rough framework for a highly decentralized family planning program that places the power of enforcement in the hands of local cadres.

The national government suggests but does not dictate the actual package of incentives and disincentives; national policy is interpreted and carried out by planned-birth committees in every province, prefecture, municipality, county, and township. Among other things, these committees, made up largely of female cadres, midwives, and other family planning workers, visit households to distribute contraceptives and urge couples to comply with family planning policy.

Decentralization has had its down side, however. Because policies become increasingly more specific as they move down the chain of command, cadres have much more power than is immediately apparent. It is the mandate of local leaders to meet regional and provincial population-size and growth-rate targets. The pressure to do so has, in some provinces, resulted in incidents of coercion, including forced abortions and the mandatory insertion of an intrauterine device following a woman's first live birth, as well as criminal penalties for its removal. While the national government has reproached cadres who move from persuasion to coercion in their efforts to reach demographic targets, it is the stringency of the targets themselves and the possible ramifications of not meeting them that can lead to abuses.

Resistance on the Farm

The one-child policy raises important questions about equity, individual choice, and human rights.

To date, many more urban than rural couples have signed on to the one-child policy; this has accentuated a difference between urban and rural fertility in China similar to that found in most developing countries. In 1983, the Chinese State Family Planning Commission estimated that 78 percent of all urban couples of childbearing age with one child had signed the certificate, as opposed to 31 percent of rural couples. Generally speaking, urban couples have lower fertility because they tend to be more highly educated and more prosperous, marry later, and hold less tightly to cultural traditions than their rural counterparts.

Apart from government policy, urban life in China offers its own built-in disincentives to big families. On average, an urban dweller has only 36 square feet of living space; often, several families live in adjoining rooms and must share kitchen and bath facilities. The high cost of clothing, education, food, and other consumer goods dissuades parents from building large families. In urban areas, either husband or wife is more likely to be working in a state-supported industry that offers social security after retirement and so obviates the need to bear sons as a hedge against poverty in old age. Perhaps more important, however, is that government control over an individual's life through the urban food rationing and employment system made gaining widespread urban adherence to the one-child policy relatively easy.

China is still a nation of farmers, however, and it's in rural areas that the battle to lower fertility is hardest to win. Cultural and economic advantages to farmers having more than one child, and at least one son, are proving difficult to counteract fully through family planning policy alone. Ironically, many of the economic reforms put in place by Deng Xiaoping, under whose leadership the one-child policy also was born, reinforce incentives for higher fertility.

In rural areas, where human labor is still the key ingredient in food production and rural industries, a family's success depends on the number of children it has to tend the fields—even more so now that agricultural reforms have largely privatized Chinese agriculture. It's in peasant homes, where sons are required to support their parents in old age, that the one-child policy faces the most resistance.

Much as they worry about fines and penalties, rural Chinese couples, like couples everywhere, are concerned about how they will fare in retirement. Unlike daughters (who generally live with and contribute to the household economy of their in-laws), Chinese sons are bound by tradition and social mores to care for their own parents. Most rural dwellers are not covered by a state-funded pension system. While rural townships are legally bound to provide the "five guarantees" (food, shelter, clothing, medical care, and burial) to elderly couples without a son, studies have shown that, even in well-off areas, this program provides minimal aid at best.

Today's current and potential Chinese parents are aware of the implications of the one-child policy on their retirement years. Demographic assessments show that the one-child family implies a sharp drop in the size of the labor force in future decades. If every family had one child, the share of the population over age 65 would reach 25 percent by 2040, as opposed to 6 percent today. Although the theoretical share is larger by an unknown quantity than what actually will bear out, since many are having more than one child, the implications for China are clear. Many developed countries with between 10 and 15 percent of their current population over age 65 already face insolvency with their social security systems. It's an open-ended question whether China will develop quickly enough to allow couples to accumulate enough of an economic surplus to care for a much larger proportion of elderly.

Interregional equity is another concern. The one-child policy has exacerbated income inequality between urban and rural areas and between advantaged and disadvantaged families within a given region, in large part because most urban and some rural areas are better able to pay incentives. In rural areas, townships must pay for benefits through the fines levied on those who have more than one child. The actual benefits disbursed range from the full menu to none at all because, in poor villages with no surplus crops, there is little if anything to redistribute from prolific couples to one-child couples.

Similarly, in urban areas where amenities are better than in rural areas, though still in short supply, "preferential treatment" becomes less meaningful when nearly everyone joins the program but shortages of housing, schools, and jobs still exist. As a result, some urban couples attempt to violate their pledges because they receive no real benefits in holding to them.

SMALL HAPPINESS

In Chinese, the phrase describing a pregnant woman translates roughly into English as "she has happiness." When a
woman gives birth to a son, she has "big happiness"; a
daughter brings her "small happiness." Making the birth of
a girl equally as welcome as that of a boy is a key challenge
to improving human rights and equity, not only in China,
but throughout most of the world.

Raising the status of women is a goal in itself. The near-
universal discrimination suffered by women in virtually
every sphere of their lives has curtailed their social, economic, and personal development, severely impaired their
health, and deprived them of self-esteem and fulfillment.
Measured in terms of education and income levels, women's
status also bears on fertility. The more opportunities women
have, the fewer children they are likely to bear. On paper,
China has done more than most countries to bridge the gender gap, but sexual discrimination dies hard. As demographers Fred Arnold and Liu Zhaoxiang note, "Sexual equality
in the political, socioeconomic, and cultural spheres of life is
guaranteed in China's constitution, but patriarchal attitudes
[and practices] are still prevalent."

A distinctive preference for sons among a large sector of
the Chinese population remains one of the biggest roadblocks to acceptance of the one-child family. Ask a Chinese
couple what sex they would like their first or only child to be
and, more often than not, the answer will be "a son." No
matter how many children a couple has, those with only
daughters are less likely to be using contraception than those
with at least one son.

Son preference varies considerably by place of residence
and by parents' levels of education, but it is evident in almost every part of the country. It is strongest in towns and
villages dominated by agriculture, where traditional atti-

tudes run deepest and the perceived importance of sons as farm workers and providers of social security is ubiquitous. Interestingly, Arnold and Liu have shown that, in rural areas, son preference is substantially weaker in nonfarm villages, where women often play a vital role in operating small factories and contributing to family income.

About 60 percent of all one-child certificate holders have a son, a fact that has disturbing implications for the status of women and equity in general. At least 50 percent more boys than girls are getting preferential treatment in schooling, food rations, health care, and opportunities to compete for employment later on under the current program—all areas where girls are at a disadvantage due to traditional discrimination. In some parts of the country, where women are caught between the demands of the state to limit fertility and the demands of the husband's family to bear a son, violence against both mothers and first-born daughters has increased.

PRODUCTION VS. REPRODUCTION

The one-child policy cannot be divorced from another campaign going on in China. The "four modernizations," as the name implies, is a drive to increase per-capita production and investment in four key areas—agriculture, industry, defense, and science and technology. The Chinese government, says Qian Xinzhong, minister of public health until 1983, is worried that if population growth continues at its current pace "we will be compelled to devote a considerable amount of . . . resources to feeding the newly increased populace. That will inevitably slow down the four modernizations."

The modernization of agriculture has taken the form of the widely publicized "agricultural responsibility" system, wherein communes and work brigades have given way to the family farm. Under this system, each family is allotted a private plot and signs a contract agreeing to sell a portion of its crop to the state at a fixed price. Any surplus crops can be sold for a higher price to the state or in the market, or used by the farm household.

The spread of the responsibility system has sounded a death knell for Chinese collectives. The share of farm income derived from producing surplus crops, raising farm animals, harvesting fruit, oilseeds, and vegetables, producing handicrafts, and engaging in small-scale industrial production has risen sharply. As the share of work points in farm income has diminished, so, too, has the power of the cadres to levy fines.

Under the responsibility system, a family's success depends on its labor resources. This has created an ironic clash between agricultural and family planning policy. In some areas, plots of land are allocated according to the number of laborers a family has, a direct conflict with the disincentives to having more than one child. Many smaller families have found that they lack the humanpower needed to meet their contractual obligations to the state and still engage in additional income-earning activities. And many farmers have found that the gains derived from having an additional child, especially a son, far outweigh the costs imposed by the one-child program.

Contradictory official signals abound. In an article entitled "How a Farm Family Gets Its Income," the same Chinese press that espouses the one-child policy described how the family of Feng Maoru, a man with five sons, has prospered under agricultural reforms. Although two of his sons (and both his married daughters) live outside the village, the three remaining at home work at beekeeping, carpentry, and farming, more than tripling the family's income. The article notes that "the two sons working outside send 300 to 400 yuan a year [to their parents] for expenses, but the couple prefers to bank it." The example illustrates how in the traditional family structure, families with sons are better able to accumulate resources, take advantage of new work opportunities, and diversify their business.

These obvious incentives to have more than one child have not escaped farmers in China's poorer regions, which lead more prosperous areas in the rates of abandoning collectivization and of reproducing children.

In response, some rural family planning committees have sought to curtail the incentives to higher fertility unleashed by the responsibility system by combining agricultural production contracts with family planning contracts; in effect they have tied the couple's immediate financial well-being (the sale of its crops) to a pledge to have only one child.

Is Two Okay?

In China, as in every country in the process of modernization, incentives to have large families will erode. As the number of farm laborers grows, for instance, additional labor on the farm yields diminishing returns. And, when available land no longer can be subdivided among new families, those children must find alternative means of making a living. The development of cities, industries, and pension plans is accompanied by smaller families. These conditions and others, such as the spread of education and opportunities for women, will push China through a transition to lower fertility.

In the China of more than one billion people, however, this natural "demographic transition" is not occurring quickly enough to avoid seriously compromising the environment. In fact, the population may be growing more rapidly than is officially acknowledged. The introduction of economic reforms has loosened the government's grip on people, made them more mobile, more economically independent, and less subject to regulations. As a result, independent sources claim that the total fertility rate in China is actually rising; contrary to government figures, it may now exceed 2.8 children per family.

The question is, How can the Chinese significantly reduce population growth without relying on increasingly coercive measures?

China experts John Bongaarts and Susan Greenhalgh of the New York–based Population Council, a nonprofit population research institute, have proposed an alternative—patterned on *wan-xi-shao*—that involves two key elements. One is a strict "stop-at-two" rule, allowing each couple to have at most two children. The second is a set of conditions under which the stop-at-two rule would operate, including a minimum age at first birth of, say, 25. Couples could marry whenever they wanted to but must delay their first birth. Second births would have to be delayed by at least four more years.

Although at first glance this proposal seems to imply a much higher rate of growth, it is actually projected to reach the same targets as the current program. By keeping one-child family incentives in place, some people still will agree to have one child. As a result of this and the fact that a proportion of the population will experience "secondary" infertility (inability to have a second child), and others "primary" infertility, the average number of children per couple nationwide would be less than two. According to the plan, late first births and delayed second ones would space children far enough apart to affect this generation's population growth rate. Bongaarts and Greenhalgh argue that such a policy would, at least partially, resolve the conflict between the government's demographic goals and individual desires. More people would have at least one son; those who had two daughters could encourage one to assume the role of provider to her parents in old age by asking her husband to join her parents' household (a move encouraged by the government).

A form of two-child policy is starting to spread. In 1984, the national government expanded the number of situations under which people may have that many children. And recent reports from China imply that several provinces have loosened their policies in a similar fashion. Although some experts point to this trend as evidence of a liberalization of government policy, others, such as Judith Banister, a sinologist at the U.S. Census Bureau, claim that despite the apparent easing of restrictions, the policy as applied still too strongly "encourages" only one child.

HOLDING THE LINE

Recent changes notwithstanding, the future of the one-child family program may hinge on the government's willingness to address mounting concerns over social security and inequity. As events in Tiananmen Square indicate, a nascent democratic movement exists in China. A backlash to family planning in China, similar to the one that occurred in India in the mid-seventies in response to forced sterilizations, is conceivable.

For now, the Chinese government can consider several steps to bring government policy more in line with individual desires. Allowing two children is one option. Establishing a rural social security system based on need might help convince more people to have fewer children. Under such a system, the central government would extend support to the poorer and middle income rural areas that cannot sufficiently meet the "five guarantees." In China as elsewhere, women still suffer discrimination in education, employment, and the application of legal principles in every day life. Making sure that government and private practices offer the same opportunities to women as to men would help erode gender bias and reduce fertility.

China entered the seventies with a clear choice: to bring population growth down swiftly through family planning policy or to allow nature to eventually take its course in the form of a deteriorating environment, declining living standards, and possible famine. In this way, China first reached a crossroads of demography and environment that many other countries—Bangladesh, Egypt, India, Kenya, and Nigeria, to name a few—are fast approaching.

With the one-child family, the Chinese have had to chart an unmapped course in the murky waters of human reproductive behavior. The positive aspects of their family planning efforts are evident: lower fertility, better health, and reduced pressure on natural resources and the economy. Several characteristics unique to Chinese society made these advances possible. The population is nearly homogenous, with a 93 percent Han majority. The closed nature of the political system, the Confucian tradition and the strong sense of family it fostered, and a 3,000-year history of allegiance to authority made the one-child family program succeed where it might otherwise have failed.

The Chinese approach to population and family planning subordinates the needs and desires of the individual to those of the society at large—a strategy that is unlikely to be tenable in such a form in many countries. Still, other countries can learn from and adapt some aspects of China's program. The barefoot-doctor program is one example. By decentralizing health care and family planning, providing it literally by villagers for villagers, countries can begin to combat high rates of maternal and infant mortality and provide the means and information necessary to plan families. Similarly, a widespread rural network can help to educate people about population and environmental issues. In addition, by codifying and enforcing laws, and offering women of every age educational and employment opportunities equivalent to men, countries can promote equity and lower fertility at the same time.

But the one-child policy raises a fundamental conflict, one that more and more countries are now facing: the rights of this generation to reproduce against those of future generations to an ecologically intact world.

Looking back, most Chinese officials probably wish the government had undertaken family planning efforts when their people numbered 500 million. None of today's rapidly growing countries can afford to wait as long as China did to act. Neither can the world.

ABORTION IN A NEW LIGHT

By Jodi L. Jacobson

Among the first actions taken by Romania's provisional government following the execution of dictator Nicolae Ceausescu in December 1989 was a repeal of the ban on abortion. The 14-year-old edict, created by Ceausescu in a fruitless attempt to raise the nation's birthrate, outlawed contraceptives and made abortion a criminal offense punishable in some instances by death.

Some six months earlier, the United States, a country with one of the world's most liberal abortion policies, took a step backward on reproductive rights. The 1989 U.S. Supreme Court ruling on *Webster v. Reproductive Services* in effect flashed a green light to those states seeking to strictly regulate abortion procedures. In *Webster,* the court threw out the trimester framework established in the landmark 1973 *Roe v. Wade* decision, which permitted states to regulate abortions only after the first trimester and to ban them only in the last. The case upholds Missouri's law declaring that life begins at conception and that physicians must carry out extensive tests before performing many second trimester abortions. Furthermore, *Webster* extended government control of private abortion facilities by upholding Missouri's ban on the use of public facilities for abortion.

Not since the Vietnam era has a single issue so polarized

public opinion in the United States. For abortion rights activists, *Webster* has been the equivalent of the Tet Offensive; it has galvanized supporters in much the same way that battle rallied opponents of the Vietnam War. But, the zeal and dedication of a highly organized pro-life minority ensures that the fight over reproductive freedom is far from over.

A careful examination of trends in Romania, the United States, and other countries illuminates several important points about the global abortion debate. One, against the backdrop of a general liberalization of abortion laws, events in several countries reveal an ominous undertow eroding recently codified reproductive rights. Two, abortion politics has become deadlocked in a no-win dispute over the ideology and criminology of abortion procedures; this has resulted in a tug-of-war over laws that don't even begin to address the complex social phenomenon of abortion. Three, this dispute postpones the day when the energies of both the prochoice and pro-life camps can be directed fully toward improving the health and welfare of women and children worldwide.

THE ISSUE THAT KNOWS NO COMPROMISE

In legalizing abortion, Romania joins some 35 other countries that have made similar changes since the late-1970s. In fact, a 30-year tide of liberalization in laws governing family planning has increased access to contraceptives and made abortions safer for millions of women worldwide. As a result, the relative number of unintended pregnancies and deaths due to illegal abortion procedures has dropped in many countries.

But groups vociferously opposed to abortion—and, in many cases, to family planning methods altogether—have kept up their fight to reverse these policies. The U.S. decision, the first major success of the "pro-life" movement, sent shock waves through the ranks of activists in Western

Europe, where the abortion debate has been far less emotional than in the United States but is becoming more polarized. Europeans from both camps have described the decision as a "wind from the west." While European pro-life groups have been "in the doldrums for a number of years . . . supporters are [now] heartened by what has taken place in the United States [and are] back in business," declares Bill Sherwin, executive secretary of the International Right to Life Federation in Rome.

The struggle over abortion rights is now a cross-border affair, with money and antiabortion protesters crossing the Atlantic from the U.S. to Europe. According to Leonora Lloyd, director of the prochoice National Abortion Campaign in London, Operation Rescue, a group that has been linked to violent tactics, is sending its organizers to England and elsewhere. Abortion rights activists in Canada, France, Italy, Spain, and Germany are gearing up for renewed battle.

Pro-life activists from the United States and Europe are supporting the growth of parallel movements in developing countries. Their agenda focuses on maintaining or reinstating restrictive abortion laws rather than providing couples with the means to prevent unintended pregnancy. However, studies show that millions of Third World couples still lack access to birth control. Not surprisingly, poor women suffer the highest rates of death due to complications of pregnancy and illegal abortion. In 1989, the antiabortion group Human Life International held its first international conference in Zambia, a country with one of Africa's most liberal reproductive rights policies. Representatives of this group are suspected of starting a widespread disinformation campaign about locally available contraceptives, causing a great deal of confusion and anguish on the part of women relying on these methods.

UNANSWERED QUESTIONS

In many ways, the goals of pro-life activists raise more questions than they answer. For example, why are so-called pro-life forces so blind to the public health toll of illegal abortion?

Illegal abortion represents a global public health problem of tremendous proportions. Estimates indicate that about 55 million unwanted pregnancies end in abortion every year, nearly half of which are illegal operations carried out mostly in the Third World. The World Health Organization (WHO) attributes the loss of roughly 200,000 women's lives annually to illegal abortions, most of which are performed by unskilled attendants under unsanitary conditions, or are self-inflicted with hangers, knitting needles, toxic herbal teas, and the like. What is more, for every woman who dies, many others suffer serious, often long-term health consequences.

By contrast, modern abortion procedures performed under proper medical supervision in countries where they are legal are among the safest of all medical procedures. In the United States, for instance, an early abortion procedure is 11 times safer than a tonsillectomy or childbirth.

Why focus on banning abortions when evidence overwhelmingly indicates that this is not the answer to the problem? History has proven that laws cannot eliminate abortions, they can only make them more or less safe and costly. Try as it might, no government has ever legislated abortion out of existence.

In Ceausescu's Romania, for example, reproductive repression was as widespread as economic privation. No woman under the age of 45 with less than five children could obtain a legal abortion. A special arm of the secret police force Securitate, dubbed the "Pregnancy Police," administered monthly checkups to female workers. Pregnant women were monitored, married women who did not conceive were kept under surveillance, and a special tax was levied on unmarried people over 25 and childless couples that could not give a medical reason for infertility.

Despite the law, data show that in the 1980s Romania's birthrate fell, before rising again later, and that the country outranked virtually all other European nations on rates of abortion and abortion-related maternal mortality. One survey showed that Bucharest Municipal Hospital alone dealt with 3,000 failed abortions in one year; still other sources indicate that well over 1,000 women died within that city each year due to complications of botched abortions. Legalization of abortion in Western Europe, by contrast, has produced the world's lowest abortion-related mortality rates. In several of these countries, public education efforts on planned parenthood have precipitated a fall in the number of abortions.

Why are pro-life groups opposed to programs most likely to prevent the greatest number of abortions? The best way to reduce the number of abortions and unintended pregnancies is to support a comprehensive family planning and health program that educates couples about birth control and lets them know where to get it. Epidemiological and social studies show conclusively that family planning improves the health of women and families most effectively by preventing the most dangerous pregnancies—those that occur in women too young or too old to carry safely to term and those that come within 24 months of a prior birth.

Family planning also affords people the means with which to exercise their basic human right to determine the number and spacing of their children. The benefits extend to children because infants who are adequately spaced tend to be better nourished and cared for than those following close on the heels of their siblings. These facts notwithstanding, pro-life groups in the United States and elsewhere have been the most vocal opponents of strategies that would reduce the number of unintended pregnancies and abortions and improve overall family health.

Politicking by pro-life groups led the United States to dramatically restructure and limit its involvement in international family planning efforts. The Reagan administration ended U.S. leadership on international family planning efforts with the announcement of a new policy stance at the 1984 International Conference on Population in Mexico City. This policy, developed under heavy lobbying from groups opposed to family planning in general, cut off U.S. funds to any private voluntary group that provides abortion services or counseling, even though a law banning the use of U.S. funds for abortions abroad was already on the books and had been stringently enforced since 1973. Blacklisted agencies include the well-respected International Planned Parenthood Federation (IPPF) and United Nations Population Fund.

Unfortunately, this turnabout has curtailed IPPF plans to expand the number of family planning clinics around the world to cope with a growing number of couples of reproductive age. At the same time, the research, development, and marketing of low-cost, long-acting contraceptives, such as implants and injectables, has also been slowed. Similar efforts in the United States and Europe have resulted in costly legal battles over family planning funds, as well as research and development of drugs such as RU-486, which terminates pregnancy in its earliest stages, when abortions are least controversial.

Given the fact that many pro-life groups harbor a strong desire to ban or restrict contraceptive methods now on the market, eliminate contraceptive research and development, and scuttle family planning altogether, just how would they propose to reduce the incidence of abortion?

If the pro-life lobby were successful in severely restricting birth control and abortion in many countries, how would it propose to deal with the regional disparities between population and resources? Without abortion as a backup to the failure, ineffective use, or total lack of birth control methods, just how would the world deal with 55 million additional (and unwanted) pregnancies each year? More fundamental to the debate perhaps is the question of how will women, forced to bear children they do not want, ever really achieve their potential as individuals?

ABORTION LAWS, WORLDWIDE

"Pro-choice" or "pro-life," few people would disagree with the idea that reducing the number of unintended pregnancies and abortions worldwide, and attempting to ensure that the largest share of abortions are carried out in the first trimester, when they are safest and least controversial, is a desirable public policy goal. Ironically, few countries have worked wholeheartedly towards this end.

The majority of the world's people now live in countries that have moved from blanket prohibition of abortion to a more reasoned acceptance of its role as a backup to contraceptive failure and unwanted pregnancy. The debate in these countries has evolved from whether or not to legalize abortions to just under what circumstances they should be available. Still, most countries relegate abortion to the criminal code, rather than dealing with it comprehensively as a public health problem.

The trend toward liberalization began in full force in the 1950s, as recognition of the need to reduce maternal mortality and promote reproductive freedom became widespread. Social justice was also an issue. Bringing abortion into the public domain reduced the disparity between those who could afford adequate medical care and those forced to resort to unsafe practitioners.

Most countries have enacted abortion laws within their criminal codes, using traditional legal justifications to indicate the actual circumstances under which abortions can be legally performed. Countries with the narrowest laws restrict abortion to cases where pregnancy poses a risk to a woman's life, although most include cases of rape or incest. Other laws consider risks to physical and mental health; still others the case of a severely impaired fetus. Some societies condone abortion for what are known as "social" reasons, as in cases where an additional childbirth will inflict undue burdens on a woman's existing family. Broadest are the laws that recognize contraceptive failure, or a simple request (usually within the first trimester), as a sound basis for abortion. Most governments leave specific interpretations (how to define "health") up to the discretion of the medical community.

According to Rebecca Cook, professor of law at the University of Toronto, several of the 35 countries that liberalized their laws since 1977 created new categories, such as adolescence, advanced maternal age, or infection with the AIDS virus, as bases for legal abortion. Cyprus, Italy, and Taiwan, for example, all broadened their laws to consider "family welfare," while Hong Kong recognized adolescence. France and the Netherlands have included clauses pertaining to pregnancy-related distress. In Hungary, one of the first Eastern European countries to liberalize abortion laws, abortion rights are extended to pregnant women who are single or have been separated from their husbands for a period of six months, to women over the age of 35 with at least three previous deliveries, and to women caught in economic hardship, such as the lack of appropriate housing.

Even countries with the most liberal laws recognize some constraints on a woman's right to abortion. Generally speaking, abortions are least regulated during the first trimester of pregnancy, during which most liberal codes permit abortion on request. In Singapore, for example, abortions are available upon request until the twenty-fourth week of pregnancy, while in Turkey only until the tenth week. A woman seeking to terminate a pregnancy after this period must show just cause under the law.

A recent review of international abortion policy data by the Washington-based Population Crisis Committee indicates that about 75 percent of the world's population (3.9 billion out of 5.3 billion people) live in countries that permit abortion on medical or broader social and economic grounds. In Ethiopia and Costa Rica, for example, abortion is legal only in cases of risk to the woman's health, while in Tunisia it is available on request until the twelfth week of pregnancy and in Taiwan on request until the fetus can live outside the womb (otherwise known as viability, the stage between the twenty-fourth and twenty-eighth weeks of pregnancy).

Another 20 percent live in 49 countries in which abortion is totally prohibited or is legal only to save the life of the mother. The category includes much of Africa, Latin America, and Muslim Asia. Unfortunately, these are also countries where women have the least access to safe, affordable means of contraception. The remaining 5 percent of the world's people are governed by laws that have added rape and incest to this fairly restrictive list.

Bucking the liberalization trend are Finland, Honduras, Iran, Ireland, Israel, New Zealand, and now the United States. Abortion laws in this group have become more restrictive since 1977. A Honduran law permitting abortions in cases where they would protect the life and health of the mother and in cases of rape and fetal deformity was rejected because it was perceived to conflict with constitutional provisions stating that the "right to life is inviolable."

Likewise, changes in the constitutions of Ecuador (1978) and the Philippines (1986) incorporated provisions according the right to life "from the moment of conception." Some of these changes have ambiguous implications. Chile's constitution, for example, protects not only the right to life and to physical and psychic integrity of individuals, but also of those "about to be born." Whether or not an embryo or 10-week-old fetus is "about to be born" remains unclear.

Because many nations' legal codes reflect social ambivalence about abortion, what happens in practice often does not reflect the law on the books. In some countries where abortion is illegal in principle, it is carried out quite freely in practice. Conversely, in other countries where women hold the legal right to abortion on demand, they find it difficult actually to procure one because of local opposition or reluctance to carry out national laws. Such is the case in the Bavarian region of Germany, where local officials have sought to circumvent national abortion rights laws.

"Liberal" laws themselves do not always safeguard a woman's ability to exercise abortion rights. A pervasive problem is that while many countries have liberalized their laws, they have not gone so far as to commit public resources to providing safe abortion services, nor do most countries mandate widespread access.

Some laws work against the goal of ensuring that when abortions do occur they are carried out at the earliest possible point. New laws in Bermuda, Kuwait, the Seychelles, and Qatar include hospital committee authorization requirements before an abortion can be performed. Yet, in most cases, these regulations, strongly supported by the pro-life community, act only to delay abortions until later stages of pregnancy, when procedures are riskier and the fetus is more developed. Such institutional and third-party authorization requirements have come under legal attack in many countries and been struck down in several, including Canada and Czechoslovakia. Unfortunately, several U.S. states may soon enact such restrictions.

The resolution of other issues under debate in countries throughout the world could have a negative effect on abortion rights. They are: when and to what extent government health-care programs should cover the costs of legal abortion; whether or not a husband's consent or notification should be required before a married woman can obtain an abortion; and whether or not laws should condition adolescent abortions on parental notification.

The question is, Will the same forces responsible for the U.S. *Webster* decision be successful in turning back the clock in other countries? The social impacts of setting limits on family planning options are likely to be staggering. Apart from the immediate health impacts of illegal abortion, experience in a number of countries shows that forcing women to carry pregnancies to term results in higher rates of infanticide, greater numbers of abandoned and neglected children, and, particularly in the Third World, a decline in health and nutritional standards. In Romania, the numbers of abandoned and neglected children soared after abortion and contraception were outlawed. Similar trends have been documented in African and Latin American countries.

A Prescription to Reduce Abortion

Only by making contraceptives safer and more available, increasing access to family planning information and supplies, and teaching children the concept of responsible parenthood will the number of unintended pregnancies and abortions be reduced. Abortion, however, will never disappear. Activists and policymakers need to begin rejecting fixed but unfounded notions about the ideology and criminality of abortion in favor of a more rational understanding of its role in the spectrum of choices within a comprehensive family planning program. In effect, this would be a strategy based on the notion that prevention is better than cure.

The first step is to remove abortion from the criminal code and address it as a public health problem. A few countries—China, Togo, and Vietnam—have already done so. In Cuba, abortion is considered a criminal offense only when it is performed for profit, by an unqualified person, in an unofficial place, or without the woman's consent.

Second, mobilize support for family planning programs. According to Rebecca Cook, a number of countries have taken this positive step by setting up programs aimed at reducing the incidence of unwanted pregnancy. Some countries now require postabortion contraceptive counseling and education, and some mandate programs for men, too. Italy now requires local and regional health authorities to promote contraceptive services and other measures to reduce demand for abortion, while Czech law aims to prevent abortion through sex education in schools and health facilities and provides for free contraceptive and associated care. Turkish law provides access to voluntary sterilization as well as to abortion.

These efforts have been successful. On the Swedish island of Gotland, abortions were almost halved in an intensive three-year program to provide information and improved family planning services. Similar results have been shown in France and elsewhere.

Third, provide support and funding for international contraceptive research and development. Making contraceptives safer, more affordable, and more widely available will reduce the need for abortions around the world.

Fourth, target high-risk groups with education programs. In the United States, for example, lack of education on family planning methods leads to one of the highest rates of unintended pregnancy among teenagers in the industrial world. That group undergoes about one-third of all abortions each year. It's no coincidence that U.S. teens lag far behind their Western European counterparts in knowledge of contraception. A common myth perpetuated by the pro-life movement is that sex education, including family planning information, leads to teen promiscuity. Data from the Alan Guttmacher Institute and elsewhere show the reverse is true.

The impact of unwanted pregnancies extends beyond the individual to encompass public health and the question of sustainable development. An international consensus among a diverse body of policymakers already exists on the adverse effects of rapid population growth on economic performance, the environment, family welfare, health, and political stability. If minimizing population-related problems is an international priority, as has been accepted by a number of U.N. legal conventions, then it is essential that abortion be available as a birth control method of last resort.

The success of abortion rights activists throughout the world will depend on their ability to make clear that abortion is a social reality that cannot be erased by legal code. Obviously, the ideal situation would be to eliminate all unintended pregnancies. In the real world, though, limited access to birth control and the inevitability of contraceptive failure, either through imperfect technologies or human error, means that unplanned pregnancies will continue to occur.

10

Reclaiming the Future

VISION OF A SUSTAINABLE WORLD

By Lester R. Brown, Christopher Flavin, and Sandra Postel

O n April 22nd, 1990, millions of people around the world celebrated Earth Day. Marking the twentieth anniversary of the original Earth Day, this event came at a time when public concern about the environmental fate of the planet had soared to unprecedented heights.

Threats such as climate change and ozone depletion underscore the fact that ecological degradation has reached global proportions. Meanwhile, the increasing severity and spread of more localized problems—including soil erosion, deforestation, water scarcity, toxic contamination, and air pollution—are already beginning to slow economic and social progress in much of the world.

Governments, development agencies, and people the world over have begun to grasp the need to reverse this broad-based deterioration of the environment. But, the result so far is a flurry of fragmented activity—a new pollution law here, a larger environment staff there—that lacks any coherent sense of what, ultimately, we are trying to achieve.

Building an environmentally stable future requires some vision of what it would look like. If not coal and oil to power society, then what? If forests are no longer to be cleared to grow food, then how is a larger population to be fed? If a throwaway culture leads inevitably to pollution and resource depletion, how can we satisfy our material needs?

In sum, if the present path is so obviously unsound, what picture of the future can we use to guide our actions toward a global community that can endure?

A sustainable society is one that satisfies its needs without jeopardizing the prospects of future generations. Unfortunately, no models of sustainability exist today. Most developing nations have for the past several decades aspired to the automobile-centered, fossil-fuel-driven economies of the industrial West. From the regional problems of air pollution to the global threat of climate change, though, it is clear that these societies are far from durable; indeed, they are rapidly bringing about their own demise.

Describing the shape of a sustainable society is a risky proposition. Ideas and technologies we can't now foresee obviously will influence society's future course. Yet, just as any technology of flight must abide by the basic principles of aerodynamics, so must a lasting society satisfy some elementary criteria. With that understanding and the experience garnered in recent decades, it is possible to create a vision of a society quite different from, indeed preferable to, today's.

Time to get the world on a sustainable path is rapidly running out. We believe that if humanity achieves sustainability, it will do so within the next 40 years. If we have not succeeded by then, environmental deterioration and economic decline will be feeding on each other, pulling us down toward social decay and political upheaval. At such a point, reclaiming any hope of a sustainable future might be impossible. Our vision, therefore, looks to the year 2030, a time closer to the present than is World War II.

Whether Earth Day 2030 turns out to be a day to celebrate lasting achievements or to lament missed opportunities is largely up to each one of us as individuals, for, in the end, it is individual values that drive social change. Progress toward sustainability thus hinges on a collective deepening of our sense of responsibility to the earth and to our off-spring. Without a reevaluation of our personal aspirations and motivations, we will never achieve an environmentally sound global community.

BEGIN WITH THE BASICS

In attempting to sketch the outlines of a sustainable society, we need to make some basic assumptions. First, our vision of the future assumes only existing technologies and foresee-able improvements in them. This clearly is a conservative assumption: 40 years ago, for example, some renewable energy technologies on which we base our model didn't even exist.

Second, the world economy of 2030 will not be powered by coal, oil, and natural gas. It is now well accepted that continuing heavy reliance on fossil fuels will cause catastrophic changes in climate. The most recent scientific evidence suggests that stabilizing the climate depends on eventually cutting annual global carbon emissions to some 2 billion tons per year, about one-third the current level. Taking population growth into account, the world in 2030 will therefore have per-capita carbon emissions about one-eighth the level found in Western Europe today.

The choice then becomes whether to make solar or nuclear power the centerpiece of energy systems. We believe nuclear power will be rejected because of its long list of economic, social, and environmental liabilities. The nuclear industry has been in decline for over a decade. Safety concerns and the failure to develop permanent storage for nuclear waste have disenchanted many citizens.

It is possible scientists could develop new nuclear technologies that are more economical and less accident-prone. Yet, this would not solve the waste dilemma. Nor would it prevent the use of nuclear energy as a stepping stone to developing nuclear weapons. Trying to stop this in a plutonium-based economy with thousands of operating plants would require a degree of control incompatible with democratic political systems. Societies are likely to opt instead for diverse, solar-based systems.

The third major assumption is about population size. Current United Nations projections have the world headed for nearly nine billion people by 2030. This figure implies a doubling or tripling of the populations of Ethiopia, India, Nigeria, and scores of other countries where human numbers are already overtaxing natural support systems. But such growth is inconceivable. Either these societies will move quickly to encourage smaller families and bring birthrates down, or rising death rates from hunger and malnutrition will check population growth.

The humane path to sustainability by the year 2030 therefore requires a dramatic drop in birthrates. As of 1990, 13 European countries had stable or declining populations; by 2030, most countries are likely to be in that category. We assume a population 40 years from now of at most eight billion that will be either essentially stable or declining slowly toward a number the earth can comfortably support.

DAWN OF A SOLAR AGE

In many ways, the solar age today is where the coal age was when the steam engine was invented in the eighteenth century. At that time, coal was used to heat homes and smelt iron ore, but the notion of using coal-fired steam engines to power factories or transportation systems was just emerging. Only a short time later, the first railroad started running and fossil fuels began to transform the world economy.

Many technologies have been developed that allow us to harness the renewable energy of the sun effectively, but so far these devices are only in limited use. By 2030 they will be widespread and much improved. The pool of energy these technologies can tap is immense: The annual influx of accessible renewable resources in the United States is estimated at 250 times the country's current energy needs.

The mix of energy sources will reflect the climate and natural resources of particular regions. Northern Europe, for example, is likely to rely heavily on wind and hydropower. Northern Africa and the Middle East may instead use direct sunlight. Japan and the Philippines will tap their abundant geothermal energy. Southeast Asian countries will be powered largely by wood and agricultural wastes, along with sunshine. Some nations—Norway and Brazil, for example—already obtain more than half of their energy from renewables.

By 2030, solar panels will heat most residential water around the world. A typical urban landscape may have thousands of collectors sprouting from rooftops, much as television antennas do today. Electricity will come via transmission lines from solar thermal plants located in desert regions of the United States, North Africa, and central Asia. This technology uses mirrored troughs to focus sunlight onto oil-filled tubes that convey heat to a turbine and generator that then produce electricity. An 80-megawatt solar thermal plant built in the desert east of Los Angeles in 1989 converted an extraordinary 22 percent of incoming sunlight into electricity—at a third less than the cost of power from new nuclear plants.

Power will also come from photovoltaic solar cells, a semiconductor technology that converts sunlight directly into electricity. Currently, photovoltaic systems are less efficient than and four times as expensive as solar thermal power, but by 2030 their cost will be competitive. Photovoltaics will be a highly decentralized energy source found atop residential homes as well as adjacent to farms and factories.

Using this technology, homeowners throughout the world may become producers as well as consumers of electricity. Indeed, photovoltaic shingles have already been developed that turn roofing material into a power source. As costs continue to decline, many homes are apt to get their electricity from photovoltaics; in sunny regions residents will sell any surplus to the utility company.

Wind power, an indirect form of solar energy generated by the sun's differential heating of the atmosphere, is already close to being cost competitive with new coal-fired power plants. Engineers are confident they can soon unveil improved wind turbines that are economical not just in California's blustery mountain passes, where they are now commonplace, but in vast stretches of the U.S. northern plains and many other areas. Forty years from now the United States could be deriving 10 to 20 percent of its electricity from the wind.

Small-scale hydro projects are likely to be a significant source of electricity, particularly in the Third World, where the undeveloped potential is greatest. As of 1990 hydro power supplied nearly one-fifth of the world's electricity. By 2030 that share should be much higher, although the massive dams favored by governments and international lending agencies in the late-twentieth century will represent a declining proportion of the total hydro capacity.

Living plants provide another means of capturing solar energy. Through photosynthesis, they convert sunlight into biomass that can be burned or converted to liquid fuels such as ethanol. Today, wood provides 12 percent of the world's energy, chiefly in the form of firewood and charcoal in developing countries. Its use will surely expand during the next 40 years, although resource constraints will not permit it to replace all of the vast quantities of petroleum in use today.

Geothermal energy taps the huge reservoir of heat that lies beneath the earth's surface, making it the only renewable source that does not rely on sunlight. Continuing advances will allow engineers to use previously unexploitable, lower-temperature reservoirs that are hundreds of times as abundant as those in use today. Virtually all Pacific Rim countries, as well as those along East Africa's Great Rift and the Mediterranean Sea, will draw on geothermal resources.

Nations in what now is called the Third World face the immense challenge of continuing to develop their economies without massive use of fossil fuels. One option is to rely on biomass energy in current quantities but to step up replanting efforts and to burn the biomass much more efficiently, using gasifiers and other devices. Another is to turn directly to the sun, which the Third World has in abundance. Solar ovens for cooking, solar collectors for hot water, and photovoltaics for electricity could satisfy most energy needs.

In both industrial and developing nations, energy production inevitably will be much more decentralized; this will break up the utilities and huge natural gas, coal, and oil industries that have been a dominant part of the economic scene in the late-twentieth century. Indeed, a world energy system based on the highly efficient use of renewable resources will be less vulnerable to disruption and more conducive to market economics.

EFFICIENT IN ALL SENSES

Getting total global carbon emissions down to 2 billion tons a year will require vast improvements in energy efficiency. Fortunately, many of the technologies to accomplish this feat already exist and are cost-effective. No technical breakthroughs are needed to double automobile fuel economy, triple the efficiency of lighting systems, or cut typical home heating requirements by 75 percent.

Automobiles in 2030 are apt to get at least 100 miles per gallon of fuel, four times the current average for new cars. A hint of what such vehicles may be like is seen in the Volvo LCP 2000, a prototype automobile. It is an aerodynamic four-passenger car that weighs half as much as today's models. Moreover, it has a highly efficient and clean-burning diesel engine. With the addition of a continuously variable transmission and a flywheel energy storage device, this vehicle will get 90 miles to the gallon.

Forty years from now, Thomas Edison's revolutionary incandescent light bulbs may be found only in museums—replaced by an array of new lighting systems, including halogen and sodium lights. The most important new light source may be compact fluorescent bulbs that use 18 watts rather than 75 to produce the same amount of light.

In 2030, homes are likely to be weather-tight and highly insulated; this will greatly reduce the need for heating and cooling. Some superinsulated homes in the Canadian province of Saskatchewan are already so tightly built that it doesn't pay to install a furnace. Homes of this kind use one-third as much energy as do modern Swedish homes, or one-tenth the U.S. average. Inside, people will have appliances that are on average three to four times as efficient as those in use today.

Improving energy efficiency will not noticeably change lifestyles or economic systems. A highly efficient refrigerator or light bulb provides the same service as an inefficient one—just more economically. Gains in energy efficiency alone, however, will not reduce fossil-fuel related carbon emissions by the needed amount. Additional steps to limit the use of fossil fuels are likely to reshape cities, transportation systems, and industrial patterns and foster a society that is more efficient in all senses.

By the year 2030, a much more diverse set of transportation options will exist. The typical European or Japanese city today has already taken one step toward this future. Highly developed rail and bus systems move people efficiently between home and work: In Tokyo only 15 percent of commuters drive cars to the office. The cities of 2030 are apt to be crisscrossed by inexpensive, street-level light rail systems that allow people to move quickly between neighborhoods.

Automobiles will undoubtedly still be in use four decades from now, but their numbers will be fewer and their role smaller. Within cities, only electric or clean hydrogen-powered vehicles are likely to be permitted, and most of these will be highly efficient "city cars." The energy to run them may well come from solar power plants. Families might rent efficient larger vehicles for vacations.

The bicycle will also play a major role in getting people about, as it already does in much of Asia as well as in some industrial-country towns and cities—in Amsterdam and Davis, California, bike-path networks encourage widespread pedaling. There are already twice as many bikes as cars worldwide. In the bicycle-centered transport system of 2030, the ratio could easily be 10 to 1.

Forty years from now, people will live closer to their jobs, and much socializing and shopping will be done by bike rather than in a 1-ton automobile. Computerized delivery services may allow people to shop from home—consuming less time as well as less energy. Telecommunications will substitute for travel as well. In addition, a world that allows only 2 billion tons of carbon emissions cannot be trucking vast quantities of food and other items thousands of miles; this is apt to encourage more decentralization of agriculture and allow local produce suppliers to flourish.

The automobile-based modern world is now only about 40 years old, but with its damaging air pollution and traffic congestion it hardly represents the pinnacle of human social evolution. Although a world where cars play a minor role may be hard to imagine, our grandparents would have had just as hard a time visualizing today's world of traffic jams and smog-filled cities.

NOTHING TO WASTE

In the sustainable, efficient economy of 2030, waste reduction and recycling industries will have largely replaced the garbage collection and disposal companies of today. The throwaway society that emerged during the late-twentieth century uses so much energy, emits so much carbon, and generates so much air pollution, acid rain, water pollution, toxic waste, and rubbish that it is strangling itself. Rooted as it is in planned obsolescence and appeals to convenience, it will be seen by historians as an aberration.

A hierarchy of options will guide materials policy in the year 2030. The first priority, of course, will be to avoid using any nonessential item. Second will be to reuse a product directly—for example, refilling a glass beverage container. The third will be to recycle the material to form a new product. Fourth, the material can be burned to extract whatever energy it contains, as long as this can be done safely. The option of last resort will be disposal in a landfill.

In the sustainable economy of 2030, the principal source of materials for industry will be recycled goods. Most of the raw material for the aluminum mill will come from the local scrap collection center, not from the bauxite mine. The steel mills of the future will feed on worn-out automobiles, household appliances, and industrial equipment. Paper and paper products will be produced at recycling mills, in which in paper will move through a series of uses, from high-quality bond to newsprint and, eventually, to cardboard boxes. Industries will turn to virgin raw materials only to replace any loses in use and recycling.

The effect on air and water quality will be obvious. For example, steel produced from scrap reduces air pollution by 85 percent, cuts water pollution by 76 percent, and eliminates mining wastes altogether. Making paper from recycled material reduces pollutants entering the air by 74 percent and the water by 35 percent. It also reduces pressures on forests in direct proportion to the amount recycled.

The economic reasons for such careful husbanding of materials will by 2030 seem quite obvious. Just 5 percent as much energy is needed to recycle aluminum as to produce it from bauxite ore. For steel produced entirely from scrap, the saving amounts to roughly two-thirds. Newsprint from recycled paper takes 25 to 60 percent less energy to make than that from wood pulp. Recycling glass saves up to a third of the energy embodied in the original product.

Societies in 2030 may also have decided to replace multi-sized and -shaped beverage containers with a set of standardized ones made of durable glass that can be reused many times. These could be used for fruit juices, beer, milk, and soda pop.

One of the cornerstones of a sustainable society will likely be its elimination of waste flows at the source. Industry will have restructured manufacturing processes to slash wastes by a third or more from 1990 levels. Food packaging, which in 1986 cost American consumers more than American farmers earned selling their crops, will have been streamlined. Food items buried in three or four layers of packaging will be a distant memory.

As recycling reaches its full potential over the next 40 years, households will begin to compost yard wastes rather than put them out for curbside pickup. A lost art in many communities now, composting will experience a revival. Garbage flows will be reduced by one-fifth or more and gardeners will have a rich source of humus.

In addition to recycling and reusing metal, glass, and paper, a sustainable society must also recycle nutrients. In nature, one organism's waste is another's sustenance. In cities, however, human sewage has become a troublesome source of water pollution. Properly treated to prevent the spread of disease and to remove contaminants, sewage will be systematically returned to the land in vegetable-growing greenbelts around cities, much as is done in Shanghai and other Asian cities today.

Other cities will probably find it more efficient to follow Calcutta's example and use treated human sewage to fertilize aquacultural operations. A steady flow of nutrients from human waste can help nourish aquatic life, which in turn is consumed by fish.

How to Feed Eight Billion

Imagine trying to meet the food, fuel, and timber needs of eight billion people—nearly three billion more than the current world population—with 960 billion fewer tons of topsoil (more than twice the amount on all U.S. cropland) and one billion fewer acres of trees (an area more than half the size of the continental United States).

That, in a nutshell, will be the predicament faced by society in 2030 if current rates of soil erosion and deforestation continue unaltered for the next 40 years. It is a fate that can only be avoided through major changes in land use.

Of necessity, societies in 2030 will be using the land intensively; the needs of a population more than half again as large as today's cannot be met otherwise. But, unlike the present, tomorrow's land-use patterns would be abiding by basic principles of biological stability: nutrient retention, carbon balance, soil protection, water conservation, and preservation of species diversity. Harvests will rarely exceed sustainable yields.

Meeting food needs will pose monumental challenges, as some simple numbers illustrate. By 2030, assuming cropland area expands by 5 percent between now and then and that population grows to eight billion, cropland per person will have dropped to a third less than we have in today's inadequately fed world. Virtually all of Asia, and especially China, will be struggling to feed its people from a far more meager base of per-capita cropland area.

In light of these constraints, the rural landscapes of 2030 are likely to exhibit greater diversity than they do now. Variations in soils, slope, climate, and water availability will require different patterns and strains of crops grown in different ways to maximize sustainable output. For example, farmers may adopt numerous forms of agroforestry—the combined production of crops and trees—to provide food, biomass, and fodder, while also adding nutrients to soils and controlling water runoff.

Also, successfully adapting to changed climates resulting from greenhouse warming, as well as to water scarcity and other resource constraints, may lead scientists to draw on a much broader base of crop varieties. For example, a greater area will be devoted to salt-tolerant and drought-resistant crops.

Efforts to arrest desertification, now claiming 15 million acres each year, may by 2030 have transformed the gullied highlands of Ethiopia and other degraded areas into productive terrain. Much of the sloping land rapidly losing topsoil will be terraced and protected by shrubs or nitrogen-fixing trees planted along the contour.

Halting desertification also depends on eliminating overgrazing. The global livestock herd in 2030 is likely to be much smaller than today's three billion. It seems inevitable that adequately nourishing a world population 60 percent larger than today's will preclude feeding a third of the global grain harvest to livestock and poultry, as is currently the case. As meat becomes more expensive, the diets of the affluent will move down the food chain to greater consumption of grains and vegetables; this will also prolong lifespans.

A HEALTHY RESPECT FOR FORESTS

Forests and woodlands will be valued more highly and for many more reasons in 2030 than is the case today. The planet's mantle of trees, already a third smaller than in pre-agricultural times and shrinking by more than 27 million acres per year now, will be stable or expanding as a result of serious efforts to slow deforestation and to replant vast areas.

Long before 2030, the clearing of most tropical forests will have ceased. Since most of the nutrients in these ecosystems are held in the leaves and biomass of the vegetation rather than in the soil, only activities that preserve the forest canopy are sustainable. While it is impossible to say how much virgin tropical forest would remain in 2030 if sustainability is achieved, certainly the rate of deforestation will have had to slow dramatically by the end of this decade. Soon thereafter it will come to a halt.

Efforts to identify and protect unique parcels of forest will probably have led to a widely dispersed network of preserves. But a large portion of tropical forests still standing in 2030 will be exploited in a variety of benign ways by people living in and around them. Hundreds of "extractive reserves" will exist, areas in which local people harvest rubber, resins, nuts, fruits, medicines, and other forest products.

Efforts to alleviate the fuel-wood crisis in developing countries, to reduce flooding and landslides in hilly regions, and to slow the buildup of carbon dioxide may spur the planting of an additional 500 million acres or so of trees. Many of these plantings will be on private farms as part of agroforestry systems, but plantations may also have an expanded role. Cities and villages will turn to managed woodlands on their outskirts to contribute fuel for heating, cooking, and electricity. This wood will substitute for some portion of coal and oil use and, since harvested on a sustained-yield basis, will make no net contribution of carbon dioxide to the atmosphere.

Restoring and stabilizing the biological resource base by 2030 depends on a pattern of land ownership and use far more equitable than today's. Much of the degradation now occurring stems from the heavily skewed distribution of land that, along with population growth, pushes poor people into ever more marginal environments. Stewardship requires that people have plots large enough to sustain their families without abusing the land, access to means of using the land productively, and the right to pass it on to their children.

No matter what technologies come along, the biochemical process of photosynthesis, carried out by green plants, will remain the basis for meeting many human needs, and its efficiency can only be marginally improved. Given that humanity already appropriates an estimated 40 percent of the earth's annual photosynthetic product on land, the urgency of slowing the growth in human numbers is obvious. The sooner societies stabilize their populations, the greater will be their opportunities for achieving equitable and stable patterns of land use that can meet their needs indefinitely.

ECONOMIC PROGRESS IN A NEW LIGHT

The fundamental changes that are needed in energy, forestry, agriculture, and other physical systems cannot occur without corresponding shifts in social, economic, and moral character. During the transition to sustainability, political leaders and citizens alike will be forced to reevaluate their goals and aspirations and to adjust to a new set of principles that have at their core the welfare of future generations.

Shifts in employment will be among the most visible as the transition gets under way. Moving from fossil fuels to a diverse set of renewable energy sources, extracting fewer materials from the earth and recycling more, and revamping farming and forestry practices will greatly expand opportunities in new areas. Job losses in coal mining, auto production, and metals prospecting will be offset by gains in the manufacture and sale of photovoltaic solar cells, wind turbines, bicycles, mass-transit equipment, and a host of technologies for recycling materials.

Since planned obsolescence will itself be obsolete in a sustainable society, a far greater share of workers will be employed in repair, maintenance, and recycling activities than in the extraction of virgin materials and production of new goods.

Wind prospectors, energy efficiency auditors, and solar architects will be among the professions booming from the shift to a highly efficient, renewable energy economy. Numbering in the hundreds of thousands today, jobs in these fields may collectively total in the millions worldwide within a few decades. Opportunities in forestry will expand markedly.

As the transition to a more environmentally sensitive economy progresses, sustainability will gradually eclipse growth as the focus of economic policymaking. Over the next few decades, government policies will encourage investments that promote stability and endurance at the expense of those that simply expand short-term production.

As a yardstick of progress, the gross national product (GNP) will be seen as a bankrupt indicator. By measuring flows of goods and services, GNP undervalues the qualities a sustainable society strives for, such as durability and resource protection; and overvalues planned obsolescence and waste. The pollution caused by a coal-burning power plant, for instance, raises GNP by requiring expenditures on lung disease treatment and the purchase of a scrubber to control emissions. Yet society would be far better off if power were generated in ways that did not pollute the air in the first place.

National military budgets in a sustainable world will be a small fraction of what they are today. Moreover, sustainability cannot be achieved without a massive shift of resources from military endeavors into energy efficiency, soil conservation, tree planting, family planning, and other needed development activities. Rather than maintaining large defense establishments, governments may come to rely on a strengthened U.N. peacekeeping force.

A New Set of Values

Movement toward a lasting society cannot occur without a transformation of individual priorities and values. Throughout the ages, philosophers and religious leaders have denounced materialism as a path to human fulfillment. Yet societies across the ideological spectrum have persisted in equating quality of life with increased consumption.

Because of the strain on resources it creates, materialism simply cannot survive the transition to a sustainable world. As public understanding of the need to adopt simpler and less consumptive lifestyles spreads, it will become unfashionable to own fancy new cars and clothes and the latest electronic devices. The potential benefits of unleashing the human energy now devoted to producing, advertising, buying, consuming, and discarding material goods are enormous.

As the amassing of personal and national wealth becomes less of a goal, the gap between haves and have notes will gradually close; this will eliminate many societal tensions. Ideological differences may fade as well, as nations adopt sustainability as a common cause, and as they come to recognize that achieving it requires a shared set of values that includes democratic principles, freedom to innovate, respect for human rights, and acceptance of diversity. With the cooperative tasks involved in repairing the earth so many and so large, the idea of waging war could become an anachronism.

The task of building a sustainable society is an enormous one that will take decades rather than years. Indeed, it is an undertaking that will easily absorb the energies that during the past 40 years have been devoted to the Cold War. The reward in the year 2030 could be an Earth Day with something to celebrate: the achievement of a society in balance with the resources that support it, instead of one that destroys the underpinnings of its future.

INDEX